ANGRY WHITE PEOPLE

COMING FACE-TO-FACE WITH THE BRITISH FAR RIGHT

HSIAO-HUNG PAI

Zed Books

LONDON

Angry White People: Coming face-to-face with the British far right
was first published in 2016 by Zed Books Ltd,
The Foundry, 17 Oval Way, London SE11 5RR, UK.

www.zedbooks.co.uk

Typeset in ITC Galliard Std by seagulls.net
Index: ed.emery@thefreeuniversity.net
Cover design: www.alice-marwick.co.uk

A catalogue record for this book is available from the British Library.

ISBN 978-1-78360-827-0 hb
ISBN 978-1-78360-692-4 pb
ISBN 978-1-78360-693-1 pdf
ISBN 978-1-78360-694-8 epub
ISBN 978-1-78360-695-5 mobi

Printed and bound by CPI Group (UK) Ltd, Croydon, CR0 4YY

CONTENTS

Acknowledgements   vii

List of abbreviations   ix

Foreword by Benjamin Zephaniah   xi

1   Born and Bred Here   1

2   Defending the Imaginary Nation   65

3   The Story of Bury Park   111

4   'The EDL Cannot Survive Here'   151

5   The Changing Faces of the Radical Right   193

6   The Colours of British Racism   235

7   The New Outsiders   287

Afterword   359

Index   369

ACKNOWLEDGEMENTS

The research of the past two years would not have been possible without the very kind sponsorship of (Sir) David Tang, whom I met when fundraising for the families of Morecambe Bay victims. David was the major donor then, and years later he offered me the financial help I needed to conduct the research for this book. He did so because he firmly believes in fighting racism. I cannot thank him enough, and only hope that he thinks the result of his sponsorship deserves it.

Many, many thanks to Benjamin Zephaniah, poet and writer and a committed anti-racist campaigner, who so kindly wrote the foreword for this book.

Big thanks also go to Anna Holmwood, who was so enthusiastic and kindly spent time editing the manuscript before I submitted it to the publisher. She was my only test reader and her help was most valuable.

Many thanks to Joseph Choonara (*Socialist Review*) for introducing me to Zed Books, for which I'm so grateful. His comradely support was and is much needed.

I'm very proud to be published by Zed Books. My biggest thanks go to Zed Book's editorial director and my editor Kika Sroka-Miller. Her empathy and commitment as a radical publisher, and her excellent editing and advice, made all the difference to shaping the book. I feel so fortunate to have such a wonderful editor and publisher!

Many, many thanks to Denis Wong, Don Flynn of Migrants' Rights Network, Barbara Storey of SOS Polonia, Abdullah Faliq and many committed campaigners and activists who have given me their support and help. Much gratitude to Arun Kundnani for his inspiring book *The Muslims Are Coming!* and great advice and encouragement throughout; and to Daniel Trilling for his brilliant book *Bloody Nasty People*.

I am so grateful to my parents, Hsiu-Hiung and Judeh, who have always supported me with their lasting encouragement and kind patience. Although we talk only by phone once every two weeks, as we're thousands of miles apart, my thoughts are always with them.

Big thanks go to Dave Barkway, who has given me companionship and much-needed support during the research and writing of the book; and to Sylvia Barkway for her lovely morale-boosting steak dinners and Michael for teaching me how to play rummy! They're like family to me and are the best example of British hospitality.

And last but not least, many, many thanks to John Davies and Leslie Hearson for their continuous kind encouragement.

ABBREVIATIONS

ANL	Anti-Nazi League
BFP	British Freedom Party
BNP	British National Party
BPA	British Patriotic Alliance
BPYP	Bury Park Youth Posse
C18	Combat 18
CxF	Combined Ex-Forces
EDL	English Defence League
EVF	English Volunteer Force
LGBT	lesbian, gay, bisexual, transgender
Migs	Men in Gear
NF	National Front
RAMFEL	Refugee and Migrant Forum of Essex and London
RAR	Rock Against Racism
RVF	Racial Volunteer Force
TNVA	The Non Violence Alliance
UAF	Unite Against Fascism
UEE	United East End
UKIP	United Kingdom Independence Party
UPL	United People of Luton

FOREWORD

BENJAMIN ZEPHANIAH

This is personal. It started when I was about eight years old. I was walking on Farm Street in Hockley, Birmingham, where my family lived. I was in my own little world, having poetic thoughts and wondering what the future held for me. Then, bang. I felt an almighty slap on the back of my head and I fell to the floor. A boy had hit me with a brick as he rode past on his bicycle. As I lay on the ground with blood pouring from the back of my head, he looked back and shouted, 'Go home, you black bastard.' I had no idea what he was talking about. I was going home. Who was black? What was a bastard? At home my mother sat me down and explained to me that there are some people in this country that didn't like people who are not white, and they wanted us to go back home. I spent the next few months wondering where my 'real' home was – I thought it was in Birmingham – and what was so great about being white, and why would anyone want to hit someone because of the colour of their skin?

I was growing up confused, but a couple of years later I felt the need to show my independence and spend some time away from my family, so I decided to visit my local youth club.

The game of choice for young boys back then was table tennis, a game that I had played a few times and was quite good at. When I arrived at the centre I went straight to the table tennis table and watched a few games; then I plucked up the courage and asked if I could play a game. I was quickly surrounded by a group of young boys and girls who started pushing me towards the door and telling me that black people should not come to this club. I was pushed and tripped to the floor a couple of times but I was relieved to see an adult arrive on the scene and come to my rescue. But he wasn't much help. He did tell the mob to leave me alone, and then he took me into his office, where he told me that it would be best if I didn't come back to the youth club because I would upset the atmosphere. He said they were like a family at the club, and I should find a family of my own.

These are just two examples of the racism that I experienced as a very young boy. I understood very quickly that I had to grow up tough and that I had to always be on the lookout for strangers who hated me and anyone like me. For the next few years I suffered many racist attacks, but I became streetwise. I learned boxing and kung fu so I could look after myself. But there was not much I could do when I was surrounded by twenty of them, and there was not much I could do when the perpetrators were the police. The police brought another level of difficulty to my life, but that's another book.

In order to escape the unemployment, the 'thug life' and the West Midlands Police Force, in 1979 I left Birmingham and headed to London. I found myself in Leyton, east London, which looked very much like the community I had left in Birmingham: working-class white people, who on the whole were enjoying the benefits of a multicultural community. The music of youth then was punk, reggae, ska and soul. Street and park festivals were popular, and (on the whole) the attitude of youth was that we had to stick together in order to overcome the miseries of unemployment, and music was a great way of bringing us together. But it didn't take long for me to realize that there were two big issues that we had to deal with day after day, and night after night. The police (who had something called the 'sus' law that they used to use against us) and the National Front. National Front members tended to have low-cut or shaved hair, rolled-up jeans and steel-capped boots, and they made no attempt to hide the fact that their main purpose was to rid the country of foreigners. They would roam the streets and viciously attack people that weren't like them. They would often crash our clubs and cause destruction, or they would wait until we left the clubs, follow us for a while, and then attack. There were many times when I had to fight my way out of clubs, or fight my way home, but one of the most violent attacks I ever witnessed happened one night at Stratford Broadway in east London.

Stratford was a place that was proud of its multicultural make-up. I felt safe there, although I knew that not far away there were no-go areas for black people. Barking and Canning Town were places we were told never to visit. They were National Front strongholds and the racists there clearly marked their boundaries. Canning Town was adjacent to Stratford, where one hot, sticky night I was walking home as slowly as I could. I noticed a couple waiting for a bus who looked as if they were passionately in love. They hugged and kissed so much that I had to lower my gaze in embarrassment. After one long kiss the bus arrived and to my surprise the boy got on the bus, leaving the girl to walk home. I know it was sexist to assume that it was the boy walking the girl to the bus stop, but that was me back then; I was learning. As the girl began to walk away, skinheads (from Canning Town) began to emerge from every nearby shop doorway. They surrounded the girl, calling her a 'nigger lover' and a 'slag'; they kicked her to the ground and continued to kick her, until I and another passer-by intervened. Intervened might be too strong a word; we distracted them just enough to allow the girl to get up and run away, but in the process we got quite a kicking ourselves.

What really struck me about this incident was the viciousness of the attack. Strong, young men, ranging in age from sixteen to thirty, kicking, punching and stamping on a girl who was no older than eighteen. She was a white like them, but they hated her because of her love for a black man. Each one of them was filled with hatred for someone they had never met, and someone who could have been related to one of them. They hated us, and they hated anyone who didn't hate us, and they had even more hatred for anyone who would dare to love us. As a young Rastafarian I was taught not to hate, and it wasn't in my nature to hate – after all, we were listening to music that was all about peace and love and bringing people together, we wanted to be living examples of how people could live together, but we knew that if we did nothing we would be killed on the streets. We knew that the National Front was a Nazi front, so our slogan became 'Self-defence is no offence', and we meant it. To defend ourselves in local communities up and down the country, black and Asian groups organized self-defence groups. These were people who would spring into action, defending (when possible) anyone who was attacked. In London we had a group called Red Action, a bunch of left-wingers who operated like an alternative police force. They would come to clubs and gatherings and make sure that the event was not invaded and that people got home safely. There were no mobile phones so they would communicate with each other using walkie-talkies, and they would react to our distress calls much quicker than Her Majesty's police force. Then there was the legendary Sari Squad. These were women, mainly of South Asian origin, who were experts in various martial arts and ready and willing to take on any racists that would try to spoil our fun. They fought with style, and would usually burst into song after seeing off any attackers.

The National Front did not hide their bigotry. They chanted racist songs, they praised fascist heroes, and they did Nazi salutes; but then something strange happened. A schism appeared. They had put up candidates in elections before but now a group within the 'movement' thought that they should now seek more respectability and concentrate their efforts on becoming a real political party by seeking power through the ballot box. We still had to fight them on the streets. But now some of them had begun wearing suits and appearing on television programmes. They even made party political broadcasts, which some argued was a major contributor to their downfall. They were a great example of a political party with no intellectual base at all. We knew that in order to make Britain more British they planned to get rid of immigrants, but now we also knew that to cut crime they were going to get rid of immigrants, to save the National Health Service they were going to get rid of immigrants, to bring inflation down they were going to get rid of immigrants, to get the traffic moving they were going to get rid of immigrants, and to improve the British weather they were going to get rid of immigrants. It was the only idea they had.

The National Front continued to argue among themselves on how racist they should be and where they should concentrate their racism, and as they did so their membership began to wane. And so Combat 18 and the British National Party (BNP) began to grow. For a while the popular face of racism was the BNP, but then they lost their thunder, and then came the United Kingdom Independence Party (UKIP) and the English Defence League (EDL). This is not a subject I studied; I was only interested in all this because I was a writer and commentator, so there were times when I would have to confront their members on TV debates, but – I'm going to repeat myself – we still had to fight them on the streets. When the racists were busy changing their names and public personas, the majority of their victims weren't concerned with what they were calling themselves. When they were deciding whether or not they should be wearing suits or boots, we were not considering how we should dress in response; we were still fighting for our lives on the streets. At various times we were being told by the racists that their enemies were the 'Pakis', or 'Jamaican yardies', or the 'Islamic fundamentalists', but whatever they say, whatever they call themselves, they have been attacking the same people on the streets, and we (those same people) still have to fight them on the streets. Nothing much has changed.

I have drawn strength and inspiration from the many people who have stood up to the racist thugs and defended our freedom to walk the streets over the years. When the police would not take attacks on black people seriously, allowing gangs of racists to roam the streets, hunting us down, and when those same police drew inspiration from a government that accused immigrants of swamping Britain, we were left to ourselves. There are many unsung heroes who really did put their lives on the line in our struggle. Some died in action, and we must always remember them. There are no monuments to them, there is no state recognition of them, but they are true martyrs. But I am saddened by some of the people who fought the racists that have now become part of the establishment; at best they tolerate racism by the establishment, at worst they become a part of it. Many became part of what was called 'the race industry'. They were skilled in applying for grants and starting projects, or they were skilled at positioning themselves to get the 'good' jobs in the booming 'race industry'. This is not a criticism of them; I just want to make the point (again) that when they were doing all that, we were still fighting them on the streets. Blair Peach, Stephen Lawrence, Anthony Walker or the girl I saw being beaten in Stratford were not in meetings when they were attacked; they were not applying for grants or running for Parliament when they were attacked; they were all walking the streets.

I have to agree with those who claim that the political elite has neglected the white working class. There are poor white people living in ghettoes all over Britain, they live in terrible housing conditions, their traditional industries have been destroyed, their schools are being run down, and governments of all colours have been ignoring their cries for help for decades. It's true. What is also true is that there are poor black people living in ghettoes all over Britain. They also live in terrible housing conditions, their traditional industries have been destroyed, their schools are being run down, and governments have been ignoring their cries for help since the creation of the slave trade and the building of the British Empire. It is precisely for these reasons that I have always thought that these poor white people and these poor black people should unite and confront the people who oversee all of our miseries. It is classic divide and rule. The biggest fear of all of the mainstream politicians is that we all reach a point where we understand how much we have in common and, instead of turning in on ourselves, we turn on them. In poetry and prose I have said that unity is strength, and that we should get to a point where we are not talking about black rights or white rights, Asian rights or rights for migrant workers; we would just be talking about our rights. As long as people of colour and minority groups are seen as the other, as long as we are being blamed for all of society's ills (including too many cars on our roads), we will keep trying to get our politicians to be honest, and we will continue to call on the white working classes to unite with us. But, if they don't, we will still have to fight them on the streets. This is personal.

1

BORN AND BRED HERE

If you want to tackle extremism, you need to put hope back into their lives. If you take away their identity, they'll be the next generation of extremists. You really need to change that. I'd like to concentrate on politicizing the next generation. They need to vote. People just don't feel like they have a say. When you have that massive disengagement, that is quite dangerous ... Labour and other parties, your fuck-ups and your experiments have created millions like me.

I had never expected these words to come from Tommy Robinson (real name Stephen Lennon), former leader of the English Defence League (EDL), ten months after we met for the first time in the summer of 2013. Back then, the EDL was in the news a lot. As a street movement, it had been receiving more publicity and public attention than any other far-right group in Britain. Since the murder of soldier Lee Rigby in Woolwich on 22 May 2013, the EDL had been growing like wildfire. The 'membership', or the number of activists calculated online, stood at 36,000. Robinson said to me in that summer: 'We don't even need to recruit people ... There are millions who think the way we think and agree with what we stand for. The amount of people who're stepping forward despite the risk of losing their jobs, I'd say there're hundreds and thousands. We've got double the online support that the Lib Dems ever got.'

The EDL exploited the nationalist and racial sentiment deepened by the Woolwich murder, intensifying its mobilization of activists and supporters in towns and cities across the country, culminating in the nationwide demonstrations on 1 June. And then, on 29 June, the group organized a 'Walk of Honour' march on Armed Forces Day, in an attempt to parade past the East London Mosque in Tower Hamlets and then Newham, areas both with a significant British Asian population. The EDL had also intended to invite two notorious racists in the USA's 'anti-Islamization campaign', Pamela Geller and Robert Spencer, to join the march (although under pressure from Britain's anti-racist groups, the two were eventually banned from entering the UK).

Cynically, the EDL used Rigby's death to further its war against Islam. Contrary to the portrayal in some of the popular media, the street movement isn't only against what it calls 'Islamic extremism', but against Islam as a religion and Muslims as a people. It works to *racialize* Islam and its believers as a homogeneous group of people, in direct contradiction of the leadership's claim that it isn't a racist movement or a movement that has been promoting racial hatred.

The EDL said on its website on 30 May 2013:

We have reached a stage where even simply acknowledging the link between Islam and terrorism makes you an

'Islamophobe' or even a racist. No wonder David Cameron refers to 'Islamist extremism', as if Islamic extremism can only come in one form and is easily distinguished from more mainstream forms of Islam ... The problem is that Islamic extremism has deep roots and cannot simply be brushed aside as if it were 'nothing to do with Islam' ... Unless the streets of our cities are to be littered with the bodies of those butchered in the name of Allah, the Islamic community must accept and acknowledge its share of the blame and its responsibility to confront and defeat extremist attitudes ... Our leaders must start addressing the consequences of their policy of unrestricted immigration or there is a very real danger that they will face the 'backlash' we all fear ... As long as we're willing to entertain the idea that Islamic extremism has nothing to do with Islam we have little chance of defeating it.

This statement is a clear manifestation of how the group attempts to link terrorism with Islam, 'immigrants' and immigration in general, without even understanding the basic fact that most terrorist acts were conducted by people born and bred in Britain. As I came to realize through my conversations with the EDL, this is a consistent current in the ideologies of far-right groups. Terrorism is directly linked to Islam and immigration in an attempt to mark British Muslims as 'outsiders', therefore attempting to racialize the religion and its believers.

This racialization had been at the heart of the work of the EDL since its formation. The anti-Islamophobia monitor Tell Mama reported, based on 2012/13 data collected before the Woolwich murder, a troubling picture of anti-Muslim harassment. There are 'incidents in the workplaces, in the street, between neighbours and particularly online, which may not always hit the headlines but can have an emotionally distressing, and in some cases devastating, effect on people's lives and their communities'. In this report, the EDL is held most responsible for disseminating anti-Muslim hatred online. It is the EDL, rather than the BNP, which is named in 49 per cent of the cases. Of 434 incidents of online abuse, 147 were directly linked to the EDL, amounting to one third of all web-based anti-Muslim incidents.

After the far-right exploitation of the death of Lee Rigby, particularly by the EDL, hate crimes such as racist abuse and violence in Britain soared within a matter of days. One hundred and thirty-six complaints of anti-Muslim incidents, including violence and online racist abuse, were reported to the police in the week following Rigby's murder. This was five times higher than the number of hate crimes recorded before his death. This torrent of hatred led directly to the murder of eighty-two-year-old Mohammed, stabbed to death in April as he walked home from a mosque in Birmingham. It was followed by an arson attack on the Somali community centre in Muswell Hill, north London, and three bomb attacks on mosques in the West Midlands.

Confidence among EDL activists seemed to be growing. This was most clearly demonstrated by their activities online, the internet being the major form of communication and mobilization for the movement. When you open the EDL Facebook page, the first line you see is 'No racism, no violence'. But you don't need to browse for long before you find the crudest form of racist abuse. A popular post on EDL London Division's Facebook page said in June 2013: 'We asked 100 people what you associated with Islam. The highest score goes to "terrorism" (28); followed by paedophilia (25), then "hate preaching" (20), "unwelcome invaders" (10), "excessive breeders" (7) and goat/camel fuckers (5).' Racism was confidently expressed here: 136 people ticked 'like' on this post. One said: 'Our country will turn into Englandstan soon and I don't want that at all.'

I was a first-generation migrant with no family relations or cultural roots in Britain. As someone born outside Britain and still a student of its society and culture, I've always been amazed by the total lack of self-awareness that racists like the above seem to display. Britain's media seem to portray them as merely a 'bunch of thugs', beyond which there seems no reason. Their faces on the TV screens and the front pages of newspapers show such deep anger, hatred and, above all, alienation, yet no explanation is ever given. I don't believe in inherent human nature or unchangeable ideologies. Surely, I thought to myself, no one's born a bigot; racial/ethnic hatred is a learned behaviour. So what are the circumstances that have driven them to adopt such ways of thinking?

In order to get a glimpse into how some of their base participants form their politics, I joined the EDL's London Division, under a false Chinese name. There, I was able to read members' communications. One wrote: 'I want Great Britain back. I'm ashamed of what Britain has become, the murder of that poor soldier lad a month ago shocked me as I never thought possible … I am also so angry, so very very angry at the way this Islam stuff has us pinned down. There is nothing wrong with anger, Jesus displayed his anger once and it's written in the bible …'

Then he spoke of his own circumstances and how he channelled his anger:

> I've had a long and glorious professional career at the highest level and then, as life does, a bitter blow was served in my personal life and everything came crashing down with it. I feel ashamed because I'm not working at the moment and the other day had a letter came from the DWP [Department of Work & Pensions]. A Big pack came through the letter box and there were pages and pages of the same letter all in different languages – I was so angry. I get 10p a week benefit after 30 years of senior manangement creating jobs and these letters in foreign languages told me that people who can't read a word of the Queen's English can get benefits, I was furious.

He then drew some conclusions as to what should be done:

> a) ALL known Islam Radicals are shipped out now and their families – no court cases or human rights, out; b) They accept our customs not the other way round – Friday is a work day for example; c) Anyone (Islam or not) who can't read and write an acceptable standard of English is out, and now; d) These rules or acceptance to British culture is imposed on all not just Islam – not just creed driven; e) Our dress code is accepted as we do when we go outside the UK, no more Cousin IT outfits; f) No more immigration (to all), we're full up. We can't care for, feed and find jobs for our own … For me, it's about starting today and going back to

good old British values. Everyone has a choice, it's our way
or the highway.

But despite activists' growing confidence in the movement's
morale, the EDL seemed to operate cautiously and treated new
online followers as potential infiltrators. In my case, they're
not wrong. So far, no one in the Division has responded to my
messages. Or could it be that I had given myself the wrong name?

I was obviously aware that, as a non-white person, it would
be difficult to reach the group's (albeit loose) online membership
and support base. But it isn't an impossible task. I wanted to
start with the group's origin.

Luton, the Bedfordshire town, won its name as the EDL
'hotbed' in May 2009 when its organization of origin,
United People of Luton, organized a 500-strong anti-Muslim
demonstration in the town in response to a group of local
Muslim men who protested against the Iraq war (an invasion
led by the USA and the UK that started in 2003) during the
homecoming parade of the 2nd Battalion, Royal Anglian
Regiment. According to the Iraq Body Count report (published
in the *Independent* in 2011), during the first two years of the
Iraq war at least 24,865 civilians were killed, 20 per cent of
them women and children. The atrocities committed during
the war were never properly reported or documented in the
UK media. During the Luton protest, the anti-war Muslim men
held up placards saying, 'Anglian soldiers: Butchers of Basra' and
'Anglian soldiers: Cowards, killers, extremists' (referring to the
killings of civilians), as the soldiers passed through.

This provoked anger from friends and families of the soldiers.

The anti-Iraq war protest was organized by Anjem Choudary, a forty-six-year-old former solicitor referred to in the British media as a 'radical Islamist preacher', 'extremist preacher' or 'hate preacher'. Choudary is a strong critic of the UK's involvement in the wars in Iraq and Afghanistan and had organized demonstrations against the interventions and the British armed forces in general. He helped form an Islamic organization, al-Muhajiroun, which organized several anti-West demonstrations, which went on to be banned by the British government. Choudary later helped form Al-Ghurabaa, which was again banned. He later formed Islam4UK, and the group was deemed illegal under Britain's counter-terrorism law in 2010. (Interestingly, the majority of the British media supported the banning of these groups, though they have never argued for the same for far-right extremist organizations in the UK.)

Following the anti-war protest in Luton, most of that evening's broadcasts and articles in the tabloid press the next day were calling the Muslim protesters 'extremists', 'fanatics' and 'hate mobs', 'Britons who hate Britain', 'the enemy within'. The *Telegraph* was particularly sensationalist on the morning of 14 March 2009: 'The Muslim extremists in Luton who jeered British troops returning from Iraq are continuing to defy public anger despite the simmering tension it has caused in a racially-mixed town.'

I knew that most media outlets didn't tell the whole truth as to what happened in Luton's anti-war, anti-army protest. So I wanted to get the other side of the story from the protest organizer, Anjem Choudary. With the negative press about him, I expected it to be difficult to set up a meeting. It proved remarkably easy, however, after a chance encounter with a teenage boy giving out copies of the Quran on a Saturday stall on Commercial Road. He put me in touch with Choudary, who immediately accepted my request for a meeting, although he was careful not to tell me the venue. Call at 9 a.m. on the day of our meeting, I was told. On the phone, Choudary was just as cautious. I was asked to come to New Road and then call him again when I reached the Costa café. I did as he instructed. Out came a woman from a café opposite. 'Are you here to meet Anjem Choudary?' she asked politely. She then led me into the café, where Choudary was sipping his coffee.

Choudary didn't shake my hand, but smiled and asked whether I'd like anything to drink. Then he introduced me to the woman who had come to meet me, his wife Umm Luqman. They had brought with them their young daughter, who sat with her mother at the table next to us. Choudary was different from the image I had formed from the press reports. He was relaxed and smiled. When asked what he thought of being called a hate preacher, his answer was calm:

> When you call for fundamental change in society, there will always be resistance ... Fifteen years ago, the [racist] agenda in Europe wasn't so much about the Muslims but more about black people and Jews ... Today the people who define themselves on the far right define themselves in relation to Islam. That's the case in France, Germany, Austria and Britain ... As a Muslim, you're always going to be part of that equation. It depends on how public you are and how much you proclaim Islam ... That is how much you'll be under attack. But I would define myself just as a Muslim.

Choudary grew up in Woolwich and attended the primary school on the same street where Lee Rigby was killed thirty years later. During his youth in the 1970s and 1980s, he witnessed the growth of the National Front and other far-right forces. 'Now the far right has become more politically astute and acceptable to society, while Muslim communities have become more empowered as the second and third generations become entrenched in this country and they're not just going to go away in face of hostility ... It's a lot different from how we grew up as the first generation ...'

Choudary said he had been looking for the meaning of life for a long time, and in his mid-twenties, after studying medicine and law, he came to discover an alternative way of thinking that took him outside capitalism and liberal democracy. He began to follow Islam strictly. He has subsequently gone on to study sharia for over two decades. He talked to me about it as a set of theological principles that, as laid out in the Quran, can be practised globally. 'It is wherever we are, not specifically about the UK,' he said, referring to his group as 'an ideological movement'.

Contrary to the media portrayal, Choudary said the Luton protest in fact also involved non-Muslims from the local white British communities who, in his words, 'transcended nationalism and patriotism' to come out against the war. 'In fact, Luton's Muslims have always got on fine with the white communities. The vast majority of local white people were fine with the Muslims and there were big demonstrations against the war where white people took part in Luton.'

He explained the real feelings behind the contentious protest in 2009:

The protesters rejected the British involvement in the murder of Muslims and the atrocities it committed in Iraq and Afghanistan ... When the army came back, they were symbolic of all that ... The words on the protesters' placards were nothing compared to what actually happened. 'Baby killers,' it said on the placards. People found it distasteful to read these words. But baby-killing did actually happen in these wars. Those people who went out there to commit murders are not conscripted ... They went out there on their own will. And yet they were paraded as heroes. That definitely needed to be opposed. For the EDL, their history might have begun that day [of the anti-war, anti-army protest in Luton]. But ours is a continuous struggle.

To counter those who say we're a banned organization and we're engaged in inciting this and that, I'd say: Nobody was blowing themselves up until the British were in Iraq and Afghanistan ... What happened in Luton was a result of what Britain was engaged in abroad ... It's all about Britain's foreign policies. And that was why there was a huge anti-war movement in this country.

However, most of the media went on in 2009 to paint Luton's anti-war protest as an Islamic issue. The seeds were being planted for the spread of anger directed at Britain's Muslim population as the imaginary enemy. It was in this context that United People of Luton (UPL) and Casuals United were born, made up of primarily white working-class young men from the Farley Hill Estate and other places in Luton. They were brought up in an enclosed, army-loyal, gang culture on the estates and see

11

allegiance to 'their own' as important. It is local identities which have shaped their emotional make-up. EDL supporter Billy Blake said in his book, *EDL: Coming Down the Road* (personally recommended by Nick Griffin to all EDL members), 'the English working-class is a *distinct ethnic group*, with its own traditions and culture'. Although they might express themselves as a 'class', their allegiance lies with their ethnicity and ethnic origin.

During the counter-demonstration organized by UPL that May, anti-Muslim sentiment led to violence in which some demonstrators attempted to attack British Asian residents in Luton. Following subsequent anti-Muslim protests organized by the UPL and Casuals United, the two groups merged to form the EDL.

The leaders of the UPL were the then twenty-five-year-old Steve Lennon (later to be known as Tommy Robinson, as I will refer to him for the rest of this book) and his relatives and associates. Robinson was a local man known among some to have formed the 'Ban the Luton Taliban' a few years earlier. He was known to be a Luton football lad who was hostile to local Muslim communities. When UPL was set up, Robinson had never expected it to expand outside of Luton and grow into a nationwide street movement. As he had been 'in trouble' and made 'enemies' in the non-political activities of his earlier life, he didn't want to use his real name as UPL was growing. At first, for fun, he called himself Wayne King, as a joke when talking to the press. He had no idea then that he would become a household name for being a far-right leader.

When UPL was formed, Robinson also set up websites called Save Luton, British Patriots against Islamic Extremism, and

United People of Luton, to get his message out to people. He also started doing radio interviews. It was at this time that a London millionaire businessman and former director of Pacific Capital Investment Management, Alan Lake, whose real name is Alan Ayling, contacted him. Lake was implicated in the inquiry into the Norwegian fascist Anders Behring Breivik, who killed seventy-seven people in the Norway massacre of 2011, and was questioned by the police authorities at the time. But when he contacted Robinson, Robinson had never heard of him.

Around the same time, prior to the formation of the EDL, Alan Lake had set up a small far-right group called March for England. Lake is known as a Zionist, and while using March for England to demonstrate against British Muslims, the nascent growth of an anti-Islamic street movement in Luton gave him hope that he could develop his own pro-Israel agenda. He therefore invited Robinson and those working with him to meet and talk at his £500,000 Barbican flat. Robinson was curious and said yes. Present at that meeting with Lake were Robinson, Kevin Carroll, Robinson's uncle Darren, Paul Ray (who later became a strong opponent of Robinson), and Ann Marchini, a north-London-based property investor who co-founded and is said to have funded the EDL.

At the time, Alan Lake saw the potential of a street movement under Robinson's leadership and wanted to 'reach out to more physical groups like football fans and get them involved'. In other words, he wanted to mobilize and use the 'masses' to do the job for him, to spread anti-Muslim racial hatred.

According to BNP leader Nick Griffin, it was under Lake's financial backing that the EDL agreed to disconnect itself officially from the anti-Zionist BNP. He said it was Lake's cash which made EDL's upcoming nationwide activities possible. It also opened the group's access to anti-Muslim, pro-Israel international networks and resources. Griffin claims that Lake named the group English Defence League to echo its counterpart in the USA, the far-right Jewish Defence League. Robinson refutes these claims, stating that the EDL has never been funded by Alan Lake and that the naming of the group was completely unconnected and that they were simply following the name of the Welsh Defence League when the movement went national. Then BNP member John Sheridan (aka Chris Renton) from Bristol provided the technology for the group to be set up online. I trace Robinson's relationship with Lake in greater detail, however, in Chapter 3.

At this point, Robinson still had no intention of revealing his true identity and coming under the spotlight. He continued to wear a mask during activities. He let Kevin Carroll, his cousin, be the first among them to speak to the camera, without disguise, about the group. In the BBC documentary *Young, British, and Angry*, Kevin Carroll spoke about how and why they got involved, giving the EDL leadership its first media spotlight.

A national far-right street movement thus began – support-ed by the wealthy, scripted and administrated by several exper-ienced far-right activists and given effect by the muscle of a disenfranchised working class. As I was to see, racist ideologies are preached and reproduced from the top down.

The ideologists and strategists of the group were able to tap into the disenfranchisement and alienation of large numbers of working-class people. As the name EDL suggests, it is the 'English way of life' which its activists and followers are led to feel is under threat and which they are aiming to defend. These men and women are motivated to mobilize their anger on an unprecedented scale. But what exactly is the 'English way of life'? What is being 'English'? Since when have those who joined or supported the movement begun to feel 'English' and under threat? When and how have they become, in their eyes, the 'outsiders'?

I prepared to go to Luton to find the answer. Before I set out, I checked up on the EDL's Luton Division and attempted to get in touch with activists. Again, no one answered. But the membership number on the webpage kept going up. The speed of growth didn't seem compatible with the group's supposed level of secrecy.

Luton was a mystery to me. A predominantly white town (68 per cent of its population of 203,600 are white and 18.9 per cent are of South Asian origin), with some of the country's worst ethnic tensions. The EDL originated here from a place called Farley Hill, a council estate built after the Second World War to replace homes destroyed in the German bombing. The estate now has a population of 11,560, of which more than 60 per cent are white British.

I arrived in Farley Hill having conjured the image of a rough, white estate plagued by far-right groups. But my first impressions were very different: it appeared quiet, and residents were going about their daily chores, keeping themselves to themselves. I looked but couldn't find the Union Jacks that you see in places like some of the run-down estates in Dagenham, east London. As I strolled around the blocks of flats, a white man with a shaved head walked past and looked at me with some curiosity. I nodded at him and went up to talk. His name was Derek, a road maintenance worker for the borough council. He sighed quietly at the mention of his job without wanting to elaborate at first. He was forty-eight, living alone in one of the flats here, although he wasn't willing to show me where exactly.

For the first five minutes of the conversation, he made no attempt to disguise his wariness and suspicion, but seemed interested in carrying on, perhaps because he rarely got the chance to air his thoughts. When asked about the variety of communities on the estate and relations between them, Derek shook his head hopelessly. 'What happens around here is happening all over Luton. Luton is no longer for the Lutonians.'

'Lutonians?' I'd never heard the term.

'Yes,' he said, frowning. 'Too many foreigners have come here in the past ten years.'

'Foreigners?'

'Yes, foreigners,' he repeated anxiously, looking into the distance with his vacant blue eyes, repeating the word 'foreigners', as if he had forgotten that I wasn't a local. 'We're losing our own culture here. Our culture is being submerged and I feel I'm being treated like a second-class citizen in my own country. I feel like an outsider.'

'But why are you feeling so uncomfortable with other cultures?' I asked gently.

'No, it isn't that I can't have other cultures around me.' He became a little nervous. 'It's just that many of them have been coming into Luton to work in the past ten years ... Now they're everywhere.'

'So they're new migrants?' I asked. 'Where are they from?'

'Mainly from eastern Europe. The Poles, etc.'

'So they're mainly white Europeans?' I confirmed.

Derek nodded, but added that it was the Muslims in the neighbourhood that he really has problems with. Despite the fact that new migration has come primarily from eastern Europe, Derek's anger has been aimed mainly at the non-whites, and he blames all Luton's ills on British Muslims, many of whom are born and bred here.

'I was at the army parade in 2009 ... and I was so angry how those Muslims could disrespect our soldiers.'

But when asked if he had joined the EDL, Derek instantly became defensive. 'No, no.' He looked at me self-assuredly. 'I'm not a racist, you know.'

Derek's awareness of the implications of association with the EDL interested me. He clearly didn't want to be branded a racist – and no one did here. The legacy of Stephen Lawrence has moved society forward by making racism *officially* unacceptable. It's become a dirty and shameful word from which even people with straightforward racist views would want to distance themselves.

I wanted to understand the issues behind Derek's anger. But often when I asked questions, he struggled for words. He rubbed his forehead uncomfortably and narrowed his eyes, accentuating his deep wrinkles. A sigh always preceded his hard-found words. As for most people on this estate, as I was to find out, unemployment is one of the major concerns. Derek said: 'Young people can't find work, you know, it's a terrible situation ... I'm lucky in that sense – my three children are all in employment ... and they've moved away from Luton.'

Since the closure of the Vauxhall car plant (which saw its peak of production in 1967) at the beginning of the century, with the loss of 2,500 jobs, and the rapid decline of manufacturing industries in Luton, many young people have left Farley Hill to seek work opportunities elsewhere. According to a local government report from 2012, entitled 'Luton's Labour market', the unemployment rate in Luton is 10.3 per cent, higher than the average rate overall for England (8.2 per cent). Skills gaps are found mainly in engineering, marketing and communication industries, owing partly to lower levels of qualifications, education and training. Many of the young people have moved to work in London, like Derek's children. Those left behind are often in low-paid service jobs and others remain jobless and on benefits. In 2013, the number of benefit claimants in both Luton North East (3.9 per cent) and Luton South East (4.9 per cent) was higher than the national total for England, 3.7 per cent. As the future looks bleak for many working-age people, it becomes easy to lay blame on non-Lutonians – or to go farther, and resort to a race-based analysis.

Before he went back to his flat, Derek shook his head again and said the words that I was to hear time and time again on this estate: 'I don't believe in these politicians any more. They do nothing for us white working class.'

At the top of the estate, I walked past a detached house with an England flag on the roof, the first one I'd seen around here. I decided to knock on the door to have a chat with the occupier. A fifty-something bald white man with tattoos on his arms opened the door. He frowned at the sight of me.

'I'm sorry to trouble you,' I said politely. 'But it's just that your flag on the roof got me curious.' I explained my research and asked whether he knew of the EDL.

He looked puzzled and kept the door half open. 'I'm not a member of any group,' he said. 'All I do is stick up for the Englishmen. That's all.'

'Stick up for the Englishmen?' I asked. 'What does that mean?'

'England is my castle. Do you understand? England is my castle.' He repeated the words with conviction, opening the door slightly.

'Englishmen are the king of the castle England. Just like this house is my castle and I'm the king of the castle ... I don't care about what goes on in the outside world.'

'What do you do for a living?' I asked.

'I work for the borough council ... Work and home is all I have and all I do.' He told me he's been doing contract cleaning for eighteen years.

I nodded. Then he looked at me and asked: 'Wouldn't you put up your flag in your country?'

'No, I wouldn't,' I said, smiling.

'But you've got your traditions over there in China, haven't you? ... with your chopsticks and all that?'

I tried not to laugh.

Then he turned serious again: 'The flag is for soldiers in Iraq. I don't think our lads should be out there.'

'So you're against the war?'

'Yes, I am. I believe the soldiers should be brought back here. I support them and that's why I put up the flag.'

'You're against Britain going to war, aren't you?' I wanted him to say more.

'Yes, as far as I'm concerned it was the US who started the war and it is our lads who died over there. I think Britain shouldn't have got involved in it. We got enough trouble already and we don't need no more. We don't need terrorism and people getting blown up. We don't need that. It never used to be like that. Never used to be terrorism years ago. We don't need people inciting terrorism over here.'

Well, at least we agreed on the war. By this point, he had opened the door wide and loosened up. I went back to my question about the EDL and his possible involvement.

'I know they hold all their meetings and rallies in the Parrot. I know they've got a fair bit of support around here. They're not all for trouble.'

'Have you considered joining the group?' I asked.

He became defensive, just like Derek. 'I'm not a racist or anything like that.'

He carried on: 'When Tommy Robinson went through Bury Park in his car, a bloke came up and slapped him straight in his face. But he didn't get up and slap him back. He's not racist ... I agree with some of the stuff they say, but I don't want to get any feedback from the council and I don't want to lose my job ... You can't join something like that if you work for the borough council. And I don't want to bring trouble for my family. I am a family man, a working man. I work for my family.'

'But you definitely support them, don't you?'

'I support groups like the EDL because they speak for us. The EDL defends the English heritage ...'

'What do you mean by English heritage?' I wanted him to elaborate.

He went quiet, looking embarrassed.

'You feel English,' I went on. 'Do you see any difference between feeling English and feeling British?'

'I don't know.' He struggled to find words, and squeezed out a nervous smile.

'What makes you most angry?'

He shook his head and said: 'Those politicians … I wouldn't vote for the main political parties. All they do is bring in cuts … I'm a working-class man and everything I've got is what I worked for. I'm angry about what they're doing to our lives.'

At this point, I totally empathized with his feelings of being deprived and marginalized by the political elite. Austerity measures have hit the working class the hardest. But he was directing his anger on to ethnic minority communities in the area – despite having moved into Farley Hill only in 2002 – and had decided to find the answer to his misfortunes in the perceived 'mixing of cultures'.

'Why do they have to build mosques in this area?' he said bitterly. 'The Kings Arms pub down the road has been bought off by a Muslim and converted into a mosque. How ridiculous is that!

'It's just they're taking over …' he carried on. The feeling of being 'swamped' seemed to need no justification.

'Do you know EDL's stance on immigration?'

'I wouldn't know that.' He shrugged, then, detaching himself from the group once again: 'Don't get me wrong. I don't always agree with everything the EDL's saying.'

'But being English and defending that identity is very important to you?' I asked.

'I just think that they stick up for the Englishmen ... because nobody else will stick up for us. Nobody's in our corner.'

I decided to go down to the Parrot, the estate pub known locally as the 'EDL pub', where the group regularly holds its meetings and rallies. It was empty. I felt thirsty and in need of a boost, so I walked up to the young barman and asked for an energy drink. He shook his head quietly. I asked for a coffee. He went in and asked a woman to come out to answer me. I guessed she was the manageress of the pub.

'Do you have any energy drinks here?' I asked hopefully.

'No,' she said grudgingly.

'Coffee?' I asked.

'No, we don't have it.' She looked concerned, and was about to walk away.

'I'm sorry,' I said. 'Can I have a Coke then?'

She turned and fetched a glass and a Coke without a word. I felt a silent hostility that I don't usually experience in pubs in London.

'Can I talk to you for a second?' I asked her politely as she handed me the glass of Coke. I explained my project and the reason why I was there. I asked about EDL's activities, but she was uneasy, a frown drawn across her face.

'Can you help me?' I pleaded.

'I know them ...' she said quietly. 'I know them from when they were babies.'

'You mean members of the EDL?'

'I mean those who run the EDL,' she said, lowering her voice more. 'But I can't talk about it. I'm not gonna tell you anything.'

'Why not? Why can't you talk about it?' I asked.

She simply shook her head. She looked so uncomfortable, as if she had been told not to speak to anyone from outside about the EDL.

'Who did you say you know?' I persisted.

'The head of the EDL.'

'Tommy Robinson? You know him personally?' I probably looked unconvinced.

'Yes, of course,' she said, holding up her mobile phone to show me his number.

'I'd like to talk to him, actually,' I said. It would be good to see the fish in his own pond.

'If you like, I'll call him and ask him to meet you.' She gave in a little.

'Really? Would he reply to your call?'

'Yes, of course!' It was a big favour, given the pressure she was under. But Robinson replied, via this pub manageress, and said that he was in an interview. I left a note and a phone number for him to call me.

On the other side of Farley Hill, several residents expressed their contempt for far-right groups. As it turned out, St Margaret's Club, an Irish pub, has a very different clientele to the Parrot. They are all Irish Catholics, and find far-right politics alien and distasteful. The mere mention of the word 'EDL' seemed to surprise the three customers who were drinking at the bar. Unanimously, they called the group racist.

'Tommy Robinson is a wanker,' one of them said, making the others laugh. 'When I saw their leaflets through my door, I just felt disgusted. I wouldn't even bother to read through it. I just threw it away. They must be joking if they think they're gonna get me on their side!'

'This side of the estate is more liberal, you see,' another regular customer explained. 'We're more friendly around here than the Parrot.'

He told me he works as a builder and has been living in the area for years. 'This is our area and Tommy Robinson wouldn't ever dare come in here. He's a racist, an arsehole.'

Another commented: 'I bet Tommy Robinson's kids must be having a very uncomfortable time at school … I mean his kids will have to interact with other kids from all sorts of backgrounds … and with a father like that!'

In the next couple of weeks, I carried on walking around the estate and came across several young EDL activists and supporters. Young people make up an important part of the group's composition. Joining the EDL is as easy as joining a local football team, and the loose 'membership' doesn't seem to require any prerequisite level of work for the group. The youth I met all seemed confident in what they believed in. Aron, for instance, an EDL activist, seemed proud to reveal his involvement. When asked his reasons for joining the group, he repeated EDL's official line without hesitation: 'We need to fight the Muslims. It's a wicked religion. We can't have the sharia law in this country.'

'Why do you think you're being threatened with sharia law?' I asked.

Aron couldn't give an answer, but said he had to go. I asked to meet him in the Parrot in an hour. He agreed, but never showed up. He sent me a text instead: 'I don't fink I can make it rite now. Sumfink has cum up. Maybe sum other time. Sorry. I'm sure you'll see sum1 in the pub neway. I've been told not to say nefink.'

The majority of EDL activists and followers seemed politically convinced but unwilling to elaborate on their personal and political history and how their ideas and activism had evolved.

Then I met Darren, an unusually open forty-eight-year-old born-and-bred Lutonian who grew up on the outskirts of Farley Hill.

I went to visit him in his family home in suburban Luton, a tranquil neighbourhood not far from the airport. He and his family live in a three-bedroom terrace house facing a green piece of land, free from the sound of droning traffic. When I arrived in the early evening, Darren had just got home from a day's work as a painter and decorator in London. He wiped his hands on his work clothes, still covered in paint, and shook my hand. Then he led me into his lounge, which looked almost newly decorated, with bright white paint on the walls. The place looked almost uninhabited, no family pictures, paintings or ornaments. I asked whether he'd moved in not long ago. 'No, we've been here for years.'

Then Darren introduced me to his wife June and two sons – the older son, twenty-five years old, was now working as a bricklayer, and the younger son, who was studying journalism at the University of Bedfordshire. They nodded at me, smiled, and said nothing. Darren led me into the dining area of their kitchen, where we sat down to talk while his wife and children sat watching TV in the lounge.

The first thing he said that surprised me was that he had just ordered my first book, *Chinese Whispers*, and had read the first hundred pages. He did this in order to know a bit about me. 'I'm telling my colleagues on the building site about the book,' he said. 'Honestly, I didn't realize … I didn't look at it from that point of view before. Now I think we've all been shafted … How come our wages have dropped this much? Lads coming over from other countries aren't getting nothing, from your book. If they can't get what they want and we are not happy with it, whose interests is it suiting?'

I listened attentively as he spoke, with a relatively strong local accent. He went on, with his calm but firm tone of voice: 'It's suiting whoever is driving the economy into this mess. No one, no one's better off. The undocumented are worse off because they're the ones who can't get out [of their situation].' I noted the word 'undocumented' (as opposed to 'illegals') which Darren had adopted – a word I use in my book which I don't see used even in the liberal press. This articulate and reasonable-sounding man in front of me didn't sit well with my preconception of an EDL activist. In the following year, I listened to his story of how his political convictions had evolved and how he came to the realization that the far right was no longer his alternative.

Darren came from an immigrant family, both parents from Dublin, where they lived in a slum. His dad arrived in Luton in the 1950s, looking for work. 'That was a time when the "no

Irish, no dogs" racism was common, and Dad came straight into all that,' he said. 'Mum followed. I was born here in Luton and grew up on Corncastle Road, which is renowned for not being very nice and probably the worst street in Luton back then.'

Darren's father died of cancer when he was twelve, and his mother, to whom he was very close, passed away the following year. The whole family was abruptly split up: one of Darren's five sisters, divorced, moved with her child to live with Darren while his two brothers went to start a new life in Nottingham. His was a childhood that required him to grow up quickly, and was full of material struggles and hardship. Life was just about getting by and surviving.

Darren's family home where he grew up was a council house, amid a diverse community of Irish, Scottish, Afro-Caribbean and Asian families. He called Luton 'a unique little place', an industrial town with all these communities that had come together since the late 1950s. 'Immigrants arrived more or less in the same five decades,' he said. 'Back in 1976, 1978, West Indian people came over and settled in the town with the Irish. The Irish went through the same bedsits as the West Indians. The Irish and the West Indians have a lot in common, not least their liking for Guinness, and they got on great ... Farley Hill as a whole was an honest community. It's so close knit and people help each other. Everyone would give you their last ten pence.'

Aside from the collective community spirit, however, Darren grew up as a lonely child. He was visited by a social worker, whom he feared would take him away. Feeling angry at the loss of his parents and his loneliness, he was often rude and in his own words 'abusive' to the social worker. She went off the scene totally after one visit, and even now Darren sometimes wonders what has happened to her. School wasn't always a happy place either; teachers weren't always kind and caning was a frequent part of the education.

The permanent feeling of isolation and solitude as an adolescent led Darren to seek comfort and company in collective sport. He became goalkeeper of the school's football team. One PE teacher who broke his nose for discipline happened to be the only adult Darren said he looked up to in his teenage years. 'I probably needed that discipline. And at least he recognized I was there,' he said with a hint of nostalgia in his voice.

Football was where he eventually found belonging. And he wanted to defend 'that something' that he could belong to. 'There, you find people who you can stick with, thick and thin.'

As for many adolescents from working-class families in the area, football became a big part of Darren's life. It made him feel alive.

Luton's a small club and small fan base, but multicultural. You had everyone in it ... The Indian lads, Afro-Caribbean lads and the white Irish, Scottish lads were all always there on the terraces. You couldn't get more mixed. I met all my friends on the terraces. It was a great place to grow up. There were very few Muslim lads, though ... maybe their dads didn't let them go. So you could never get to know them on the terraces ... It was when we played local football that we got to know Muslim lads that way. Some of them were trying to introduce football into their community and get linked to local clubs ...

Darren enjoyed the active social life built around football during all those years. Before and after each match, lads would go down the pubs and drink together. They'd almost always end up in the Mad Hatters, a notorious 'rough' nightclub opened in the 1970s by an athlete and popular among football lads in the 1980s. Good old days, those were.

But growing up on Luton's football terraces wasn't always easy. It wasn't exactly a kind environment for a young boy. In the early 1970s, as Darren recalled most distinctively, football was very violent and racist. 'In the 1970s it went unchecked ... You have football violence in 1970, 1971 to 1973 ... then the far right started moving in during 1974–77 as they thought it's great, there's a vehicle here [football], we'll jump on it. They organized them. Then they came to towns like Luton, which was very multi-ethnic ...'

Luton fans were then watching big, well-supported teams coming to their town. 'They're calling it their big day out. Millwall, for instance, they used to come in, in the 1970s, and they were better fighters and very well organized. They would stand in our ends, keep it low, and when they decided, they'll kick off and beat everyone up. Truly, there's a difference between a working-class lad and a Millwall.

'None of us wanted to have a fight at that stage ... I was only a kid. I was watching it for a good five seasons. Then when I was getting a bit older, I saw all these older blokes getting beaten up and running away. The Millwall fans were stabbing people. It was just all-out violence. We had 1974 when Millwall went to the Luton end and stabbed two Luton supporters ... and we had

Millwall down here in 1975 doing the same. There were some real horrific injuries. Luton supporters got hurt all the time.'

Then Darren touched his back, from top to bottom:

One of my friends from Farley Hill, for no reason at all, was slashed for that long; he needed fifty stitches. That was the West Ham boys. They did it at your back; you wouldn't know he was behind you. There was someone getting killed somewhere every week at football. I got beaten up loads of times by West Ham ... West Ham, Millwall, Chelsea, Arsenal. It was always when the teams come out ...

West Ham, racist, Millwall, racist, Chelsea, racist. Chelsea had a big racist element but they were more subtle ... They wouldn't want to declare it until they were doing it. You wouldn't be able to work them out as easily as with West Ham, because West Ham came in with massive numbers. Arsenal in the 1980s had their racists come down and infiltrate. But that went away fast as they had a lot of black supporters ... And there were some northern racist teams as well ...'

I remember watching 5,000 West Ham supporters coming in and you had about 1,500 strong men singing Gas the Jews ... 'I've never felt more like gassing the Jews than when West Ham wins,' they sang. They hated black people, too. If you were white and standing with your mates who were black to fight West Ham, these men hated you the worst, a strange pecking order of hate. They see you as a race traitor. My friends who I grew up with, four out of ten are black. You couldn't let your mates down, so you had to stand with them. So then you got targeted for that ... So everyone became a target. That's how that solidified ...

Darren was only fifteen then. Out of that culture of football violence, a new generation of Lutonians was coming through, who fought back at that violence and starting defending their own town. A local gang culture was coming into being. Looking back now, Darren said with rational distance, he doesn't want to romanticize it because there's nothing romantic about violence. But the football gang, in his eyes, acted as the defenders of the people who couldn't fight for themselves in football grounds. Along with other lads from Farley Hill, Darren started a local gang called Migs (Men in Gear, referring to their clothing preferences, such as Burberry, Nike, etc.), primarily a white and West Indian gang. Lutonians called it the biggest gang outside the British Pakistani community gangs. This was the beginning of a localist sentiment in Luton.

Darren described how much the formation of the gang began to change things:

> The teams would come and they were asked to get out of the Luton end, instead of the Luton supporters running and being scared and trying to get out. Some terraces are very dangerous; if you fell over you could get tramped over. I remember this particular time when I came in thinking it would be the usual, and it wasn't. They [the other team's supporters] were trying to get out. So then you feel like you're taking control of your own community ... That was a turnaround. Luton got put on the map of football gangs. It meant all the Londoners couldn't come to Luton and do that [violence] ever again. We're a lot smarter than you think.

Football gang culture continued. Gang rivalry grew, and working-class neighbourhoods continued to be affected by it. In the mid- to late 1980s, the Migs clashed with the local Pakistani youth gang, Bury Park Youth Posse (BPYP). As these two were the biggest gangs in town, the feud went on for quite a while. By and large, it was young guys fighting for territory, mostly in the form of turf wars over drugs. Little fallouts and grudges snowballed, which kept the youth of the two communities apart from each other. Occasional gang fights became the only interaction between them.

However, Darren believed that Luton never had a problem with the local Pakistani community (until quite recently), and that fights between gangs were simply a youth matter that people in both communities have long grown out of. After all, the two gangs were born out of similar contexts. Although not football-based, the BPYP was formed out of their need to defend themselves, just as the Migs organized to defend themselves from outside football team supporters.

Despite the high level of violence, there was a strong emotional need for Darren to remain in the football scene in the early days. He smiled as if he was amused by the memory: 'There was a strange thrill about it all. I was making all these new friends and allegiances, so it was a social thing for me … I was drawn to it, even though I feared getting beaten up. It was like we all suffered together … You could smell burger, fear, urine, beer, sweat, all in the air. Strangely, I felt alive …'

I saw for myself that social space that Darren needed so much when I joined him for the Luton versus Braintree match in April 2014. It was the biggest match he'd seen that year, attended by over 10,000 fans, who were all eagerly hoping that Luton would finally rejoin the League after five years. That day, on meeting me in front of the town hall, Darren handed me an orange-and-white Luton scarf and a T-shirt that he'd prepared for me to wear, in support of his team. My name was written on the back of the T-shirt. His younger son came with him, and we walked to join the others at the White House, a pub frequented by Luton fans before the match. There, Darren's older son and six-year-old grandson were waiting for him.

The morale among the fans was high. The White House was so packed with fans that it took us half an hour to get through the queue and get our first drink. I was introduced to many of Darren's mates whom he'd gotten to know over the years through their mutual love of football. Like Darren, they were family men now, Migs in name but not in deed. One of his best mates is a local man of West Indian parentage, nicknamed Barty, who's known Darren since their school days decades ago. Darren and his wife June have always said to me that Barty hasn't changed one bit since he was nineteen. Barty told me his main job is organizing and promoting music events and doing some DJ work. Darren and June used to go to gigs with him.

Barty's love of football made him a name in a book titled *Mig Down,* * published in 2005 and written by a man with the same name as the EDL's Tommy Robinson. This Tommy Robinson was also a Migs member, who wrote about the Migs and the Luton football scene without anyone's knowledge. The book apparently depicted a variety of Luton football characters

---

* *Mig Down*, published by Pennant Books, UK, in 2005, 'the story of Luton's Mig crew as told from the sharp end of football's frontline'.

unfavourably, to the anger of Stephen Lennon, EDL's Tommy Robinson (although Lennon himself was described as a 'natural-born leader'). Therefore, as an act of revenge, Stephen Lennon decided to use the author's name – also without informing him – when he became the EDL leader. Rumours say that the original Tommy Robinson has moved out of Luton and is now living in Spain.

Barty said that, like other Migs members, he only found out about the author making a character out of him in *Mig Down* after the book was published. But Barty in the book is a 'trustworthy mate', as many would describe him in reality. As Darren puts it, when you've been through so much on the terraces, getting beaten up together, you're mates for life.

Barty told me that Darren had introduced him to EDL events in the early days of the group in 2009. He didn't know what it was all about, and went on one demo in Luton. He quickly felt it wasn't for him. But if you ask Barty his views, to find out exactly where he drew the line, his answer is cheeky and elusive: 'I'm a lover, not a fighter.' As his mates would say, he's middle of the road. But eventually for Barty, EDL was just 'too right-wing'. As Darren explained more bluntly, 'When there's white racism, obviously a black man feels it first.'

The football ground is situated in the middle of Bury Park, the part of Luton with the highest concentration of British Asians. It felt a little awkward to be walking through this neighbourhood with a huge crowd of Luton football fans, especially as I knew I didn't look part of the scene. But Darren carried on talking to me in a relaxed manner as we walked through the streets. He described the old days when he used to come down here.

'When I was a kid, I used to come here for the only chicken shop in Luton, for some chicken and chips type of thing. Back then, you had a place called West Side Centre, a shopping complex. And we used to come down to a place called Funky Junction, to get our funky belts and jeans ...'

But that was before the 1980s when things started to change. Local white residents began to want to move out, as Bury Park was less and less of an attractive place to live, owing to the location of the football ground and the trouble and violence it had seen over the years. The neighbourhood bore the image of low-cost housing with low standards of living. Also, as cross-community relations began to deteriorate, some white residents moved out in favour of whiter neighbourhoods. As a result, shops in Bury Park gradually stopped catering for people of Darren's background and fashion tastes, and, as it happened, youngsters like him began to lose their interest in coming down here. He saw his favourite place, Funky Junction, shut down, amid the departure of many white residents from this area. As people started moving out through the 1980s, the high street began to look more 'Asian', with British Asian shops gradually becoming the majority.

Darren noted the changing ethnic landscape of Bury Park.

It happened with the old Irish community, too. As the community got older, some moved back to Ireland. So that community shrunk and shrunk. Young Irish always go where the work is. Anywhere. Nowadays it is Russians and Poles who settle down in Bury Park [owing mainly to its low housing costs. You can, for instance, rent a three-bedroom flat for £250–300 a month]. From 1985 onwards, for about twenty years, everything becomes more settled down and you have mostly South Asian population living in Bury Park. This is us, this is you, everything becomes fixed.

As we walked on, Darren said he is still recognized by some passers-by, from the old days of the Migs. He himself still spots faces of those involved in the drug scene in competition with the Migs. 'There's no more grudges now. We're all grown-ups. Sometimes we might give each other a nod as we walk past.'

But much more difficult is being recognized as part of 'the Carrolls in Luton'. During our second meeting, Darren revealed to me that he is the cousin of Kevin Carroll, the then deputy leader of the EDL. He told me he is Tommy Robinson's uncle. No one knows that Darren absolutely detests Kevin Carroll and they do not talk to each other, as I will elaborate on in later chapters. He doesn't get the chance to say that he has left the EDL. Everywhere Darren goes, the name of 'the Carrolls in Luton' will continue to sit heavy on his shoulders. When people at work talk about Kevin Carroll and he admits he's related, people look at each other and go quiet. When he goes into a pub and someone asks about Kevin Carroll, Darren is always worried that he might be asked what his surname is. 'If I reveal my surname, I would be talked to as if I were Kev Carroll. I don't get a chance.'

But as soon as Darren told me that he was one of 'the Carrolls in Luton', I couldn't disassociate him from that either. On many occasions, I repeated questions, probing as to his real thoughts and feelings. We often talked about race relations in

Luton. I wanted to understand what it all meant to him. Without exception, he always traced it back to the football culture in which he grew up.

Through the late 1970s, you had the National Front [NF] and British Movement who were jumping on our football. At the time I just understood it as them not liking my black mates and them not liking me because I got black mates. Looking back now, I understand the bigger picture: it's all contesting politics. You had white lads through this era adhering themselves to both the NF and the British Movement ... I was at school when NF affected my life for the first time. I saw black lads started fighting with the white lads. It was the first time I came to make a decision. It was all easy well up to then. We all went to football and enjoyed the game. Sometimes there were fights, other times none. But it was always black and white together. Then when NF made big inroads on the terraces and infiltrated all the communities with leaflets, whether you liked it or not, you had to be involved. You had to choose your ideology. You had to work out which side you're on. The black mates felt very threatened. At first, I remember saying to them, what is all this about? They said, 'You don't know because you're not black.' If you sat on the fence and watch your black mates getting abused, that wouldn't be acceptable. So you find out who you are, without ever thinking you had to do that.

When it was West Ham, you wouldn't get the NF going to home games, because they'll be less tolerated. You'll get NF coming to places like Luton and attach themselves to

West Ham. One time we were playing West Ham. West Ham had come down in force, massive, 5,000–6,000 of them ... There was all NF up there. They always came down in big numbers. The police didn't let us out, so we all got to go in. We all thought we're gonna get battered. What happened was the NF were urinating on everyone. We were all crammed and couldn't move. They were pissing on our heads. To this day, I still carry some of that humiliation. The most humiliating thing for me was they were all laughing when urinating on us. It was the laughing.

Darren looked indignant, saying he'll never forget this past, pointing to his head. 'I save it all up here.'

One time, he got chased by the NF, from Hazelbury Crescent to Biscuit Mills, normally a twenty-five-minute walk. He was running with ten other friends, among them his West Indian friend who was a bricklayer, with the NF men shouting behind, 'Get the nigger, get the nigger lover!' Darren was behind his friend at one stage, and he could hear the flap of his friend's boots. Overtaking was out of the question, as he had no laces in his boots. Luckily, in the end, they got away.

Then, in 1985, Millwall came down, with 10,000 hooligans, for the Luton Town versus Millwall match, in the sixth round of the FA Cup. All the London fans turned out. A lot of people got hurt and even a police officer was kicked to death. The *Guardian* in 1985 called it 'a night football suffered a slow death': 'Droogs charging across the Kenilworth Road turf, hurling seats and golf balls at policemen in full retreat. A knife thrown at the home goalkeeper ... The soccer special with its ceilings torn off and innards gutted so completely that a British Rail spokesman said it was like a bomb had exploded inside some of the carriages.'

Darren remembered: 'We came up against proper skinheads, boots and jackets, loads of them everywhere, from Millwall. West Ham and other racist groups were also sticking together. I thought we were gonna get murdered there.'

With the subsequent crackdown on football violence, that level of trouble in Luton was never again repeated, although street fights between Luton fans (the younger generation of Migs) and racist Millwall fans have continued to this day. Otherwise, football matches can be peaceful. The day I joined them, there was a lot of excitement among the fans, but they seemed to behave in an orderly fashion throughout the match with Braintree. Even when Luton lost and was delayed in its promotion back to the League, its fans were civilized enough to applaud the winners as they walked off the pitch.

I visited Darren regularly at his home. He has a firm routine: after work, he returns home around five, has dinner with his family and spends the evening resting in front of the TV. When I was there, his wife June never spoke much, but always smiled and made me coffee, leaving us to talk in the kitchen. This time, I tried to talk to her. 'Your house is spotless,' I said. 'It's a change from my place.'

She giggled. 'Oh, that's because my job in town is part-time [at the airport] and I have plenty of time to clean the house!' She brought me a cup of coffee and Darren a tea. Then she pulled the door shut behind us.

Darren and June have gone through a lot together. She has struggled through bad times with him, for which he's grateful. Since the early 1980s, Darren has been working in the building trade. That didn't come easy.

I went straight from school into a twelve-month equal opportunity, a government-run scheme, down the road in Bury Park, in 1982. They promised me a job, but I didn't get one. It was slave labour: I got picked up six in the morning ... We worked all the top quality work in London ... They picked us up at 7.30 p.m. again and sent us back to Luton, where I had to do more work, till around 9 p.m. The company worked me at least thirteen hours a day, and I was paid only £25 a week. I thought I might get an apprenticeship at the end of it. They said, if you want that, you'll have to go self-employed and get yourself to a college. So I worked and paid my college ... I thought I'd better go cheap, to survive ... £15 a day I worked for, in those days, on domestics and building sites.

After moving from one rented flat to the next for a long while, Darren and June managed to get a mortgage for a house, for £20,000, back in 1985, and later on, with two children, moved to a slightly bigger house which cost them £36,000. 'We were raising the two young sons there. With a big mortgage, we were broke. With the mortgage, we had nothing,' he recalled. In 1989, during the recession, Darren couldn't get any work for a while. It was a tough time. When he managed to get some casual decorating work in London, he used to hide on the train to work

40

because he couldn't afford the train fare. Each time, he went to the toilet just as the ticket inspector came into the carriage. Sometimes he got caught, and had to plead with the officer. One of them took pity on him and let him off several times.

Darren always remembered this period of his life with a sigh – almost a sigh of relief that he had got through. He was accustomed to hardship, and never ceased to see himself as a working-class man. 'My dad was a dustman. I'm working-class; it's in my breeding. And we all voted Labour in the old days. We wouldn't even mention Tories in our house.'

Darren looked back at the 1980s as if it were a black-and-white era, without any colour. The struggle remained fresh in his memory, as he described the 1980s as a 'real hardcore decade for the working class', following on from the Winter of Discontent of 1978/79, which was characterized by the nationwide strikes over pay rises. At the time, he felt too young and immature to understand it all. Looking back, he realized that, in the past, individual working-class people were never afraid to stand up and have a say.

> We used to spend a lot of our time in the Luton Labour Club, men and women, talking and debating about what went on in politics and society … We'd had that since the 1970s and all the way to the 1980s … There was very much a community spirit back then. We had the Toxteth riot of 1981 … We had the miners having a say … At the Luton Labour Club, the miners used to come in and collect …'
>
> But it's been different since. The community spirit was all smashed during the Thatcher years … Now there's only

the Tory club in town, no more Labour clubs. For years now, you feel you have to keep your head down all the time. And for the first time, many working-class people were feeling that they've been written off. They felt lost. They lost their pride and collectiveness ...

That decade saw the beginning of a continuous contraction in manufacturing, with thousands of job losses in Luton. Falling living standards and poverty deepened divisions between communities, which paved the way for the infiltration of far-right groups. According to the anti-racist campaign Hope Not Hate, the 1980s saw an increase in serious racist attacks here. Then came the three-day Luton riot in July 1981, a response to a time when the working class were on the defensive: there'd been a higher level of surveillance and more powers for the police. Back then, Luton saw black and white youths in working-class neighbourhoods joining together against injustice. The resistance against racism and racist attacks was formed by both black and white Lutonians.

Darren remembered that the NF came to town again that day, adding to the number of local NF skinheads. Together, over a hundred of them entered a cafeteria in High Town. There was a feeling that something big was going to happen that night as skirmishes built up around town during the day. A British Indian man Darren knew at school picked up a brick and threw it through the café window. The skinheads came out and Darren recognized some of their faces. Around twelve of them had swastikas in the middle of their foreheads and on their necks. They'd been walking around town. The owners of the café, two middle-aged Italian men on their own, didn't invite the skinheads in but couldn't just turn them out.

That night, everyone was out in Luton. The man who had led Darren in his apprenticeship was arrested during the riot. But because of football, Darren said he didn't want to get involved. I was puzzled. Because of football? Darren looked slightly embarrassed, and explained to me that football was everything to him. 'I thought, if I get nicked for rioting here, it'll affect my football. That's what I lived for, you see. The rioters were people who didn't go to football. They were out against the then Home Secretary William Whitelaw's Sus law. I know black lads who were affected by it. I didn't used to know about the Sus law until the black lads told me. I only knew of racism on the terraces ... They were also out rioting against the NF stirring up communities ...'

Although not there himself, Darren was well aware that the riot was 'black and white together'. At this point he sounded almost proud, raising his voice slightly: 'White lads all joined in the riot, too. The Luton riot was purely a copycat from Brixton and Toxteth riots.'

As for the NF, they petered out, at least in Luton. They even changed their dress and tried to be more casual, to fit in on the terraces. But skinheads are skinheads through and through. Darren said: 'They didn't quite cut the mustard with the wear, so it was a big giveaway ... They were still there in the mid-1980s. But by the late 1980s, the NF was gone from football ... Prior to that, it was all political and racism. The Casuals, multicultural and multiracial, took a foothold and defeated the NF. Since the Casuals, it was all about who looked the smartest. It was like a new order coming ...'

Sadly, despite the multicultural composition of the Luton fan base and the history of fighting the racist teams, since the 2000s Luton's football scene and the Migs have gradually developed an antagonistic relationship with the local Muslim population, a spillover from gang fights in the previous decade. A large part of that negative sentiment was focused on culture and cultural differences. As Muslim youth were outside the local football culture, where allegiance to the local team is paramount, it seemed easy for Islamophobia to grow among the football fans. Street fights, some ferocious ones, between the Migs and the local BPYP gang increased. 'All you need is twenty lads on one side of the road and another twenty on the other side, and it goes off. Simple as that. The fights went both ways: sometimes the BPYP lads started it, but Migs were no angels.'

The relationship between the Migs and local Muslim youth deteriorated through the 2000s as news of Luton men killed in Afghanistan reached town. At one point, Migs members even attempted to offer support to the Plymouth gang (the Plymouth Argyle fans), the Central Element, to help them fight the Muslim youth in Bury Park.

BPYP later faded out into two main gangs, the Yellas and the Gabinos. Meanwhile, the first-generation Migs have formed families and gradually fell out of the gang culture. Darren said: 'Nowadays, the lads are all grown men … When they walk past me on the street, they sometimes still call me by my old nickname, Ging. But no more fights.'

I wondered how Darren, centrally involved in Luton's football scene, sees the link between Luton's football fan base and the EDL. For instance, Casuals United is part of the EDL and calls itself 'uniting UK's football tribes against the Jihadists'. Darren told me that Casuals United has nothing to do with the original Casuals who fought the NF. They are in fact two different groups. He said:

> In Luton, there isn't that necessary connection between football and groups like the EDL. Some of the EDL people don't even go to football … It's easy nicking the name and calling yourselves Casuals, because then you got lads coming to the band of the Casuals. Like the old NF skinheads nicked the Reggae movement look, didn't they? The original Casuals [which defeated the NF] were just geezers, of all ethnic backgrounds. But these boys, the Casuals [United], they're braindeads, aligned to the political far right. They are not even at football. They're only Casuals in name but not by nature. They're tricking young minds with their name.

Darren sounds much more a regionalist and localist than a nationalist.

> Originally football lads were the first to be part of the EDL, but that soon went – it went as soon as it arrived, because it's not everyone's cup of tea. When it [the EDL movement] stopped being Luton, forget it for me. A lot of the [football] lads were just testing the water and seeing what it was all about. They soon left, after a couple of demos, for the same reasons that I did [see Chapter 2]. Yes, in Luton, there was the football connection [with EDL], but it wasn't always there. You just couldn't go on those demos and come back to tell your black mates all about it.

Good or bad, football was what shaped Darren. I asked him whether he ever regrets his involvement with the Migs and the football gang culture. He lowered his head and paused for thought. Then he spoke, clearly and slowly: 'When we were doing it, you think when you've had enough, you grow up and it's all over. But it hasn't. That's what I learn about life as well – the legacy gets passed down, so you've got to be careful. I was too young at the time to realize that.' Today, the Migs are still around as the youth hear stories of the past and want to emulate it. They want to belong to the football scene, and take up the name in order to forge that connection.

'Even to this day, when I go into town, people come up to me and want to shake my hands, asking me if I'm all right. Because of my age, I find it an embarrassment to be recognized as one of the founders of Migs. And above all, my son has had trouble when he goes to school where people say to him, "Your dad is a Mig." But you are who you've been; it follows you. There's nothing you can do about it. The legacy, it has legs of its own.'

'I can't leave Luton. I just love it. I just feel I've got to be here for it. Sometimes not Luton for me, but me for Luton. My church. My family ... Just can't leave the place.' This is what Darren said to me one evening on one of my visits. But his strong localist feelings were tested when he witnessed changes to the town that he wasn't prepared for.

Drugs have become a huge problem, across the board, in Farley Hill where Darren grew up. No matter what drugs. 'Opposite the Parrot pub, you have some lovely little council flats. The council just put crackies in there. It was never like that. Heroin was creeping in. It's all about greed. If you're not working, you're gonna be taking or selling drugs.' And Darren is only one among many who expresses this frustration with the deteriorating environment of the estates.

Luton's post-war estates like Farley Hill were already in decline in the 1970s as the local government stopped investing money. Affordable social housing was in limited supply and estates became overcrowded and fell into disrepair. As a result, these neighbourhoods became slums, where crime grew and gang culture prospered.

'And Vauxhall's out the window. And with the lack of education, a lot of young lads feel defeated. When I was fifteen, we had a bit of an affluent time … and then all of a sudden there's the feeling that you're not working hard enough …'

Darren became more emotional as he spoke. He showed genuine concern for his community, as many do in Farley Hill. 'The government doesn't care about young people. Gordon Brown talked about apprenticeship; my son is twenty-four and is one of the few lucky ones who got apprenticeships. There's none for his generation. All my son's mates are out of work, desperate to get an apprenticeship. They want progression. They want to do something. They want to be called something.'

I nodded in empathy. He crossed his arms, sighed once again, and continued: 'Luton's been regenerated … and at the moment there're big contracts going on but you can't get on that … The council's going on about Luton this, Luton that, and everyone's happy and we all stick together. But there's no folk doing work in Luton.'

At this point, I was wondering whether he was going to start talking about immigration for the first time since I'd met him. He said: 'There're no local lads because all the labour's imported. And I don't mean from Poland or China, but from English companies, bringing Welsh lads in. Where's work for Luton lads? There should be a percentage of people from local. There's workforce out there. They're not work shy. But there's a 20 per cent ratio for Lutonians on the jobs. So they know the money isn't gonna go back in to Luton. So the local lads go to London for work.'

'Is it because companies find it hard to recruit local labour, or there simply isn't enough local labour to do the job, and that's why contracts are given to people from outside?' I wondered.

'Yes,' he said. 'But I also know many people who want to work and can't.'

I can understand Darren's concerns here, because this is the same story that I've heard from many in Farley Hill. The young on this estate are just feeling lost.

'You can't just stay at your dad's house. You have to earn the money somehow … London's always been a draw on Luton so that's where young people go. If we were in Stoke, no chance. That's why houses go downhill and started getting boarded up [in Stoke]. You won't see that here, only because of London.'

Darren said he's lucky because he was able to leave Farley Hill early, in the late 1980s, to move to the suburbs.

There's no investment since it [the estate] was built. All they [the council] want to do is to move people with social problems, maybe through drink, drug, care-in-the-community types, there. And they're quite happy living there. But other people get caught in that trap and they can't get out. Yet the council expect it to be all right. Luton has been forgotten. The government forgot about Luton; the council won't make Luton people feel part of the change ... There's nothing you can do because they [the council] were voted in. I voted Labour all my life. But now I'll never vote for them again ... It all changed because we've been lied to.

This was by far the angriest I've seen Darren. These are clearly the issues he cares most about.

The constant fear of not having a say about the changes happening to his community paved the way for Darren's decision to move to Australia to try a new life. In his words, it's like 'running away from a predicament', a tendency that's been ingrained in him since childhood. And growing up as an orphan equipped him with the emotional capacity needed to migrate and step into new possibilities. He wanted a better environment – not the gang culture and levels of crime they were witnessing around them – for his then ten-year-old and twelve-year-old sons to grow up in.

'I'd felt for a long time that it wasn't the place for working-class people to speak and question things ... I thought that even if life abroad doesn't work out, when I come back, I won't be so fearful of anything or anyone,' he said.

I take up Darren's story farther, in Chapter 2.

On Farley Hill estate, there is a white European group of residents who either actively or passively support the EDL. They have either lived most of their lives in Britain or have grown up here, sharing the same loyalties as the white British EDL followers. In almost all cases, they were drawn to the ideology of the group by its propagation of a racialized attack on Islam and British Muslims.

I was directed by several local residents to Alfredo (not his real name), an Italian-British barber at the corner of the estate's row of shops. Someone refers to him as 'the soul of Farley Hill'; 'if he dies, Farley Hill dies'. This is not least because he runs a football team that many residents are part of. He's also an outspoken resident and claims to speak for the estate.

His barber shop was busy as I looked in the window from outside. I could see a middle-aged, slightly overweight Italian-looking man serving a customer, with several others waiting. His shop assistant was busying herself with cleaning the floor in the background. I returned to his shop a couple of hours later, when it was quieter. I went in and asked whether I could talk. He politely pointed to the chair for waiting customers: 'Have a seat.'

'I am an Italian English,' he introduced himself to me while carrying on trimming a customer's hair in front of the mirror. 'I've been living in Britain for fifty years.'

'You speak like a native,' I said.

Still with scissors in his right hand, he pointed to the framed pictures of an Italian football club on the wall above the mirror. 'I am very proud of my cultural heritage. Italy is my spiritual home. Even though I was born here and I've lived most of my life here, I feel Italian instead of British. I still see myself as Italian before I see myself as English … I brought up my children to be proud of their Italian heritage even though they were born here and have English partners. They still feel more Italian than English …'

I found it interesting that, with his strong cultural identity with his origin, Alfredo is nevertheless seen by people on Farley Hill as representing their feelings and views. From what he shared with me, I gathered that his lasting identity was partly shaped by his early experience of racism upon arriving in Britain.

'I used to be called a "wog" by local people,' he said, smiling. 'You can't do anything about it; you just get on with it.' Alfredo managed to reconcile himself with that initial hostility. Over the decades, he built his family life here and refound his own loyalties. He now tells everyone that he is proud to be English, proud of his community and of Farley Hill. 'I will defend Britain because it is the country that feeds me. My children's mum is English. I will always defend Britain.'

His patriotism for Britain has been strengthened by the discomfort he has felt towards the changing landscape of the population on the estate. Back in 1963, he said, there was only one Asian family on the whole estate. Most residents were Scottish and Irish. 'There were only two Italian families; that was myself and a bloke who used to work here. Now, in fifty years, sixty or 50 per cent are non-white.'

As conversation turned to the EDL, Alfredo became cautious about being associated with the group. 'I have never been to any of their group meetings … I've not joined because there are too many fanatics in that group … Some of them just don't even know their own history. They hold St George's in the Parrot pub, but they don't realize that it's not even English! And there are people in the EDL who are basically racist and there's no doubt about it.'

At the same time, he was open about his empathy with the anger shared among EDL activists. 'I know many people in the

EDL. One of the reasons why the EDL started in this town is obviously the reaction when the soldiers marched through the town ... and how people felt ... I don't always agree with what they say, although I agree with why they started and why they have those kinds of opinions.'

Alfredo was to return to that passive support for the EDL throughout our conversations. 'My view is that it's got a lot to do with the fact that many people are getting preferential treatment ... This is now happening with a lot of the Muslims ... I know the person who runs the EDL, Yaxley, and I have to be honest that the basis of some of the things they say is quite right ... It's how other people view it and take it on. That day when the soldiers marched through town – why did the council allow the Muslims to pass the supporters of the soldiers? Why did they allow them to express those points of view? This is when people are getting fed up.'

'But surely they have the right to protest,' I said.

'The right to protest?!' Alfredo became frustrated, raising his voice slightly. 'Wait and see when they're in power; they'll take away that right for you. They'd be introducing sharia law in this country.'

Alfredo used to be a 'Labour man', as he phrased it. He supported the Labour Party for forty years and had voted for them at most elections. But in the past decade, he has become increasingly frustrated with mainstream politics and feels that 'they don't care about the working class'. However, he draws the same conclusions about 'who is to blame' as many in the EDL.

While claiming there are no ethnic tensions on the estate, Alfredo believes that Muslims and 'their attitude' are the reason why there is so little interaction between the white and Muslim residents on the estate. 'The Muslims want to keep to their own community ... I don't use the word that they should "integrate", but they should "interact" ...' he said. 'I hear about Muslim groups saying how they are family-oriented and they are a close community, but that is only their community and they don't interact with anyone else ... I got a football team and all the Muslim kids, as soon as they get to fifteen or sixteen, they go back to their own little group ... Nearly every one of them sees themselves as Muslim and not British.'

'Well, if that is the case, perhaps it's because there's little acceptance and tolerance towards them?' I asked again. 'Fear of rejection pushes people back to their own communities. No?'

'But why is it that they feel so strongly about their religion?' Alfredo became agitated. 'Why is it that they only seem to be defensive when people are against their religion?'

He carried on, still agitated. By this point, he was finished with the customer who had been sitting listening in silence as he had his hair trimmed. Alfredo was relentless: 'And then you get this situation with these paedophiles ... Those Muslims who groomed white girls for sex ...'

I was beginning to feel I was listening to an EDL broadcast. I kept calm, but felt more and more infuriated with his speech about paedophilia and the Muslim community. My views must have been written on my face, as Alfredo looked more and more uneasy, and angry, too. There is absolutely no historical or cultural link between paedophilia and Muslim males and by extension between paedophilia and Islam, in the same way that there is no link between paedophilia and Christian males or paedophilia and Christianity. (Did Jimmy Savile do what he did because he was Christian?) Yet this line of argument is frequently repeated among EDL followers.

Tommy Robinson, the then EDL leader who led the propagation of the myth, later said to me: 'Ninety-five per cent of convictions for grooming are Muslims – that's a fact. The men share young girls with their brothers, their uncles, their colleagues. The usual paedophile keeps it a secret. They can't go to their brother and say, "Do you want to shag this kid?". With this grooming, they specifically target young girls, get them hooked on alcohol and heroin, and pass them around their communities ... It is specifically Muslim. It is a Muslim problem.'

The far right propagated the myth that somehow these crimes are mandated by a sharia law that endorses sexual exploitation of non-Muslims. The myth established the assumption that there is a direct link between the grooming issue and Muslim communities. These myths have been reproduced in the British media, creating a synonymy between the words 'grooming' and 'Muslim' in the public mind.

However, research has confirmed that the link is false. A research report for the children's commissioner in 2012, as Vikram Dodd reported in the *Guardian* in 2013, found that 545 of the 1,514 perpetrators were white, 415 were 'Asian' and 244 were black. Just 35 of the 415 Asians are categorized as originating from Pakistan. Only five are recorded as coming from a Bangladeshi background. Therefore, Muslim men were a minority in these figures. A 2011 study conducted by the Child Exploitation and Online Protection Centre that looked at the 2,379 potential offenders caught grooming girls since 2008 found that, of 940 suspects, 26 per cent were Asian, 38 per cent were white and 32 per cent were categorized as unknown. According to *Guardian* journalist Vikram Dodd, these figures for 'Asians' (of which Muslims are only a part) is best explained by the demography of the offenders and the make-up of the night-time economy (i.e. vulnerable young women happen to fall prey to potential offenders who work nights, such as taxi drivers). There is no association between these crimes and religion or Islamic culture at all.

Yet this level of racialization has been consistently endorsed and promoted by parts of the tabloid press and right-wing broadsheets. For instance, in November 2013, Rod Liddle said in the *Spectator* that there's probably 'something within the religion or ideology of Islam which somehow encourages or merely facilitates extremist Muslim maniacs to maim or kill non-Muslims'. The *Daily Mail* reported on 14 June 2011 on a Derby case of sex trafficking: 'The sexual predators – both British-born fathers of Pakistani origin who had arranged marriages in that country – cruised the streets of Derby in either a Range Rover or a BMW looking for vulnerable young girls to prey on ...' The report quoted retired Lancashire police chief Mick Gradwell saying that 'pressure not to appear "institutionally racist" led to a culture of silence over Asian sex gangs' and that he 'worked on operations which had been set up to tackle, amongst other things, an element of Asian men who saw white girls as easy meat, as Jack Straw rightly put it ... It was a persistent issue.'

Through misrepresentation in popular media, the false link between paedophilia, street trafficking of young women and Muslim men has become a socially acceptable assumption. Meanwhile, the terms 'Muslim men' and 'Asian men' have become freely interchangeable, as repeatedly reported in the British press. As with the case of the nine men who were involved in a child exploitation gang in Rochdale, Greater Manchester, in 2008 and 2009, and were sentenced in 2012, when the words 'Asian men' were used in many British newspapers, despite the fact that one man came from Afghanistan and the others from Pakistan, hardly representing the entire 'Asian' male population. The BNP and EDL were then able to exploit the case and picket the court during the nine men's trial, making the child exploitation issue an 'Asian' and Muslim issue.

I tried to point out to Alfredo that his views are identical to those of the EDL, even though he wouldn't want to admit it. 'The EDL see Muslims as a problem. Do you?' I asked.

'No, I don't see them as a problem, but I see that if they don't deal with certain aspects of their life, it could become a problem ...' he said. Then he added: 'Too many of them hide behind British passports, but actually oppose everything about Britain.'

Moreover, it's easy to see here that 'integration' has been used as moral justification for the far right today to label British Muslims as a social 'problem'. Integration (or the 'lack of integration') is also a theme widely accepted in mainstream political discourse. David Cameron has consistently argued that British Muslims are not properly integrated into society and there is a 'growing problem of cultural separatism'. The national media is filled with this finger-pointing, that British Muslims are unwilling to be part of society. (Such examples are plenty, such as in the *Daily Mail*, on 8 May 2009, where it was reported that 'only one in ten Muslims in Britain see themselves as integrated into the rest of society'.)

The opposite is true. As Dr Leon Moosavi, a sociologist of race and religion at the University of Liverpool, said on 3 July 2012: 'In Britain today, there is a mismatch between how non-Muslims often perceive Muslims and how Muslims typically perceive themselves. This disconnect is down to a tendency by non-Muslims to assume that Muslims struggle with their British identity and divided loyalties ...' A research paper titled 'Understanding society', by the University of Essex, actually found that British Muslims identify with 'Britishness' more than any other Britons and they express a stronger sense of belonging than any other group. The research finds that 83 per cent of British Muslims are proud to be British, compared to 79 per cent of the general public; 77 per cent of British Muslims strongly identify with Britain while only 50 per cent of the wider population do; 86.4 per cent of Muslims feel they belong in Britain, more than the 85.9 per cent of Christians; 82 per cent of British Muslims want to live in diverse and mixed neighbourhoods compared to 63 per cent of non-Muslim Britons. The research concludes that there is no issue with British Muslims wanting to be part of British society.

Interestingly, the research also shows that the problem lies with the social perception of Muslims by non-Muslims: 47 per cent of Britons see Muslims as a threat; 52 per cent of Britons believe Muslims create problems; 55 per cent of Britons would be concerned if a mosque was built in their area; 58 per cent of Britons associate Islam with extremism; only 28 per cent believe Muslims want to integrate into British society.

As found in my communication and dialogue with the sympathizers and supporters of the far right, 'integration' rhetoric is a cover-up for exclusion and racial discrimination. Among the

EDL followers, the 'integration' theme also goes hand in hand with blatant scapegoating of ethnic minority communities for crime, one of the city's major worries.

Alfredo talked of the Muslim youth he knows on the estate, and became more and more emotional: 'Their mothers and fathers don't want to mix with local English, but they are quite happy to mix with people who're selling drugs in this town … and killing our kids.' It turned out that he has a very personal reason for this conclusion: he lost his son to drugs six months before our talk. The man who sold drugs to his son happened to be Muslim. Now he believes all of the drug dealers in town are Muslim. I wanted to know more about what happened to his son and the story behind it, but at this point Alfredo's anger prevented me from asking.

Drugs are clearly the town's biggest problem. It is said that you can't move around this estate without encountering a drug dealer. And all over town, a turf war is under way between white, British West Indian and Pakistani gangs. But it's not a problem specific to any ethnic group. As I found out later in Bury Park, Alfredo's idea that the drug scene is dominated by Muslims is a myth based on prejudice. Many Muslim young people learned about drugs through their white friends, too. And like most parents, Muslim parents have found the prevalence of drug use a serious problem about which they are extremely concerned.

The born-and-bred Lutonian Lenos Wilson, founder of The Non Violence Alliance (TNVA), a non-profit charitable organization based in Luton's communities, refuted the claim that the local drug problem is worse among Muslim youths. 'You'll find drug problems in all communities. This is not a race issue at all. It applies to all, white or Asian.'

But Alfredo went farther, attempting to associate the drug problem with immigration: 'I don't mean that I hate these people for that. Just like I don't hate the Italians because the Mafia come from Italy ... But drugs do come from outside [of Britain] and we have to accept that.'

His personal experience may have made up his mind for him. He seemed determined to link the growing level of crime to the presence of 'Asian' youth, despite the fact that the majority of residents in the Farley Hill estate do not see drug and crime as a race issue. In fact, the incidents of crime quoted by the residents I met were largely concentrated on damage to business premises (such as shops run by Pakistani men who suffered from the damage). The perpetrators were, contrary to Alfredo's claims, by and large white youth.

Lenos Wilson of TNVA told me that in fact the current problem of escalating crime rates does not necessarily have much to do with drugs. 'Gang crime has deteriorated in the past few years, with reprisals and territorial control being the main cause,' he said. A large part of TNVA's work is crime reduction in Luton, which he said is a serious cross-community issue.

Farley Hill isn't the worst place to be in terms of crime, its residents said. They talk of Marsh Farm estate, not far away, as 'the roughest estate in Luton'. Marsh Farm is notorious and, again, its residents do not see crime as an ethnicity-related issue. The estate is multicultural with a white majority. Its history and current level of crime have nothing to do with immigration.

Marsh Farm estate has a population of 10,000 and was built around the same time as the Farley Hill estate in the late 1960s, with a mixture of flats and houses, as part of the post-war expansion of Luton. The estate became infamous in July 1995 when the build-up of social problems on the estate culminated in three days of rioting involving up to 500 locals. More than 250 police officers, with the help of the Met riot squad, were brought in to bring the situation under control. In response, around 500 teenagers attacked police with bottles, bricks and petrol bombs.

Years of poverty-related issues on the Marsh Farm estate led to plans for redevelopment and £50 million of European money was made available to that end. However, the intervention seems insufficient and the estate still looks run down and continues to be known as one of the worst areas for crime in Luton today. It is still plagued by violence caused by cross-estate fighting between rival gangs. Between January and July 2013, there were nine shootings in four months and sixteen gun crime incidents recorded. In May, a member of the Marsh Farm Gang, who was associated with drug dealing, was sentenced to twenty-four years for murdering a former friend who belonged to the rival gang on the nearby Lewsey Farm estate.

This is why, in May 2013, police armed with Heckler and Koch G36 assault rifles capable of firing at a rate of 750 rounds a minute were sent into the estate to crack down on gangs. However, the armed police patrol does not seem to have solved the problems and has provided only a temporary calm. Fear permeates and circulates, amplifying the bad name that this estate has garnered. Those living there seem more than aware that the fundamental problem remains: some of the young people simply don't know any better than gang culture. Little education, few facilities and services that cater for their interests or betterment, few employment prospects, and little hope for a real future. These are the most important issues shared among estates like Marsh Farm and Farley Hill, and heavy policing isn't going to end the cycle of crime for them.

Alfredo wanted to lock up his barber shop for the day. He ended our conversation with an extended critique of 'the unwanted', taking in another social group: the travellers. 'The other group I can't stand because sometimes they have the same attitude [as the Muslims] is the travellers ... The travellers always say that they are very good family people and they love their community. But they love only their community ... People feel threatened because they see these groups being given [a lot] ... and that's why we go to fanatical groups. But are those groups really that fanatical?'

The support, active and passive, received by the EDL gave the movement confidence to grow. This development has caused concern among certain ethnic minority residents in Farley Hill. A catering worker, whose name and ethnic origin cannot be revealed for safety reasons, told me that the growth of the far right is affecting future plans for him and his family. 'I've been living and working here for more than ten years ... I'd like to continue living and working here. But there are a lot of EDL activities around. It's worrying to bring up my children here. I don't know what to do. I don't think we will be able to settle here permanently.'

However, it would be simplistic to assume that Alfredo's views represent the majority on this estate. The spectrum of perspectives is in fact wide ranging and fluid and reflects the complex formation of an individual's beliefs and opinions, which are often contradictory and in constant flux, whether reinforced or challenged. As I have observed when talking to people in Farley Hill, their views are often mixed and inconsistent, and people often shift their ideological positions when responding to changing circumstances.

A single mother with an eight-year-old boy outside the estate shops was chatting with her fifty-something mother. They were approachable and open, albeit politically uninformed. 'I'm not interested in politics,' the young mother said. 'I don't really know what groups like the EDL are up to, but I wouldn't go near them.'

She said she wasn't aware of the 2009 conflict, and saw no problem with living alongside British Muslim residents. 'This is quite a mixed estate … Although my neighbours are all English, my landlady is Asian. We have no problems with anyone.'

Her mother said there's been change of population on the estate in the past few years. 'Since they built the mosque around the corner two years ago … and the high school … there's been many more Turkish people … and Pakistani people around here. Also, there's quite a few Polish people coming in, doing shop work and factory work through agencies. I don't know any of them. Each group is separate from each other.'

She displayed a lack of interest in community relations and seems to feel that holding no position about things is safest. 'Once, before Christmas, we saw the EDL people having a fight with several Asian people outside a pub opposite the town hall, the pub where the EDL people usually hang out. We only go into town once a week and we just happened to see the fight. We were frightened. Luckily the police dealt with it quickly so it didn't escalate, but it was quite scary … Apart from that, I occasionally get a leaflet through my door from the BNP, but not the EDL. We just ignore all that really. We want no trouble.'

She carried on: 'As long as the EDL leaves me alone, I've got no real opinions about it. Some of what they say might be right. I see the EDL in the papers and on television sometimes, and I know that Kevin Carroll [the then deputy leader of EDL] lives up here. But I'm not really interested. They do what they do and we have nothing to do with them. We don't want no contact with them ... We keep ourselves to ourselves really.'

She is more concerned by local issues. 'Luton has changed ...' she said. 'It's been harder to get jobs since the past two years. And you look around and you see people hanging around on the streets here when they should be working ... The last time I voted Conservatives and I wish I hadn't. I voted for them because I was working with one of the Conservative MPs and thought I'd better keep him happy. But really they've done nothing for us.'

I came across another single mother, in her early forties, on the estate. She frowned at my mention of the EDL. 'To be honest, I don't think the main issue around here is about Muslim culture or anything like that. I'm not bothered if they want to integrate or not. The real problem here is the lack of facilities and places for kids to go. Young people hang around the estate most of the time and they don't learn anything from anyone.'

The lack of venues for social education is the one thing that every parent seems to talk about here. 'What do you think will happen when kids have nowhere to go all the time? That's why the crime and drug abuse is such a problem around here,' she said angrily. 'There used to be a youth centre around but that's gone. The government just cut services back all the time. And unemployment is bad here … My son and daughter can't find work.' There was a deep sense of fatigue and helplessness in her voice. The burden of raising children on her own must have been a heavy weight on her shoulders. She has little to feel hopeful about. Where do people turn when they feel they're losing hope?

2

DEFENDING THE IMAGINARY NATION

I ran into Derek, the road maintenance worker, again another day as I walked around the estate. He was wearing a baseball cap, an England T-shirt and his bright green work trousers. He was also carrying a bag of clothes. 'I'm heading to the laundry,' he said with a smile, a 'Support Our Heroes' bracelet hanging from his left wrist. This happened to be one of his days off in a long sixty-hour week.

'Can I come with you?' I asked, hoping for a conversation.

'Yes, sure.' He appeared in a better mood today. 'I just finished my morning shift. Have to do this laundry. But we can talk.'

So I sat with him in the estate laundry just across the road. An acquaintance of his, Betsy, who works the morning shifts in the laundry, said hello to him.

'Come and meet this woman.' Derek waved to Betsy. 'She's writing stuff about our estate.'

The eighty-something, white-haired Betsy turned around and didn't say anything. She was clearly uninterested.

'Things aren't the same around here any more, ain't it, Betsy? It ain't used to be like this,' Derek said to her.

'Yes ... They aren't the same no more,' she murmured lifelessly as she looked out of the window.

'Everything has changed beyond recognition on the estate,' Derek said, shaking his head at Betsy. 'Ain't it?'

She nodded quietly. She appeared dejected. Half a minute later, she turned to me: 'The biggest problems are crime and antisocial behaviour,' she said, pointing to a shop run by a British Pakistani man across the road. 'The other day someone smashed the shop window over there. Loads of police came. It was frightening. Things like that happen a lot these days.'

Although these problems on the estate have nothing to do with immigration, Betsy has convinced herself that they are linked. She sighed, a nostalgia for the 'good old days' without immigration. 'Those Pakistanis kept coming in ... I have Pakistani neighbours and they're a real nuisance.' She has received a lot of letters addressed to the Pakistani neighbours, thus assuming that they are misusing her address.

'Do you live alone?' I asked her.

'Yes.' But even then she prefers not to communicate with her Pakistani neighbours.

Derek repeated the same words: 'It ain't the same any more.'

His 'Support Our Heroes' bracelet hung so prominently on his wrist that I had to ask him. 'So what is this about, then?'

'This? This is to support our army and our soldiers,' he said with indignation in his voice. 'Lee Rigby was attacked wearing the same thing. Any of us can be attacked wearing this. But I am not going to stop wearing it.'

Then he suddenly remembered to tell me: 'Did you read *Luton News* today? It makes me so angry! My blood's boiling … The council is banning an army parade in town!'

'Really?'

'Yes, they're doing that for fear of offending the Muslims! Why should we be afraid of offending them? This is our country! Our army!' he claimed, raising his voice and waving his fist.

'Do you think it's a good idea to carry on wearing this?' I pointed to his shiny bracelet.

'Why shouldn't I? I am born and bred here and I'm proud of our army. I'm not going to hide away from my beliefs.'

Derek was no longer shying away from expressing sympathy for the EDL as he had last time. The growth of the group in recent months had given him confidence. 'I grew up with Kevin Carroll; he's a nice bloke,' he said to Betsy and me.

Kevin Carroll, the then deputy leader (or joint leader as many see him) of the EDL, told me he'd never been politically active prior to 2009. As a self-employed builder, he said his aim in life had always been to secure work and support his family. But his life changed following the anti-war and anti-army Muslim protest in Luton in 2009, and the five years since have been like 'running 1,000 miles per hour non-stop'. He became a central figure in a street movement that he claims is against 'Islamic extremism' and 'Islamification'.

Back in 2011, Kevin Carroll and Tommy Robinson formed an electoral pact with the far-right British Freedom Party (BFP), a splinter party of the BNP registered in October 2010. Robinson became BFP's deputy party leader in April 2012, and Kevin Carroll became head of the BFP in January 2013, with the aim of pursuing systematic anti-Muslim policies. Under the agreement made with the BFP, the EDL leaders were able to run as election candidates in the party's name.

Kevin Carroll said in an election statement when running as a Police and Crime Commissioner candidate on behalf of the BFP in winter 2012: 'I am Luton born and bred, fiercely proud of my home and country ...' Among his policing priorities were 'zero tolerance for extremist and terrorist activity in Bedfordshire', 'an end to so-called "honour" crimes' and 'an end to politically correct policing' aimed at ethnic minority communities, particularly the Muslims.

I paused for a few minutes. I couldn't think of anything to say in response to Derek's praise of Kevin Carroll. I sat facing him, as he stared at the empty space outside the shop. The only sound we could hear was the turning of the washing machines.

Then the silence was broken as a forty-something bearded man came into the laundry. He said hello to both Derek and Betsy, and introduced himself as Adrian. He was originally from Cyprus, and runs a busy chip shop next door.

On seeing Adrian, Derek started where he'd left off, talking about Kevin Carroll, and asked Adrian to give his opinion. 'You know them, don't you?'

'Yes, I drink and socialize with EDL guys,' Adrian said with a broad smile. 'They're all right.'

Like Alfredo's, Adrian's support for the EDL is based on 'the Muslim question'. He's a Catholic and seems to feel animosity towards Muslims. His religious beliefs have led him to respond to the EDL's strategy of driving a wedge between the 'non-Islamic population' and the Muslims, replacing the old far-right approach of creating divisions between 'white' and 'black'. It was looking as if the group had successfully exploited social prejudice against Muslims and gathered a certain support even among Brits who had origins abroad.

'I've been in the UK for forty years and see myself as Cyprus English,' Adrian told me. 'All my friends from Cyprus living on this estate think the same about the EDL. We don't think they're racist.'

Adrian reiterated a statement I would find typical of the EDL's supporters: 'The problem we have about the Muslims is that they don't integrate.'

'How do you expect them to "integrate" if what the EDL wants is for them to close down the mosques, practically banning their religion?' I said to him.

In February 2012, BFP and EDL leaders held a meeting during which they discussed policies that the EDL was eager to put forward on the BFP platform. These policies – such as the key demands to ban the burka, limit Muslims in the building of places of worship and developing new madrasas (Islamic schools), and an end to immigration (migrants must undergo health checks, have a sponsor, have sufficient funds to support them and their families and must be able to speak and write English) – indicated that the group's focus was all Muslims (and by extension migrants), not only 'Muslim extremists' as they claimed in the press.

'I support the EDL and voted for them when they stood for BFP in the last elections,' Adrian carried on without hesitation.

'Are you aware of their stance on immigration?' I asked.

He shook his head. That didn't seem to concern him. 'They are the least bad among all political parties. That was why I voted for them.'

The BFP didn't last long. It was deregistered by the Electoral Commission in December 2012 after failing to return their annual registration form and the £25 fee.

Adrian's wife came into the laundry at this point. 'We can have a drink at the Parrot some time if you want to talk more about this,' he said, smiling, and left with her.

The churning of the washing machines was still playing its accompaniment. I turned to Betsy and asked what she does outside of work. She said she used to visit a community centre on the estate. 'Just down there,' she pointed down to the right, 'but the council has cut down on the staff and the place isn't as good as before any more. You'll get nothing trying to ask any questions there.' Once again, the lack of facilities and social venues was given as a common concern among the estate's residents. But far-right groups like the EDL, despite frequently using the phrase 'working class', have never addressed these local concerns and would never mobilize on these grounds, i.e. to save local services, or to fight against government cuts.

Derek was looking miserable and vacant. The absence of an alternative way of thinking and analysing one's own situation has left a vacuum for far-right ideologies to fill. Looking for easy scapegoats has become the only option offered to him. Thus his tendency to turn that anger against anyone who might seem to do slightly better. 'Those people on benefits ...' he said, frowning bitterly, 'I'm really angry with them ... They're getting help from the government and are better off than me.'

Derek told me the main concern that stops him from joining groups like the EDL is that he doesn't want to risk his job. 'I just don't want more trouble in my life.'

I saw that he is alone with this deep, unaddressed anger. In a quiet moment he sat, looking saddened and lost. I asked him about his children. He was content enough to say that they're doing all right, but didn't want to elaborate. Then he revealed to me that he's divorced and that his ex-wife didn't appreciate him. 'You don't know how good your man is before you lose them,' he said quietly. 'But then, you don't know how good your woman is before you lose her.'

He feels his life is empty and the isolation is eating away at his spirit. But he isn't doing anything to break out of that isolation. His two sisters live in the same town, but he rarely sees them. He isn't interested in building a social life, even around the like-minded. 'I used to go to the Parrot, but not any more, because I can't afford drinking much ...' he said. 'Anyway, it's best to keep myself to myself. I don't trust people.'

Most of his old friends have moved out of Luton for work. I asked whether he ever travelled to see them. 'Yes, a few times,' he said. 'I went to visit my friend who lives in Bermondsey, south London. We used to be in the Migs together and grew up with it. I remember all the violence on the terraces when Millwall came down. Now he's in London, he's shifted to support Millwall ... But yeah, it was all right to see him.'

His laundry was done; Derek had to go. He suggested I visit the other end of the estate, to talk to people.

'I'll walk you,' he volunteered.

On the way there, I asked him about his memories of growing up in Farley Hill.

'I didn't grow up here,' he said, sounding dispirited once again, 'I grew up on a travellers' campsite in Luton ... Not far from here. My parents were Gypsies. Dad was a boxer ...'

I was surprised, as I know the EDL, for whom he feels much sympathy, wouldn't say a good word about travellers of any origin. I wanted to ask him more, but he simply looked down and said: 'I wanted to move out of that life. My parents had passed away.' I looked at him and saw that his eyes were turning red.

One person Darren talked about on numerous occasions was his wife June's Scottish grandmother. She saved their lives, he kept telling me. Back in the 1990s, life was a real struggle, particularly with the recession in 1992. 'A lot of people lost their houses; our friends did, too. Everyone just walked up to the estate agent and gave them the keys. It would have also happened to us if it weren't for Nan.'

Darren was barely able to support the family with his income, so they moved to live upstairs in the grandmother's house while they rented out their own house. They stayed for three years. She shared everything with them. 'I love her to bits. She's really old-school,' Darren said. 'If it wasn't for her, we wouldn't have been able to pay the mortgage ... It was one of the biggest things anyone's ever done for me. She had a real tough life ... She helped everybody in the family. Everybody. Because everybody was having it hard. You had to hold on to what you had ...'

It was during that time that many working-class men and women became embittered and gradually turned rightwards – with some eventually drawn into the ranks of far-right groups. Ethnic tensions came to the fore as divisions deepened further between communities. It was at this time that the BNP won its first council seat in a by-election on the Isle of Dogs, east London. The year was 1993. There, Derek Beackon, an unemployed lorry driver, defeated the Labour Party candidate, taking the traditionally Labour Millwall seat. The BNP's share of the vote had also risen from the previous year's election result of 20 per cent to 33.9 per cent in 1993.

In Luton, until then, ethnic tensions had never been a major issue. But the past two decades of local industrial decline and the 'divide-and-rule' internal and foreign policies of successive governments had begun to weigh heavily on working-class communities, white and non-white. In the early 1990s, cracks were beginning to show.

Britain's wars abroad began to divide communities locally and it proved to be the decisive turning point in the town's ethnic relations. Darren witnessed this transformation. 'Every one of us comes from an immigrant background – black, Asian, white immigrants. We're all immigrants. I work with Albanian Muslim lads, African Muslim lads, Christian lads. Either you get on with it or you don't, and I choose to get on with it. We're used to diversity. Luton's problem is more to do with what's going on in the world.'

The mood in Luton changed in 1991. Darren felt it, and he knew something big was growing. He put it down to the Gulf War invasion.

Back then, we didn't care about politics of the world. The world never comes to Luton. Back in the 1980s it was all about football and the gang ... and then all of a sudden, politics came in the 1990s ... Before the Gulf War, if you asked me where Islamabad is, I'd say Arabia. I wouldn't have a clue. But since the Gulf War, things started changing and, whether we like it or not, we have to get clued up.

In the old days, the aggression towards each other, between BPYP and us, it could all be sorted out. We could all grow up from it. It was just a lad's thing, if you like. Everyone played by rules ... But then the Gulf War happened, and there seemed to be some very sensitive things happening in Luton ... There was a level of aggression from some Pakistani youth since 1991. It didn't visualize at first ... just hostility ... and then the violence came. Angry lads ... There was the feeling that it was the West's fault what was happening in Muslim countries. At street level we got the backlash ... People started getting used to it ... making sure that if a car pulled up, you wouldn't look up from the pavement. Beatings on the street.

While Darren was feeling the impact of that perceived change, the reality in the British Muslim communities in Bury Park was a growing hostility and violence inflicted upon them by local white people. There was a rise in racist incidents throughout the decade and the violence continued into the 2000s. The majority of racial crimes have been committed by white people, and in most cases British Asians have been the victims. In 2005, in particular, police dealt with 171 reported race hate incidents, a 50 per cent increase over the previous year. Most victims were Asian (42 per cent) while most offenders were white (40 per cent). Bedfordshire Police's 2010–14 records show a worsening trend. In 2010, the number of racial crimes totalled 227, of which 124 were committed by white people and 36 by British Asians. Out of the 124 cases committed by whites, 72 were white-on-Asian (Asians being the victims). In 2011, out of a total of 228 racial crimes, 103 were committed by white people and 16 by Asians. Fifty-eight cases were white-on-Asian racial crimes while 10 cases were Asian-on-white. In 2012, out of 213 race crimes, white offenders accounted for 114 and Asians 23. Fifty-six of the cases were white-on-Asian while 7 were Asian-on-white. In 2013, out of 222 racial crimes, 104 were committed by whites. Fifty-seven cases were white-on Asian; 15 were Asian-on-white. Between January and July 2014, out of a total of 191 racial crimes, there were 94 committed by whites, out of which 46 were white-on-Asian. There were 14 Asian-on-white cases.

Despite facts, the media preferred to report Asian-on-white violence. It's not difficult to see how people can draw one-sided conclusions, especially if the violence is inflicted on someone close to you. Such as Darren, who lost his close friend, Mark, in 1995, when he was stabbed to death on a street corner. Darren's family was horrified. His wife June told me he was killed on her mum's street. 'The kid that did it lived next door to my sister,' she said. 'They were only kids. I just couldn't believe it, how much kids have changed.' Darren said he has yet to come to terms with his friend's death.

Darren believes that the growing conflict and resentment between white and Muslim Lutonians is the direct result of 'radicalization' among some of the young British Pakistani population. 'Radicalization' has become the new way of seeing British Muslims since 9/11. However, in contrast to the main-stream radicalization theorists (found in most British media, for instance, as well as EDL followers) who base their argument on religion (i.e. the 'vice' inherent in a particular religion, therefore making a person who practises that religion automatically prone to 'radicalization'), Darren sees it as rooted in politics, i.e. Britain's foreign policies and their consequences.

'Back then we were unaware of what they were angry about. But looking back, you can see lads were radicalized by what happened since 1991 and saw the war as all about oil and money ... That was just way above our heads. We're living our street level ...'

Usama Hasan, a former Salafi activist, part-time imam and ex-leader of Jimas (which preached a conservative interpretation of Islam), told me that activists like himself numbered only around a dozen families in Luton in the 1980s, a tiny minority in the local Muslim community. For him, it was part of a wider social context in which British Muslim youths were becoming gradually politicized. It was difficult growing up as a Muslim, he said, faced with a great deal of hostility and isolation from mainstream society. Rejection and social isolation led to an identity crisis and a gap to fill. 'Eventually, the [Muslim] youths joined radical groups as a reaction to all the racism ... and they were seeking an alternative identity,' he said. 'Therefore, in the 1980s and 1990s, there was an increase in the number of people turning to political Islam, looking to a Muslim identity ...'

However, there is no evidence to suggest a link between street violence and the 'radicalization' of young people. Although the politicized mood among those youngsters cannot be ignored, the growing gang culture in town continued to play an important role in the deepening antagonisms at street level. Darren acknowledged that the gangs did play a part in the growing violence all over town. 'Every generation has males growing up thinking they're the lads, the protector of their community, like it happened to us. We stood up to protect our community of football ... The gang thing is not done and dusted because Migs are still there ...'

Meanwhile, following the events of 9/11 in 2001 and the Iraq invasion of 2003, the relationship between the white British and Muslim communities in Luton began to deteriorate, just as was happening all across the country. Throughout the 2000s, Muslim communities were being disproportionately targeted in political activity and victimized via terrorism laws and stop-and-search measures. Home Office figures showed that in 2002 and 2003 there were 32,100 searches in total under the Terrorism Act, up from 21,900 the previous year. British Muslims accounted for the majority. In 2003 and 2004, 12.5 per cent of searches under the anti-terrorism laws were on British Asians, even though they make up only 4.7 per cent of the UK population. On 2 March 2005, the then Home Office minister Hazel Blears went even farther to justify the level of victimization by saying that 'UK Muslims should accept that people of Islamic appearance are more likely to be stopped and searched by police'.

As Arun Kundnani well documented in his book *The Muslims Are Coming!: Islamophobia, Extremism and the Domestic War on Terror*, the new thinking on 'radicalization' became the basis for the Preventing Violent Extremism programme, known as

Prevent, 'one of the most elaborate programmes of surveillance and social control attempted in Western states in recent decades'. It was launched by Blair's government in 2006 and set out the national framework for the monitoring and surveillance of British Muslims.

In this hostile political climate, the monitoring of community life for Britain's ethnic minorities has intensified, impacting most negatively on the lives of many British Muslims. According to CAGE, an independent advocacy organization that has been working with communities impacted by the War on Terror for more than a decade, among those arrested for terrorism offences, only 1 per cent were eventually convicted. Eighty-four per cent of those convicted did not even go to trial and pleaded guilty for a lesser sentence. The British anti-terror laws allow people, when arrested, to be detained and repeatedly interrogated for up to fourteen days without charge. The raids, arrests and detention have had a tremendous impact on the individuals involved, most of them traumatized, having had their family life disrupted and their sense of normality taken away. Such actions by the police and intelligence services in the name of the War on Terror have deeply alienated Britain's Muslim communities.

One of the turning points for Darren was his decision to come home after a year in Australia, in 2004. I met him and his wife June for dinner on the tenth anniversary of their return from Australia. It also happened to be St George's Day. Sitting in their local diner, the Brache, the couple talked with amusement about that period of time. They looked at each other as they spoke, as if seeking approval and mutual understanding. Emigration to Berwick, near Melbourne, in Australia, was a first-time adventure for them, and, as they set out, they made the promise that 'if one member of the family does not like it out there, then all of us will come back'. The idea was to stay together.

As it turned out, the couple didn't find the Australian life-style easy. They had a small social circle and, as Darren put it, there wasn't a lot to do. 'Dull' was the word he used to describe living there. His elder son, then fifteen, also found it hard to adjust. Darren said that his son is more like him in his nature, more home-bound. 'He's always gonna be a Luton lad,' he said, looking at June. Besides, the work environment was a challenge for Darren. His building site was filled with 'typical white Australians', he said, who seemed to resent the British as well as the Aborigines. Overall, the experience wasn't pleasant enough for them to stay.

When the family decided to return to Luton, June feared the difficulties they would face coming back, and she refused to get on the plane until Darren found a place for them to live. So he came back on his own first, feeling a great pressure to rent a place quickly. He remembered it with a forced smile: 'It was a tough time for everyone. No one could give a hand ...

'It was a general rough old period ... Old wounds get opened up,' said Darren thoughtfully. On his first day back in Luton, he took a walk around town. Having been detached from the local scene for a while, Darren was shocked by the changes. One of the first things he saw was a group of white Lutonian men burning a Black Banner, or what they called an 'al-Qaeda flag', in a local pub, in protest at the fact that some Muslim residents were preaching on the streets of Luton. He suddenly found himself in the middle of the beginnings of an anti-Islamic far-right movement, the first of its kind in Britain.

At this time, just as Darren and family were returning, Britain saw the first wave of migration from Poland as the EU enlarged. 'The Poles were coming in,' said June, remembering how people felt there weren't enough jobs to go around. It was at that time that immigration became much more of an issue locally, with growing hostility towards outsiders.

Darren soon found and rented a maisonette from a West Indian family in Luton. He then tried to get back on the ladder and get his work back on track. June arrived back in town a couple of weeks later with their sons, and went back to her old job in the post office. She giggled as she remembered the first thing that she found hard to get used to back in Luton: 'It was the smell of the place. So awful and dirty, the High Town, where I grew up.'

Then she sighed and said: 'It's one of the oldest communities here, the High Town. They've tried to change it into a more bohemian kind of place, full of artists, and I guess it will be all right eventually ...'

There were changes in town that the couple couldn't ignore. June recalled growing community conflict, gang violence and a general increase in crime. 'It was hard adjusting back to the life here, in our own country,' said Darren.

But it wasn't until 2009 that the nascent far-right street movement Darren had witnessed on his first day back in Luton was realized, when a group of (primarily) Muslim men protested against the returning soldiers parading through town. Divisions were most serious among the working class, and for the first time in this town they were cut mostly along ethnic lines. British Muslims who opposed the war were brought face to face with their working-class counterparts in the white communities from which the soldiers came. State policies began to poison the lives of everyone involved.

'At first I thought, we need to respond, to give white working-class a certain voice ...' Darren said. 'The soldiers come from working-class backgrounds. We know the Anglian troops. They are mates. Those soldiers from Luton come from Farley Hill, from working-class families ... Middle-class people get nice jobs with a nice wage, or they go to captaincy in the army ... But working-class lads had their lives ruined, like my boy's mate, he lost his leg ... I'm decorating his house now. It all comes home to roost ... It wasn't a war film. I stand there having a beer, that young lad comes in with a false leg for a pint ... It all comes home to roost.'

In retrospect, Darren now sees the suffering for both white and British Muslim working-class communities. 'Like the Pakistani community and their boys ... we started to feel some of the pain ... Those boys are from our community ... They lost their legs and they're dying ... If you feel like that, you must understand we feel like it too. We didn't vote for the war. Why don't you go to tell that gobshite Tony Blair in number ten? He started it!'

Darren said he took part in protesting against the anti-army demonstrators because he felt it was the right time to tell the world how the people of Luton live. When dozens of Muslim protesters went through the town, he got a call from a friend saying, 'Al Mujahidin kicked off against the troops'. He felt the urge to be there. When he got there, he said, there were many local Muslim residents and older women surrounding and supporting the protesters. 'The Luton crowd was all saying you should support our troops and calling them scum, and the Muslims were shouting "rapists". It was very sad really ... I know a younger lad who died, from Farley Hill. He was an Anglian and he wasn't there at the parade because he was dead.'

I wanted to know how Darren truly felt when he saw the protest for himself. 'Gutted,' he said without hesitation. 'Gutted.'

Then he paused and said: 'I've been thinking ... Where did the divide come from? We're all Lutonians. We all live in this country. We know some of the Anglians didn't come back – one Luton man didn't come back. My feelings are always with Luton. When you realize the people who'd gone to the same school as you and grown up here don't want to be part of Luton, and see the troops as the enemy, it's too much to take ... I look at these [Muslim] lads and think, you're not Luton, you're like West Ham. It was then I felt I have to respond.'

Darren's localist sentiment seemed much more important than his nationalist emotions. I asked him whether, for him, Luton comes before England. He said yes, but added that the majority of EDL members don't share that strong local allegiance. For them, he said, national identity and nationalism stand way above everything else.

At the time, March for England organized a protest in Luton as the town came into the national spotlight, and far-right groups all wanted to make their mark there. Although Darren didn't know who the organizer was and only guessed it was 'someone from Brighton', he decided to take part. He said it felt as if the group had genuine concerns and he thought it was the right thing to do. Along with hundreds of young white Lutonians, he marched from Park Street to the war memorial to lay poppies. Darren himself did not see anything beyond making the point about paying respect to the soldiers, which he believed was completely legitimate. However, the march turned violent and Asian shops were attacked by demonstrators. A British Indian man was mistaken as Muslim and was hit on the head. But Darren wasn't aware of these incidents and was guided simply by his strong desire to support the soldiers.

Then, United People of Luton, made up of people from estates all over town (which later formed the EDL), organized a protest in town and planned to march to the town hall. Darren was there. 'A lot of lads got together and decided, well, the council facilitated and brought the Muslim protesters into the town hall ... They'll be able to facilitate our demo ... We wanted them to know that not everyone in Luton hated the troops ...'

June and her sister, out of curiosity, also went on the march. They wanted to see what it was like. She told me:

Working in a post office you have all communities there ... It was the first time I felt that they [local Muslims] didn't actually see themselves as Lutonians. I knew of the march, and thought I agreed with what they're saying ... But none of us expected the group to grow like that, that fast and nationwide. When we got to the protest, we were just stunned. There were so many supporters, men and women, and older people. I was so shocked to see my colleagues

83

from the post office. They all came out. And my friend who's a traffic warden, I was surprised to see her come out to the demo, too …

To avoid the police, Darren followed the others to organize. They made up signs and banners in secret, and loaded them on to a van. Then everyone met at the Crown pub at 3 p.m. the next day and picked up the signs: 'Troops are Heroes', 'We're not the BNP', 'You're the Devil'. 'We were planning to hand in the petition and get them ASBO-ed and banned in the town centre, because we didn't like the fact that they were taken into the town hall while abusing the soldiers,' he said. 'We got thousands of petitions. But the police stopped us and said, you're not going anywhere … They kettled us for three hours. They sent in their horses. I got stepped on my foot by a horse. Then demos were banned. We started contesting it.'

Police tactics provoked more anger. As the first demo was made up primarily of residents of the town, there was a feeling that the policing was unjustifiably heavy-handed against the 'ordinary families of Luton'. Following the protest, the police went to fourteen houses to arrest those involved on public order offences. They were banned from the town centre. In response, football fans were brought in on the second Luton protest. Many claim that if the police hadn't responded in the way they did, those first protests wouldn't have exploded into a movement, and there would be no EDL.

It was at this point that Darren was drawn closer into the formation of the EDL. His localist allegiance and empathy with the soldiers were converging with the nationalist, pro-West sentiments that he had seen in EDL activists and followers. 'The Muslims were having their marches for a good year or two prior to our demos in Luton ... All anti-Israel stuff ... The Al Mujahidin guys were there every Saturday, shouting about the West, about Bush and Blair, about Cameron, about us being voters and taxpayers funding the war machine against the Muslims ...'

I couldn't help questioning Darren at this point: 'But don't you think you might have something in common with them about the wars?'

'Oh yes,' he responded without a doubt, 'we don't want any of that war. We don't want lads fighting in Afghanistan ... It's hard to have a discussion with anyone about it. I bought a *Socialist Worker* once when they were selling it in town and read about it ...'

Interestingly, Darren isn't pro-Israel like many in the EDL. He visited Palestine during a family holiday to Jerusalem, and saw pictures of martyrs who were suicide bombers. He was particularly struck by the female ones. He walked around local neighbourhoods and received great hospitality from many Palestinians. Having seen the impoverished community on constant security alert, he felt sympathy for the Palestinian cause and said he hopes Palestine will flourish. During his time in the EDL, he experienced a constant contradiction between his own ideas and those of the group, a tension he resolved only once he decided to leave it.

In truth, the street movement grew too fast, too suddenly and too strongly for Darren to grasp. He followed the tide, and was soon swept along by the unchannelled mass anger. For him, the Muslim protest against the soldiers was the 'straw that broke the camel's back', the one incident that confirmed his previous perceptions about the growing divide between his and the Muslim communities. 'Then a couple of lads set up Facebook sites ... Then people from other parts of the country said, look, there's this similar group in Luton ... I was uninterested in politics and wasn't involved in any political group before the EDL was set up ... All of a sudden, I became active and was fundamental to its activities at the beginning when it was founded in 2009. It [the movement] went national. Suddenly I felt that if I were part of an organization, I might get listened to ...'

A large number of local working-class men who joined the ranks of the EDL were in the construction industry. Some were ex-army. At the beginning of the group's formation, many took part in activities with a wait-and-see-what-happens attitude. Few had made up their minds about their political views, and as a result they were often not only misguided but also inconsistent. Many turned to the ideologies of the EDL as an answer to the misfortunes in their own lives, but during the course of its development, those with more of a stake in society tended to be driven away by the violence and extremism they witnessed in the EDL's street activities.

Darren wasn't aware of the implications of racism when he first got involved with the group, before it went national. He believed he was engaged in the defence of the soldiers against 'Islamic fundamentalists'. But what fundamentally angered him wasn't the Muslim protest. 'I wanted Luton fixed. I love Luton ... I'm not like those who jumped to the EDL wanting to shout, "This is our country," with a can of lager. And you got people who see Islamism as the problem and they came out with a lot of racism – it all turned out to be bigger than me. But all I cared about was Luton.'

However, the Birmingham demonstration in August 2009, his first EDL demonstration, challenged him deeply. He was told by those in the EDL that a demo was being organized because Anjem Choudary had forcibly converted a twelve-year-old lad called Shaun. He decided to go with another ninety people from Luton to protest against it, although he secretly didn't like some of them and was still wondering whether this level of activism was for him. His wife June said she didn't really like the idea of Darren going on a march outside of Luton, but didn't try to stop him because she knew that was what he wanted to do.

It was Darren's first experience of street politics, and naively he took his son with him. 'We nearly got murdered – by half of Birmingham.' He looked frightened even by the memory. 'On a football match, no one wants to kill you. They just want to beat you up. But on a political demo, they can kill you. I could hear the roar [of the anti-racists] in the middle of a ghost town vacated by the police.'

Darren still speaks about the experience with mixed emotions, and with regret.

My first shock was when Salma Yaqoob, a very eloquent lady with a left-wing agenda, was shouting the NF was coming. I fought the NF. I fought the British Movement. I was shocked I was called one of them.

It was my first day on a demo … It was terrifying. I shrunk within myself at that demo … If I think I'm right,

I stand up. I'd take the beating if I think I'm in the right. Or I'll say my piece if I think I'm in the right. But I wasn't understanding it. I didn't feel comfortable at all ... I was at the forefront of the demo, holding my banner saying 'black and white, unite and fight' ...

To this day, Darren can't shake off the shame he felt when two white middle-aged women walked past him and spat in his face, shouting at him, 'Nazi scum, get out of Brum!' He guessed that they were probably from the contingent of people from Unite Against Fascism (UAF), an organization he came across for the first time that day.

'That was really difficult for me,' he said. 'I could cry. I felt instant shame. At that moment I just wanted to fall between the cracks in the pavement ... but I was there and I couldn't just disappear. I just took the spit and I couldn't speak. I felt my whole life just being turned upside down.'

Paul Sillett, organizer of UAF, recalled:

The EDL's early days in Birmingham in autumn 2009 were disastrous, as hundreds attended a UAF counter-demonstration and drove EDL away from the city centre ... UAF put calls out to say the EDL should not be allowed to spread Islamophobia in the city, and many answered this by mobilizing in their hundreds. The local TUC backed the initial mobilization, as did other union members of core supporters of UAF, e.g. PCS [Public and Commercial Services] and NUT [National Union of Teachers] members.

It is a great memory I have of EDL literally being run out of town, pursued by locals, of all colours, faiths, creeds.

In the next couple of days, Darren's shame turned into more anger. He thought to himself: 'Who are you to tell me who I am? You don't even know me.' To be spat on by two white-haired middle-aged women was like his mother spitting in his face, he said. But he knew who he was. At this stage, he wasn't yet ready to admit that he'd taken the wrong route to voice his deeply held frustrations.

He carried on this political path, stubbornly, even knowing that it wasn't right. Persuaded by others in the group, he went on the second demo in Birmingham. He was soon to see that the street movement was filled with what he calls 'the NF type'. He said to Tommy Robinson, the then EDL leader, that he didn't like them.

Robinson asked him: 'Is it because they don't come from Luton?'

Darren replied: 'No, it isn't that. They're just real rottens. They looked to me like old skinheads ... I grew up through all that. I'm not happy with it.' But his words were ignored.

In fact, the EDL's response to the disaster of the first demo in Birmingham was to bring in crowds of football fans to its second demo, held in the same city. They came from all over the country, but in particular Luton. It was the EDL's show of force. As Robinson himself later confirmed, it was his own friends and acquaintances in the Luton football scene that formed the main part of the Luton EDL, although the football fans didn't last in their involvement. Soon, they came to the conclusion that the political character of the movement wasn't to their liking. Their involvement also prevented fans of other teams, like Millwall, joining EDL activities.*

Darren was the only one in the EDL to make a 'black and white unite' banner. After the second Birmingham demo, he wasn't sure whether it would go down well with the EDL crowd. From then on, he saw the banner as a sort of test. Some British West Indian lads from Luton got involved in EDL activities at the beginning, simply through the football connection, Darren told me. Their presence was the reason why Darren felt he had to have the banner up. As he put it, the West Indian lads dipped their toes in, but very soon found that the group wasn't for them and that they couldn't hang around. And according to Darren, the number of Luton football fans on marches after the second Birmingham demo decreased significantly.

---

* Paul Sillett, organizer of Unite Against Fascism (UAF), said that many of the EDL's initial foot-soldiers were from firms, or around firms, from Portsmouth up to Newcastle. 'Their numbers varied on the size of firm, e.g. Portsmouth EDL initially had around a hundred supporters, many from the old 6.57 crew. Newcastle was another division which enjoyed support from a number of "Gremlins", the hooligan firm of Newcastle United. Show Racism the Red Card did and continue to do sterling work undercutting the likes of the EDL support, in the North East, particularly ... At the Stoke demo, in 2009, over twenty firms were in support of the EDL ... The firms gave the EDL, for the first two or three years, some strength and were a key support base. This was not to last as inter-firm rivalry often broke out, and, along with arrests rates and opposition from anti-fascists, melted away, after a period of time.' He also commented: 'There exist many people who used to do stuff at football, had reactionary ideas and now look back, and think, "Was that me?" Breaking from racism takes imagination and, at times, some courage ... Being in a firm, of course, is a bonding experience. Any serious firm has to trust each other; failure to do so can lead to disaster, or, at the least, a serious kicking. Challenging others' racism in a firm is often just not the done thing, even now.'

UAF has done a great deal of work around the firms. 'EDL had tapped into racist and Loyalist hooligans at different firms and were growing. I spoke to other anti-fascist football fans and at clubs where the EDL either had or were trying to get a base. We decided to leaflet. Initially, we went for straight UAF anti-EDL leafleting. But then through a contact at Kick It Out, we got permission to use their logo and some words to bolster our message. Some places were easier to do than others.'

The British West Indian men didn't feel safe; the presence of neo-fascists on the demos frightened them. 'On the demos, Luton lads stuck with Luton; because then you know you're safe. And if anyone comes to you for your black mates, you know what to do. At demos, we had the football mentality where we all stuck together. No one's touching my mates. Just like being on the terraces.' Darren remembered an NF skinhead with a Union Jack jacket from Sunderland on the second Birmingham demo. As police were blocking the roads, the skinhead happened to be trapped among Darren's West Indian friends and couldn't get out. 'He Sieg-heiled in front of my black mates. "Do one." I asked him to leave. I didn't want any Nazi salute around. He tried to provoke us and we were gonna beat him up. But my black mates said, let him go. So I said to this skinhead, "The reason why you haven't got a good kicking today is because the black lads say not to." He got all teared up, starting to kick around. My black mates never went back to any EDL demo.'

Millwall was at times lively, but when they saw we had support, that element backed off. Man City, Leeds, Villa, Birmingham City, and others followed. Orient was the place where we had the most trouble – a few EDLers attacked leafleters and were helped by certain stewards ... A few months on, with the help of Orient fans, the EDL there were silenced, on and off the terraces. The local Supporters Club hosted the brilliant Steve White band ... to get the message over ... We had some great support from fans at all levels. Fans at clubs like Wellington FC, Luton and Leeds, where EDL had a small measure of success, refused to bow to intimidation and won through. Luton was surreal. On one occasion, EDL members had hired an executive box and were coming out with Islamophobic abuse ... Casuals United threatened us one time and said we were in real trouble. We always took such threats seriously. Truth is, though, that the leafleting could only go so far. We were small fishes in a big pool. We had no illusions that we were important. We just thought, "We have to do something." What was great, and went miles beyond the likes of us, was when highly respected stars in the game spoke out against racism ... To his credit, Jamie Barton did criticize the EDL. His comments were reprinted on an R's fans-against-the-EDL leaflet, at QPR's next home game ... EDL at QPR are few and far between, now. However, they haven't entirely gone away at grounds, and some will be looking to regroup. On Guard must be the motto.'

As Darren puts it, people with a trade or a job didn't tend to stay long in the EDL.

Many family men tried to find out what will happen in the next decade of their life … They want to know what the future holds … They try to predict the future for their families. They would come to see that it [what EDL stands for] is all a lot of rubbish …

Then you got other lads who are just basically not able to hold a job. Since the second Birmingham demo, the EDL pulled in a lot of people who were just crying for help … A lot of them can't articulate how they feel, so they let someone else speak for them. These lads have never had a job. Never visited a dentist in the last twenty years. Around 30 per cent of the EDL was made up of unemployed lads. I could see them going out looking for hope. And what is presented to them is just like that video *This is My England* on the EDL website that you and I were talking about: It's a mirage. The beautiful landscape and the pretty things they see of rural England on that video, about their country, their nation, are not within their reach … It's not theirs. But they followed it. They acted out their feelings. They follow their instinct looking for some meaning. But they'd been defeated years ago. Just defeated.

'Defeated?' I repeated.

'Yes. They haven't got a dim hope – that's the reality. Some of them just generally need help, mentally and physically.'

Darren didn't want to be counted among the alienated

individuals whose lives are so without future prospects that they eventually resort to racial hatred. He felt the shame of being associated with them. The Birmingham demonstrations were his introduction to the EDL, and where he started seriously considering leaving the organization.

But why didn't he? Darren went on to two more demonstrations, in Bradford and Dudley. Was it because Kevin Carroll is his cousin and Tommy Robinson his nephew? He felt compelled to, he said. It was a compulsion from within. It was almost like testing his limits. Did he want to back down? The answer at this point was no.

Meanwhile, EDL's growth and strength were causing UAF much concern. Its organizer, Paul Sillett, said:

> For us, alarm bells started ringing after the EDL's Manchester demonstration in October 2009. We realized that they were mobilizing large numbers at short notice, on this occasion, around 700. UAF outnumbered the EDL in Manchester, but it was clear that the EDL were operating a 'march and grow' strategy – recruiting supporters and building up momentum for the 'big one', to march on places such as Bradford, and Tower Hamlets in east London.
>
> The early EDL demos set a pattern for their future; their marches were characterized by huge levels of lumpen aggression, full of the often drunken assumption that 'sharia law' was soon to be huge in the UK, and that Islam was seeking world domination. Hardened racists and not a few fascists were always the main core of EDL demos. On some demos, NF members openly sold badges and other tat ...

In spring 2010, Darren got on a bus with sixty others – some of whom he knew from the terraces – from EDL's Luton Division, to join the thousand-strong march in Dudley. He felt he had to go to Dudley to join the protest against Saudi Arabia's financing of a local mosque. It was Saudi Arabian money coming to Dudley and locals didn't want it, because they believed the sect of Islam was not 'integrational'. The rationale was that they believed it couldn't be good for the community, and thousands of people signed a petition against it. Stopping the building of mosques has always been one of EDL's key activities. But why would the building of a mosque in Dudley concern a localist Lutonian like Darren?

'How could it have affected you?'

'I felt threatened,' Darren said, looking straight at me. 'Scared.'

I nodded, and tried to understand what he meant.

'Without having somebody to sit down from the Islamic community to talk to you … you don't know and you feel threatened. No man wants to admit that it is driven by a level of fear.'

'What did you fear?' I asked.

'Fear of domination,' he said, sighing. 'It's the mood in the air … You hear it a lot in the media. You hear Anjem Choudary, and Abu Hamza; they were saying what they felt. But I'd never felt like that in my lifetime. I started to fear. Fear for my kids, for my family.' The fear that what he had built hard all his life could suddenly be taken away from him and his beloved.

Once again, Darren was met with anti-racists, this time in Dudley, and once again he had to confront this image of himself as a racist. It was a shock for him, because he'd believed he was on the other side. When the naming became consistent, the shame became unbearable. He had to find ways to deal with it within him. This conflicting sense of self made him very unhappy and confused. As time went on, remaining in the EDL began to make him feel more and more anxious.

When Tommy Robinson was making his speeches on stage, Darren would look around the crowd and watch them chanting and shouting. 'This is not right,' he would think to himself, time and time again. He started to question what the group was really about and asked himself why he was still in it. Apart from the constant self-doubt and questioning, he was under considerable social pressure, too. When he went on jobs on building sites, people would comment on his involvement in the EDL as news travelled. Colleagues would ask him whether he'd been on any EDL demos lately. He became known as the 'EDL bloke'. And soon he began losing work. He'd been asked to leave jobs because of his association with the group. Other people traced him, found out where he worked and called up the companies and informed them. There was nowhere to run, nowhere to hide.

This public disapproval fed back into his self-image. Darren had to face up to being a racist, not only at work and in public, but also within himself. It became an internal battle. The unbearable confusion turned into more fear. Darren was afraid of what he heard and saw. He was afraid of what was said about him. It came to a point where the biggest thing for him was how to break the fear. 'Many of us were keeping our heads down. Scared if you open your mouth and your faces get seen, what's gonna come. Scared of what people might be calling you ... They've never met me before and never sat down to talk to me. They could say anything about me. It was very scary.'

Eventually, it felt like a thick cloud of paranoia was hanging over his life, and Luton too. 'It felt like al-Qaeda's gonna jump out of the woodwork and kill us.' What was feeding that paranoia? The media, he said.

Throughout 2010 and 2011, the EDL street movement was growing. This was a difficult time as anti-racist campaigners were working out strategies to combat it. One important barrier against the campaigners in their resistance was the state's Prevent policies. UAF said:

> Our strategy had to take in another important factor, the state – with today's levels of surveillance, intelligence teams, CCTV cameras, the Prevent strategy used to intimidate communities, and anti-terrorism laws that targeted young Asians, especially. In the 1970s it was common for anti-fascists to take a more 'direct' approach. However, you cannot simply replicate the past; you have to take into consideration new conditions and new factors. On the successful Cardiff UAF demo, in 2010 ... Asian young men were argued with by those implementing Prevent, to leave the UAF mobilization ... When the EDL marched in Preston [in 2011], in Lancashire, the police used the government Prevent strategy to instruct all mosque goers not to join the UAF counter-mobilization ... On that day we only managed to turn out some 200 people, including some councillors, led by Michael Lavalette, while around the corner EDL had some 2,000.

The general one-sidedness of the police became a feature. Money was thrown at curbing effective anti-fascism, whilst free coaches and pubs were the order of the day for EDL. We were also outnumbered in places such as Dudley, in 2011. Though we had around 800, the EDL had around 3,000 … Hundreds of them broke through barriers and went for UAF and others. They were beaten back, but this was a sign that to stop the EDL, we needed to broaden our forces and deepen UAF's base.

The EDL called a series of marches over the summer of 2011, targeting areas from Blackpool to Plymouth. 'We insisted that UAF groups had to mobilize from within communities and the labour movement. In this way local groups began to sink deep roots …' said UAF.

Leicester was a test case in 2011 for this. Our people worked with the local TUC, some Labour councillors, and key individuals from the main mosques and PCS and CWU unions … Some veterans had played a key role on the Anti-Nazi League against the National Front and their links in the City were important in mobilizing for what turned out to be a successful 700-strong protest. This mattered; the next year when the EDL arrived, many more councillors joined the protest and UAF held a march in the city against EDL. Not a few who had argued against UAF twelve months previously joined Leicester UAF on this occasion, including the Lord Mayor!

When the EDL organized in Liverpool in 2012/13, UAF adopted the same strategy. Through working closely with Unite the Union and members of the local Irish community, UAF organized a 5,000-strong march there to counter the EDL in 2013. 'The North West UAF organizer worked from Unite's office, and enjoyed good links with all the major unions across the region,' said UAF. 'This was vital in work undertaken to oust Griffin and undercut the EDL across the area. Those who played a major part in kicking Nick Griffin out were also the backbone in undermining the EDL in the North West ...'

Meanwhile, Darren's doubt had led him to detach himself from the social side of the EDL's activities, which many saw as important. He talked to a total of half a dozen people during his entire time in the group, including a couple of army men. He was always very cautious and didn't trust those around him easily. If he didn't get a good feeling from the first few seconds, he would stop talking to them. He pulled the shutters down, as he put it, didn't let anyone in. Others, therefore, thought him mysterious and difficult to work out, despite his being related to the leadership.

His localist feelings continued to dominate. He trusted the members from Luton more, because he 'knew their blueprint'. It was self-protection. He found a few members with the same concerns, 'those who saw it as a way to make a point about us in Luton', 'those who were there to say, "We're here, too."' But those people started drifting off slowly, as he was to do himself eventually.

Tommy Robinson wasn't aware of Darren's feelings. He was too involved in leading the group and fighting rivals. At one point, he came to Darren's house to ask him whether he'd like to be the co-leader of the EDL. Darren said no to the offer without a thought. He knew he was the first person Robinson approached. Clearly, he was trusted because he wasn't making much noise about what was going wrong in the group and he was one of the few able to articulate his ideas. Robinson needed someone like him. But Darren knew there was no way he could accept; he was thinking of leaving. Robinson went straight to Kevin Carroll, who accepted the position of co-leader without hesitation.

Darren was embarrassed about his association with the forty-four-year-old Kevin Carroll. Being Kevin's cousin, Darren was once seen by others in the group as being close to the 'core power'. Despite describing Kevin as a good uncle to his children, Darren has never approved of his conduct since his involvement with the far right. 'If you got a big ego, your ego believes things you shouldn't believe … I tried to give him advice, but his ego is driving him … The EDL has turned him into a narcissist.' Darren and Kevin are completely different characters. Darren describes himself as 'more of a soul lad' whereas 'Kev was coarser'. Kevin Carroll grew up on the other side of Farley Hill and the two came together only later in life, when Darren was about thirty-five. Darren said Kevin was propelled into the limelight by the events of 2009 in Luton. 'He just wanted the camera in front of him … It was the lack of emotional education really. He was just being used … After a while, I just kept quiet and watched him carry on.'

Darren's disappointment in Kevin Carroll gradually turned into anger and disgust. He watched Kevin change himself to suit the EDL. He saw how Kevin tried to play down his origins in order to appease the neo-fascists in the group. One day, Darren saw Kevin making a speech and holding up their grandfather's war medal, in the middle of an EDL demo. It was a medal the grandfather won in France during the Second World War. Kevin Carroll was showing it to prove to the EDL crowd that he was British, in response to comments by EDL activists that 'he's not even English; he's Catholic and Irish' and 'you can't be English and Catholic'. Darren shook his head at his cousin's conduct: 'And he capitulated to that, telling people how Grandad spilt blood here and there. I sat there looking at that, feeling disgusted. He was showing Grandad's medal to a load of dickheads. They were cheering, "Hero, Hero", to him. I thought to myself, how very sad ... Grandad went through all that war, for Kev to stand in the Midlands somewhere, to try and prove to the EDL crowd that he's British. I'll never forgive him for that.'

Worse still, Kevin Carroll started making noise about Darren's maternal grandfather, whom Darren himself has never met but who also won a war medal. He was doing this, again, to appease the EDL crowd and strengthen his own position within the group. 'You're not even bloodline,' Darren challenged him. 'This is the other side of the family.' But his complaint was ignored.

Soon after that, owing to pressure from his critics, who were making him extremely uncomfortable with regard to his background, Kevin Carroll began to denounce Catholicism and say it had never done anything for him. He was a Protestant, he announced. He even avoided St Patrick's Cathedral on his holidays in New York, just to avoid criticism from EDL activists.

For Darren, Kevin had gone from bad to worse. When he was running as the police commissioner candidate for the BFP,

Darren saw him handing out leaflets and talking to passers-by in town. Darren went up to him and asked for a leaflet, trying to engage him in a discussion about the BFP. Kevin Carroll refused to give him one, or even reply.

'You're not talking to me?' Darren said to him. 'I'm your constituent.'

Kevin Carroll ignored him.

'Surely, as your constituent, I have the right to ask you what your manifesto is,' Darren continued. Again, he was ignored.

'Your problem is that your mouth engages before your brain. You are just a useless idiot,' Darren said, and left.

On another occasion, he witnessed Kevin Carroll telling an EDL crowd that 'Palestine doesn't exist'. His words were filled with pro-Israel hatred.

Darren shouted to him: 'Who put that speech in your hand? Have you actually been to Palestine? Who are you to say all that? If you haven't been there and don't know the smell of the country, what are you shouting about?'

Kevin Carroll went quiet. He wouldn't tell Darren who actually wrote the speech for him. He didn't write it.

As time went on, Darren became increasingly frustrated with the neo-fascist elements within the EDL. He had always been anti-BNP, but several founding members of the EDL are known to have been BNP members – for example, Davy Cooling from Daventry and John Sheridan (aka Chris Renton) of Weston-super-Mare were both full-time BNP members. Alan

Spence, one of EDL's Newcastle organizers, stood as the BNP parliamentary candidate in Newcastle East in May 2010.

Many activists in the EDL were drawn to the BNP, whose members infiltrated the group from the beginning in an attempt to bring it closer to the party. Tommy Robinson also revealed this to me later when we met. For instance, Stuart Bates and Michael Fritz from Birmingham are both EDL activists, while being members of BNP's West Midlands security team. (According to Hope Not Hate, Stuart Bates was once drafted in to provide security for Nick Griffin on the BBC's *Question Time*.) BNP supporters have been out at most EDL demos, forming a decisive presence at EDL's Walsall demonstration in 2012, for instance. They spread rumours about Robinson – who was on a stag weekend and wasn't planning to attend the demo – that he didn't care about the Midlands. Robinson had to make an appearance as a result of the pressure.

The infiltration was successful, as Robinson himself acknowledged. Tony Curtis was an influential face in the EDL, but was later found to be working with Nick Griffin. Curtis rose to the top of the EDL and started a whispering campaign that the EDL needed unity with the BNP. Among the twenty or so regional organizers across the country, more and more were arguing for unity with BNP. Therefore, at the Walsall demo, Robinson made a speech to the EDL crowd and asked those who wanted to unite with BNP to make a show of hands. As he expected, no one dared. Robinson then looked at those who advocated unity and said: 'I don't want to hear another word about unity with the BNP.' That speech silenced the BNP faction for a while, but, as Robinson himself would admit, the intentions remained.

UAF adopted the strategy of fighting EDL and BNP on two fronts:

EDL were looking to piggyback on the streets on the back of the BNP's then relative strengths [BNP had two MEPs elected in June 2009]. UAF's resources were focused primarily then on thinking through how to combat Griffin in his target seat of Barking and Dagenham, in May 2010. UAF members put in huge efforts, alongside other anti-fascists, and were ultimately successful in ensuring not just that Griffin was not elected but that the BNP suffered, greatly. They were thrashed in their two key parliamentary constituencies of Barking and Stoke Central. Its record number of council and parliamentary candidates didn't make a breakthrough and only two out of twenty-eight BNP councillors standing for re-election were elected.

By then the EDL were established and looking to instigate conflagration in cities such as Bradford and boroughs such as Tower Hamlets. UAF faced thus two major challenges, looking to defeat the BNP electorally and opposing with broad forces the EDL's potential street threat. In this, joining forces with wide coalitions of anti-racists and anti-fascists was going to be critical if the BNP and the EDL were to be neutered. This, we set out to do, with urgency.

... It was clear that EDL demonstrated in areas where BNP had support, Stoke being a case in point, in 2010. BNP councillors of the time joined forces with the EDL ... EDL, BNP and Ulster Loyalists would combine in their violence. UAF meetings were attacked in Brighton, Manchester,

Leeds, Barking and Leicester. In Liverpool, EDL members tried to attack the Unite the Union office ... whilst in Wales, a TUC May Day event was targeted by thugs, who tried to shut it down.

For the Lutonians, the BNP came into view around the mid-1990s as individual supporters began to appear in town. But Darren believes they were never significant enough to be a collective, because a collective wouldn't have been tolerated in multi-ethnic Luton, with its strong British West Indian community. Darren believes that at least the West Indian Lutonians would have stood up to it.

According to Darren, the lads who wanted to join the BNP did so because they felt it was 'the last straw'; they were drowning. They felt no one was listening to them and there was no alternative, just as Tommy Robinson did, in 2004.

Robinson remained in the BNP for a while until he attended a meeting with his British West Indian friend. The BNP wouldn't let them in. That was when he turned against the group, Darren said to me. But could Robinson have been so naive about the BNP before?

'Sometimes at a certain stage of your life, you only hear what you want to hear,' Darren reflected.

Sometimes you need an experience to even open your ears and eyes. Maybe you don't want to hear it. You want an answer to how you're feeling. I did point it out to Steve [Tommy Robinson]: BNP's no good. Read their manifesto. From point one to ten, if you love your country, you might be able to reconcile most of it. You thought it looked all right ... They'll tell you what you want to hear. Do you feel like you're a stranger in your own country? they ask. People are gonna feel disenfranchised when they're not listened to ... And the reason why you're feeling disenfranchised is because of the politicians, not because of the family moving in down the road. The BNP rhetoric around it becomes very clever. Because many people can't articulate why they're feeling disenfranchised. BNP knows how to make you feel, which the NF could never do.

But if you read on and get to point eleven and twelve of the BNP manifesto, you'll see something like, 'You can't be a member of the BNP if you're black, but we can take your donations.' [Their tone becomes] just like the NF. You'd put it in the bin straight away ... They say all the fluff and flannel, but you've got to dig for what they're really about, and not everyone digs enough. Some people joined without even looking at the manifesto at all.

Darren said that when Kevin Carroll got involved with the BNP, they fell out for the first time. Then he heard that Kevin signed the nomination papers for the 2007 Luton council elections for BNP candidate Robert Sherratt. Darren felt disgusted: 'I just couldn't understand it. Kev's daughter is bi-racial and he raised her from six months of age ... When she was upstairs, we had an argument about it. Kev just went on about how no one was listening. I said to him, anything's better than the BNP.'

Later, when I met Kevin Carroll, he denied any involvement with the BNP and said he would never go near someone like Nick

Griffin. He told me that he only went to a BNP meeting once, with Robinson, 'just to see what it's like'. Kevin Carroll seemed approachable, but his answers to my questions always sounded like prepared statements. He was secure about his activism in the EDL and felt little regret. 'It's all worth it,' he said, even when giving me lengthy descriptions about the threats he'd received from local Muslim men.

To my amazement, one of the few people I heard praise Kevin Carroll was Lenos Wilson, a local activist of West Indian parentage (mentioned in Chapter 1). Wilson said he was surprised to find that Kevin wasn't exactly the 'racist thug' he had imagined. Part of Wilson's work for The Non Violence Alliance (TNVA) involves the prevention of violence by extremist individuals. He and his colleagues work with the borough council as well as the police. When the EDL was organizing a demo in Luton in May 2011, Wilson and his colleagues intervened and talked to Robinson and Carroll, with the aim of having the demo cancelled. 'We went to speak to them and tried to dissuade Tommy and Kevin from holding the demo. Fortunately they were quite polite about it and agreed to cancel the demo,' he said.

'I'm proud to say that TNVA managed to have the demo cancelled and saved the public a great deal of policing costs. People from the local Asian communities came up to shake my hands and said, "Well done."' Since his intervention, Wilson has managed to get Carroll and Robinson to come out to help with his night patrols a few times. However, Wilson said that the threat of violence from extremists has not gone away. 'The EDL will be coming back to try to hold a demo here in the near future. We're definitely going to stop them again.'

Meanwhile, Darren continued to find it a struggle to stay in the EDL, surrounded by neo-fascists of all descriptions. Each time he stood at a demo, he looked around and felt it difficult to tolerate. 'There are so many hateful people ... Half of the people in the EDL are open racists and you have an extreme far right element attached to it ... You can't beat these people coming. They got their own agenda. Steve [Tommy Robinson] told me he was scared that it [EDL] could be hijacked and his name would be attached to something that got out of control around the country ... I just didn't feel I could be part of the group at all. I felt alienated. I began to shut conversations down with people all the time.'

Darren said that Robinson had tried to control the growth of the neo-fascists in the EDL. But Darren knew it wasn't going to work. He started considering leaving the EDL properly by cutting all ties because he felt it was irreversibly going down the wrong path. 'I looked around and saw that it was for the stupid, and the brave ... You couldn't just stand up and speak to no one, and in the end, all the extremist idiots come, and it's a slow change over a certain amount of demos. And then you stand there speaking to yet another load of neo-Nazis.'

At one of the demos, Darren saw the neo-fascist types turning up with T-shirts with skulls on them. He knew it'd be related to some sort of Nazi calendar. These guys started causing a lot of trouble; they got organized and turned up in bigger numbers. Those who disapproved of their presence ended up fighting them physically. Demos were therefore filled with punch-ups between groups of men. Then the neo-fascists came with screwdrivers.

The Blackburn demo in 2010 was one of the worst. Fifty men who belonged to splinter groups Northwest Infidels and Northeast Infidels arrived dressed in eighteenth-century-style clothing. They got into a fight with Robinson's men. Robinson's then head of security Steve Eddowes had to shield him from an attacker with his back and managed to get Robinson out. After that march, fighting between mainstream EDL members and the neo-fascists came to a head, until the neo-fascists left the EDL and formed splinter groups. The Northwest Infidels and the Northeast Infidels are much closer to the neo-Nazi far right than the Robinson-led EDL. Like most neo-Nazis, they support the Ulster Unionist cause. The Northwest Infidels was run by John Shaw, who protests against halal meat on the basis of 'animal welfare', but was found guilty in April 2012 of cruelty to animals as he deliberately starved his llamas to death. The Northeast Infidels is headed by Paul Duffy, EDL's former North East organizer. He was found guilty of firearms offences in March 2013 and was given five years in prison. On EDL demos, the Northwest and Northeast Infidels often appeared with banners with Nazi slogans, and didn't hesitate to use violence.

EDL's regional organizers have always been relaxed about the violent, neo-fascist elements gaining force within their ranks and have never seen them as a problem. They have always worked with groups like the Racial Volunteer Force (RVF), a violent neo-Nazi splinter group of Combat 18 (C18). Formed in 2003 under the leadership of Mark Atkinson and John Hill following a split in C18, they have in fact maintained close ties with it. RVF advocates aggression against non-white people and is close to the NF. Mark Atkinson, from Egham, Surrey, is a white supremacist who was involved in the NF from the age of fifteen and has proudly claimed an association with the Ku Klux Klan. In 2005, Atkinson and four others were jailed for a total of fifteen years under the Race Relations Act. The court heard that his group paid tribute to the Soho nail bomber David Copeland with instructions on how to make a bomb. The five had admitted conspiracy to publish *Stormer*, RVF's magazine, to stir up racial hatred. Even in prison, Atkinson didn't stop disseminating his vicious racism: 'I have definitely seen a difference between North and South jails. Southern jails are full of negroes and Muslims whereas the Northern jails are predominately white, which is much better for me.'

In March 2009, Atkinson opened a whites-only pub in the Glasgow area, claiming 'it will be a place where all white people will be welcome apart from the reds and other white scum'. Atkinson said: 'It will be the only place in this country that will go back to the good old days of the colour bar and the non-white will definitely NOT be welcome.' He told supporters that they were looking to open more such pubs all over the country.

These were the neo-Nazis Darren was telling me about.

One of the few divisions that was loyal to Robinson at the time was the Anglian Division. Darren observed that 'they stood with him' and fought Combat 18 and the other neo-fascists. 'Some of the lads from the Anglian Division were army lads, you see. They fought the Nazis.'

3

THE STORY OF BURY PARK

Tommy Robinson, head of the EDL until October 2013, has been described as a legend-like figure in Luton and nationwide. The popular media have given him a near-charismatic aura, some making him the spokesman for the underprivileged white Briton. Media interviews always seemed tinged by embarrassment, as if trying to balance a commercial desire to give him column inches/airtime and a sense of guilt at giving him space to express his views.

A week after I tried to get in touch with Robinson via the pub manager in Farley Hill, he sent an email via his PA, Hel Gower, asking for a contact number. But he never called. Weeks later, through a contact of mine, I managed to get hold of his mobile phone number and called him. On hearing my foreign accent, Robinson sounded suspicious. 'Do you write in English?' he asked. 'Have you published in this country?'

He said yes to my interview eventually, and asked to meet at the Icon Hotel, Luton. Given his reputation as one of the most notorious racists in this country, I had no idea how our meeting would turn out. I even told myself to be prepared that the interview could be cut short. With all this in mind, I was a little surprised to see Robinson in person; he wasn't quite what I'd expected. He had arrived early and was sitting on a sofa in the hotel lobby, with two crutches next to him. He looked somehow smaller in real life, almost shrunken in comparison to the bloated, confident image that I'd seen in the press. Had the media made him look bigger than he really is? I couldn't help smiling at the thought.

I nodded, instead of shaking his hand, as I approached him. He nodded in reply without any movement in his face. There was ice to be broken. 'What happened?' I asked, pointing to his crutches.

'I had a fight with some football fans out of town,' he replied, turning up his trousers to show me his injury. 'But it's nothing to do with the EDL.'

Robinson had adopted various different names throughout his life and, intentionally or otherwise, created a mystery surrounding his personal story in the press. He explained: 'I was born under the name Stephen Yaxley. Yaxley was my real father's name. I haven't seen him since I was eleven years old. I was adopted by my father now, whose name is Lennon. So I got the two names together. Up until the age of eleven or twelve, everyone knew me as Yaxley ... Then when I got to sixteen [having left school] and as I grew older as a man, I thought, do I want my children to take my name Yaxley? I don't. So I got rid of Yaxley, and just kept the name Stephen Lennon.'

Since he was a young boy, Robinson has followed the Luton Town Football Club along with many of the people he grew up with. He saw football as his community, like Darren. But unlike Darren, his resentment against the town's Muslim population developed during his early, football days. Even then, he was involved in fights between football fans and Muslim residents in Bury Park. He set up 'Ban the Luton Taliban', in 2004, at the age of only twenty-one. Contrary to the official story, Robinson's anti-Muslim feelings did not originate with the 2009 anti-army Muslim parade; they reached farther back to the early years of his adulthood.

He adopted the name 'Tommy Robinson' after having organized a 'Ban the Luton Taliban' protest in town. 'At the time I was talking about girls being groomed and all that,' he said in a casual manner, without looking at me. 'And the fallout of that was that I was under attack … My house was attacked … All the Muslim gangs wanted to get me. When they abused our troops six, seven years later, I wanted to make a stand and say something, but I didn't want to get all the threats against me, so I wore a mask and used a different name, Tommy Robinson.'

Rumours said that he had adopted the false name under the guidance of the supposed 'mastermind' and financial backer of the EDL, Alan Lake. But Robinson told a different story about his relationship with Alan Lake to the one I knew from press reports. Claims that Lake put up money for the group are nothing more than a groundless conspiracy theory, he says.

'I've never met anyone like him,' Robinson said.

He's different to everyone I've ever known growing up with … There's no middle class in Luton.

We drove down to meet them in Alan's Barbican flat. Ten of them met with a few of us. When we met, I thought they were a million miles away from who I am, in the sense of their wealth, their background, their upbringing, their intelligence ... They were all intellectual people. One of them was like a strategist, nuts, talking all the time about Roman manoeuvres, telling us how we should organize ourselves to outmanoeuvre the police ... I said to him, we don't want to outmanoeuvre the police. All we wanted to do is protest and tell people what's going on. I thought to myself, who the hell are these people? Are they Freemasons or the MI5 or what? What's their interest in what we're doing in Luton? What was all that about?

Alan knows a lot about Islam and everything, far more than us. But he was nervous about things, like about when to run a demo, etc. He was trying to strategically plan things. We just thought, shut up, we're gonna have a demo and that's what we were doing. Alan offered us support at the time, helping with education around Islam. But we were just miles apart. I knew that even after the first meeting.

He's never funded the group. What the press said was all bullshit. They invented it because they couldn't explain how something could come from nothing – how a Luton protest could develop into a nationwide movement. So they said it's funded by the Jews. Absolute bullshit.

Robinson continued:

The first time Alan was seen with us ... he turned up in a suit. He doesn't look like one of us. They [the press] saw an upper-middle-class eccentric talking to us, and they assumed he's the brain and he's the backer. He isn't. He's never financed us. All he did was pay for a PA system, £240, and he asked for the money back. We funded ourselves, selling merchandise [e.g. the EDL T-shirts, jumpers, badges] – I used to run the merchandise like a business, generating £600–700 a week, which was enough for us to pay for banners, placards, etc. And we also relied on donations from individuals. The EDL grew from nothing into a national movement. Imagine if we had his funding!

Alan wanted to promote his own group, Four Freedoms [which argues that Islam is the main threat to 'secular democracy']. He came to our protest and promoted Four Freedoms, which was just a lot of talk. What we wanted was to go out there and do things. It's an illusion that he gave us any guidance about anything. He came to our first few demos, in Dudley and Newcastle, for instance, but he couldn't talk to people on the street. He wanted to do a Shakespeare play. I said to him, if you do that, you'll get battered. You're miles away, I said. The wavelength is just too different ... He's very knowledgeable, but when it comes to life experience, he hasn't got a lot ... We got different visions ... Alan's very angry with the left, whereas it didn't bother me. For me, it wasn't about that. The difference between me and Alan is the class difference. It just doesn't work between us ... So we parted company.

Later, Paul Ray also commented on Alan Lake's connections and how far away he is from the masses of the EDL: 'Alan Ayling aka Alan Lake has some serious protection in this earthly realm, protection that is not afforded to us mere mortals lower down the social ladder who do not have the added wealth or family background to walk in such circles who we can call upon to protect us from the law ...'

Alan Lake didn't respond to my request for an interview, so I was unable to confirm either way if he had funded EDL's early activities.

I wanted to know how the early years of Robinson's life shaped his identity and his deep-seated resentment against Muslims. I wanted to know about his family background. He told me: 'My mum's from Ireland and she came to Luton with her family at the age of four ... I used to live in a completely Irish area but I didn't go to a Catholic school. I broke away from that and I don't see myself as Irish at all. I've never been to Ireland. My real dad's English. I feel completely English.'

Robinson's stepfather, Lennon (whom he calls Father), worked for Vauxhall for years, and Robinson used to help out, working alongside him on Saturdays. His father was made redundant in the early 2000s and had to work abroad, doing pipework, in Germany and Mexico.

He added: 'Everyone in this town is an immigrant. But we all class ourselves as English.'

Despite insisting on being 'English', Robinson, just like Kevin Carroll, was constantly criticized for not being 'proper English' by Paul Ray and his supporters. Paul Ray was one of the co-founders of EDL and is a neo-fascist blogger who calls himself Lionheart (borrowing the soubriquet of King Richard I). His views are said to have influenced the Norwegian fascist Anders Behring Breivik. During Robinson's time in the EDL, Paul Ray launched an attack on Robinson, calling him 'Irish Tommy', and arguing his leadership was ideologically impure. Not only was he Irish, but a Catholic, and for some this undermined his legitimacy as leader of the EDL.

Despite this, Robinson insisted on using the word 'English' to describe himself and his allegiances.

'What is English?' I asked, expecting a planned answer that he'd probably prepared for every interviewer. But he paused.

'What is English?' I asked again. 'And what are you defending?'

'Defending England,' he answered firmly this time. 'When I say being English, it's like if you come here and you embrace this country and love this country ... and you have children here and your children will be brought up feeling English. Then you're English. Look at Ian Wright; I look at black footballers and I say of course they're English.'

'So what's the difference between being English and British, then?' I asked.

'I don't feel British. I feel English,' he said, looking embarrassed as he couldn't explain the difference.

'So, when a British Muslim identifies himself or herself with this country and adopts the culture, would you see them as English?' I asked.

He shook his head, looking for words. 'But they don't see themselves that way. You will not find one of them that will carry the England flag or wear the English cross, because it's got the cross of St George.'

'You mean someone has to do all that to be called English?' I asked again.

'Look, I mean, when you see a Muslim, say a Muslim boxer, he has the Union Jack ... but as soon as he makes his money, he gets rid of the Union Jack and gets a Pakistan flag! Amir Khan, a Muslim boxer, used a British flag, but as soon as he made a career, I hope he doesn't, I bet he'll get himself a Pakistan flag.'

Robinson said his street movement aims to defend 'a way of life'. 'This year, St George's Day was cancelled,' he said bitterly. 'Armed Forces Day, cancelled. Christmas, cancelled. Fireworks night, cancelled. There were no fireworks.'

'Christmas was cancelled?'

'Yeah. There's no Christmas lights,' he replied, looking genuinely angry.

'So you want Christmas lights back on.' I tried to conjure up the image of a Christmas lights campaign run by the embittered ultra-nationalists.

He went on: 'The council is slowly neutralizing our special days, our festivals. This Saturday, for Eid, there will be massive celebrations. Massive. And what about us? Our identity and our culture? It's all just been pushed to …'

I tried to stop his predictable Anglo-centric ranting about his culture being invaded, and to move on to other questions I wanted to ask. But he carried on about Christmas.

'The council's saying they haven't got the money to put up the Christmas celebrations. There'll be no Christmas lights, no Christmas trees, for the first time, in 200 years. Christmas is not being celebrated in Luton!' he said. 'And slowly, everything we hold dear is disappearing. Everything that is sacred to our culture, our way of life, is eroded. And all we see flourishing is Islam …'

The erosion of 'English culture', the dominant culture in this country, is plainly a false fear. Looking at his town with its white

British majority, you do not get the impression that it is being 'taken over by incoming cultures'.

'So what you're saying is that you find it uncomfortable to live alongside people of different cultures,' I said.

Robinson looked defensive, and said everyone gets on great and he has no problem with other cultures. 'I just find it uncomfortable to live among Islam,' he said anxiously. 'What upsets me about the Muslims is they force [their practices] upon me ... and their way of lifestyle encroaches on mine.'

I wondered what Robinson's early years were like, how he interacted with children of other cultural backgrounds at school, and how he began to see other cultural practices as an encroachment. He said ethnic relations were not a problem until after junior high school. But once everyone started at senior high school, students began to break into groups along ethnic lines. He began to feel a great discomfort about Islam. 'I recognized it [the discomfort] since Putteridge High School. I realized that there's something different about Muslim children. Around 25 per cent of the students were Muslims, like the percentage in Luton town itself. They had this sort of confidence, togetherness, and hostility towards non-Muslims. As you grow up in the town, you always wonder what it was ... why they were like that ... At the time I thought it was just a Pakistani thing ...'

Without any interaction with children from Muslim backgrounds and no school education about multicultural living, Robinson simply formed his own conclusions in his young mind: it must have been religion that made some kids seem 'cooler' and 'different' to others. Having not befriended Muslim children of the same age, he assumed that it was the Quran that taught them, in his words, 'not to be friends with Christians or Jews'. These ideas, without being challenged by schoolteachers or his peer group, only strengthened as he grew older.

When Robinson left school, he started working as an aircraft engineer at Luton Airport and was in an apprenticeship for five years. When I asked him whether he had any Muslim colleagues during that time, he simply shrugged his shoulders and said: 'No, because Muslims don't really work in skilled jobs.' Later, he trained as a plumber and set up his own plumbing business, and then, in 2007, opened a sunbed shop just over the road from the Icon Hotel where we were meeting. Throughout his working life, he has never had any contact with British Muslims. In fact, his only interaction with the community came after he began his activities on the far right in the mid-2000s.

Despite his deep dislike of Islam, it was years into his anti-Muslim activities before Robinson eventually tried to read the Quran, during a prison sentence in October 2012. He found it difficult to make sense of what he read. 'It's not in numerical order ... not in the order of history,' he said to me. 'But I tried to read the whole thing and listed out the verse about things like friendship with non-Muslims.' In other words, Robinson attempted to comprehend the Quran by pulling sections out of context and interpreting them in a way of his own choosing.

Robinson's rough reading of the Quran only served to strengthen his previous prejudices against Islam and Muslims into a set of views based on popular racial myths already existing in Britain's mass media: e.g. 'foreigners are getting a better deal' (as Robinson said, 'We're highlighting a complete two-tier system in this country when our communities are treated with an

iron fist and everyone tiptoes around the Islamic community');
'Muslim men are culturally prone to sex grooming' (see Chapter
1); 'Muslims don't integrate' (Robinson calls British Muslims
'just Islamic ghettoes'). These myths often extend to other
groups of 'outsiders'. Robinson said: 'Our kids have to pay 9K
tuition fees when the Welsh are paying fuck all.'

With his focus on cultural practices and the inherent differences between contending cultural groups, Robinson's politics
of race bears more resemblance to the old-fashioned 'centre-
right' racists of British mainstream politics than to the traditional
far right such as the BNP. His views resonate with, for instance,
those expressed by tabloids such as the *Daily Mail* and politicians
of the likes of Godfrey Bloom, UKIP's MEP for Yorkshire and
Northern Lincolnshire, famous for describing countries receiving
foreign aid as 'Bongo-bongo land'.

Tommy Robinson and his circle began their activities against
the local Muslim community in Luton years before the
EDL was formed. Their views were formed by years and years of
demonization of British Muslims by the same popular tabloids
which had always portrayed Luton as a 'hotbed of extremism'.

The rationale is that an unusual number of Islamic extremists
came from – or in some cases, more accurately, have spent time in
or passed by – this town. The 7/7 bombers from West Yorkshire
met at Luton station on the day of their suicide bombing in
2005 and abandoned their cars in the car park. Taimour al-
Abdaly, the twenty-eight-year-old bomber who blew himself up
in Stockholm in December 2010, studied physical therapy at

the University of Luton (now the University of Bedfordshire) between 2001 and 2004, and appeared at the Luton Islamic Centre during Ramadan in 2006 or 2007. There is no real evidence that Taimour al-Abdaly became radicalized there. But, since then, the mosque, as well as entire communities, have been blamed for one man's extreme act.

Instead of putting money where it is needed, i.e. building sorely needed local services to benefit particularly women, the youth and the elderly in Luton's Muslim communities, the Home Office's Preventing Violent Extremism scheme expected members of these communities to spy on each other and to report the names of 'those likely to commit violent crimes so they can be put on an at-risk list'. When no one was willing to do so, the tabloids launched an attack on the entire community. On 13 December 2010, the *Telegraph* ran the headline 'Sweden suicide bombings: Luton synonymous with Islamic extremism and racial tension', and the report called the town 'home to one of the main concentrations of extremists in the country', concluding that 'the concentration of extremists has exacerbated racial tensions'. And on 18 December, the *Daily Mail* proclaimed, 'Muslims in bomber's town get £500,000 to combat terror but don't give police a single tip-off.' Media reports like these provided justification for the propagation of racist ideologies and laid the groundwork for street movements like the EDL.

The media has also consistently attempted to equate 'Islamic extremism' with far-right ideologies, and in doing so has played down the extreme racism propagated by far-right organizations. An example of this is Stacey Dooley's BBC documentary *My*

Hometown Fanatics, broadcast on 20 February 2012, a report so favourable to the far right that the EDL and many EDL-friendly groups have put it up on their website as publicity material. In the documentary, Dooley, who also came from Luton, legitimized EDL's views by selectively talking to some local Muslims with more radical perspectives. She also endorsed the EDL line that Luton has changed beyond recognition through the presence of ethnically diverse communities. She acted alarmed upon hearing chanting from the mosque, saying: 'I heard something that reminds me how diverse this town has become.'

Then she turned to ask a Muslim man walking next to her: 'What is this?'

'It's the prayer,' he said.

'I wonder how the white working-class folk here feel when they hear this?'

'No one has complained yet,' the man replied.

Her presumptions that different cultural practices would automatically cause tensions and fuel discontent are false and filled with racial undertones. Her programme completely ignored the fact that Muslim Lutonians have been the main target for racism for the past decade, and it did not address the level of racial abuse they've suffered as a result of the growth of far-right ideologies.

As I came to visit Bury Park and spent time talking to its residents, I witnessed first-hand that the reality here could not be more different to the one portrayed in the popular media and by the far right.

Stacey Dooley said of Bury Park: 'You can be easily mistaken that this is not English ... not a place in England.' However,

British Asian people have not always been so concentrated here and Bury Park was not always known as an 'Asian area'.

Bury Park, and Luton in general, was transformed when the Vauxhall car plant opened in 1905. Insufficient local labour at the time meant that the industry pulled in not only workers from nearby London but also from Ireland, Asia and the West Indies. At its peak in the 1950s, the factory employed 30,000 people. It was a multicultural workforce, which reflected the ethnic composition of the town. Multicultural living was the norm. But when the plant closed earlier in this century, it shut down the most important means of livelihood that families in *all* communities had depended on for a hundred years. That closure created bitterness and deepened divisions that were to last. It also led to the decline of communities like Bury Park.

Abdul, in his late twenties, described the outflow of white Lutonians from Bury Park as it ceased to be an attractive choice of residence: 'There used to be English people living in Bury Park in the old days. But some of them didn't like living in this area any more because they thought there were too many "foreigners" … They didn't want to live alongside Muslims. They wanted to stick to their own culture and their own group. So they gradually moved out of the area since the late 1990s … Eventually, Bury Park became our area.'

With popular media providing the ammunition, the far right was confident in acting out its racism. In the past few years, attacks on Muslim communities in Luton have increased, among them the attempted arson attack on the Al-Ghurabaa mosque following written threats in May 2009, the attack on Medina mosque in July 2011, the arson attack on Bury Park Jamie Masjid in Bury Park Road in April 2012, and the attempted arson attack on Al Hira Education Centre in October 2013.

I tried to get a general sense of how local people see their security and well-being here and how that has been affected by recent developments in the race politics of this town. I talked to several workers who were raising money from passers-by for the Hockwell Ring Masjid, a local mosque ten minutes away from the centre of Bury Park. One of them told me that their communities self-fund the refurbishment of their mosques and rely on volunteers like himself to do fundraising on the streets.

He said he's been living in Britain for three decades and has only begun to feel concerned about the well-being of British Muslims in the last few years. Since the rise of activities organized by the EDL in Luton, he has felt threatened and worried about not only the security of the communities as a whole but also his own personal safety. 'I'm a law-abiding person,' he said quietly. 'I spend all my time working and helping others. I work as a warehouse worker four days a week, and spend the rest of my time doing voluntary work for the mosque.'

He told me that since the Woolwich murder, the number of racial attacks and the level of abuse in the town have increased. 'I kept hearing about cases of verbal abuse,' he said. 'About twice a week these days. People talk about it all the time.' His fellow fundraiser, who was standing next to him, nodded gently in agreement.

When they went off-shift, a woman and a teenage girl took over the fundraising stall. They were no less outspoken than their male colleagues. They tried to engage passers-by about their cause.

Komorum is in her forties, her daughter now seventeen. Komorum works full-time as a schoolteacher and is committed to her work. 'Contrary to popular prejudice against Muslim women, many of us work and lead a life just like women of other faiths,' she asserted. She also does voluntary work for the Hockwell Ring mosque, organizing workshops for girls and teaching Islam there.

Komorum said she has not always lived in Bury Park. She was born and grew up in Birmingham, and moved down to Luton when she got married. She doesn't hesitate to define her identity and is confident in exposing her feelings to a stranger like me. 'I see myself as a British Muslim. First and foremost I see myself as British,' she said. 'Like me, many Muslims are born and bred in Britain and feel completely British. We're very well integrated.'

In her full-time job as well as voluntary work for the mosque, Komorum has always worked with and alongside non-Muslims and befriended many of them. At this point, her daughter interrupted: 'I have many friends from all religious backgrounds and religion has never been an issue.' She's British through and through, even more so than her cultivated mother. Such an open and polite girl, well spoken, she will most likely grow up to embrace a future filled with plenty of opportunities, I thought to myself. She will probably go to university and become a professional, be successful in her career and bring up a family of her own. Surely, she would be a citizen to be proud of in any nationalist's 'British dream', the future of this country.

Recognizing their own wholehearted effort to 'integrate', Komorum feels angry with the way her community is being targeted and victimized. 'The growth of racism has had a very negative impact on Muslim communities,' she said. 'The portrayal of Muslims is totally unfair and wrong. They try to create the image that every Muslim is an extremist.'

Komorum believes that the demonization of British Muslim communities in the media and society at large has led to an increase in attacks and abuse based on both skin colour (when recognized as of South Asian origin) and religion. 'I have continued to hear about these attacks and abuse in the past year,' she said. 'This is largely a result of the growth of groups like the EDL. Their existence has made me feel unsafe to go out of my area.'

'You mean you fear leaving Bury Park?' I asked.

'Yes, I really don't feel safe outside of Bury Park,' she said. 'Not only that – Muslim residents have often been warned by others in the community not to go out during the EDL activities such as when there's a rally in town; we also try not to go out of this neighbourhood even when there isn't such a warning.'

What can be done about the ongoing demonization of British Muslims? Komorum said that re-education of British young people is the way forward. Ignorance breeds fear. The younger generation needs to be provided with the knowledge to enable them to learn to live in a multicultural society. However, before that happens, Komorum resorts to 'keeping ourselves to ourselves'. 'It is the only way to protect ourselves in a hostile environment at the moment,' she said.

Across the road from the Islamic Centre, I walk past a sweet shop and get talking to the owner, a friendly and approachable man. His name is Abdul, and he invites me to sit.

Abdul is what would generally be considered a relatively successful second-generation British Pakistani – hard working and law abiding, like many in the British Chinese communities who migrated from Hong Kong to Britain in the 1960s and 1970s. All Abdul has ever wanted to do is to make a good life here for himself and his family. His father migrated to the UK, leading the way for the family's eventual settlement here – he opened fourteen shops in Southall, south London, and was very successful for a while. In the mid-1970s, however, he made losses and became depressed. He finally decided to arrange for Abdul, sixteen years of age at the time, and his mother, to come to join him in England.

So Abdul arrived in the UK in 1979, hoping to run businesses here as his father did, and helping with the family's livelihood. Abdul followed in his father's footsteps and set up his own catering business in Southall. By this time his dad had set up a new sweet shop in Luton. As Abdul's business was doing well in Southall, he began to expand it, and set up another food shop in Green Street, popular for its South Asian cuisine, and garment businesses in Upton Park, east London. Although it wasn't doing badly, Abdul later felt that the competition was too fierce for him to handle. 'So eventually, I decided to take over my father's shop in Luton,' he said. 'I moved my family up here and together we started a new life. Running a business was far too complicated in London. I found Luton a good place for that.'

Abdul described Luton as 'providing a better quality of life'. He concentrated on work and settling his family. Unlike many of the Pakistani workers who arrived to work in the Vauxhall factory in Luton, Abdul had some resources at hand, thanks to his dad's hard work.

But even for Abdul, life wasn't without difficulties. He recalled the conflicts that existed between different communities in the early days, the tensions he referred to as 'between the white locals and us newcomers'. He looked out of the shop window and pointed to the right, saying, 'The football ground over there … used to pull in crowds of hostile locals.'

Then he pointed to a café across the road. 'There used to be a nightclub right opposite this shop … and there used to be a lot of hell … The club-goers often found trouble, particularly with Asians, and once my shop windows were smashed.'

Abdul said that trouble like that occurred a lot in the 1990s. There was a lot of fear among British Asian residents in Bury Park as there always seemed to be people looking for a fight. 'There were skinheads around,' he recalled, shaking his head. 'One time, four to five hundred skinheads came to this area to make trouble. Can you imagine that? Four to five hundred. The police were called and came in the end …'

Abdul said that this kind of trouble tends to happen outside of Bury Park these days, as Bury Park has become a British-Asian-majority area where probably even skinheads might find it difficult to 'make a scene'. And this means that Bury Park is the only place where British Asian residents feel safe in Luton. As he explained: 'Most Asians don't tend to leave this area. It's safe here. And this is the reason why we don't often feel that the problem of racial tension is serious – because we're protected here in our neighbourhood.'

Racial attacks and abuse over the years, particularly through the 1990s, have created the current reality of two segregated communities; the white British community and the British Asian community stay out of each other's way. They are two worlds that don't meet. 'We live our own lives away from the white communities,' Abdul told me, 'and we concentrate on doing our business and raising our children.' Isolation has shaped the British Asian communities here, and a self-sufficient 'community economy' has developed over the decades.

Abdul raised his children to value education. He has two daughters and two sons: the elder daughter is twenty-six years old, a science graduate; his eldest son is an accountant and the younger a doctor. 'The four of them all see themselves as British Muslims,' he said. 'They received a good education and are contributing their skills and talents to society. They're completely and thoroughly "integrated".'

What have become of the skinheads that were active around here when his children were growing up? Does he still see them on the streets and are they still a threat? 'Not around here any more,' Abdul said, and smiled. 'I think they must have grown up by now.'

Abdul has a different way of looking at the far right. He obviously saw the skinheads as 'children', kids who had nothing better to do and were misguided. He felt no grudges against them and their hatred, and seemed only want to smile it away. 'Their parents, I believe, would have taught them right and wrong and how to become good human beings,' he said, sipping his tea. 'You see, education is very, very important.'

Holding no grudges and wanting to get on with life doesn't always protect British Asian Muslims from racial harassment and the unjust portrayal of their communities. I wondered what Abdul thinks is the way out of social prejudice and the stigma imposed upon British Muslims. He resorted, once again, to education. As in my experience with the British Chinese community, ensuring a good education is one of the main ways for ethnic minorities to resist hostility and racism. Many also believe it to be the key to changing the minds of the indigenous population.

In Britain there is a lot of misunderstanding and misconception about Islam and Muslims. I think education is the way to get rid of prejudice. If people know more about Islam and Muslims, they would not think the prejudice they do.

There are many merits in Islam. One thing I always see as important is the idea that the haves in society must share their wealth with the have-nots. I deeply believe in the importance of giving ... and there is a lot of giving in the spirit of Islam. In our community, the wealthier people are obligated to give 2.5 per cent of their profits to the poor. The capable ones have a duty to look after those in need. We do this by conscience. We rely on conscience for the wealthy in our community to practise this and for them to donate the correct percentage of their wealth to the poor.

Mohammad, employed by Abdul to look after the shop, nodded in agreement as he listened to the conversation. Perhaps he has learned to reconcile class differences with his employer as they share the same difficulties being Muslims in Britain. The hostility from British society has bound them together, members of an isolated and victimized community. I had observed the same process at work, the same cycle of ethnic community life, among Britain's Chinese communities: isolation and victimization lead to a self-sufficient and enclosed existence, which leads to yet further isolation and victimization.

A large proportion of Bury Park's low-skilled and semi-skilled workforce is made up of an army of transient migrant workers from South Asia. Their experience of interaction with other cultures can be more intense than that of the older generation of immigrants. As part of the manual working class, they are likely to experience racism first-hand and therefore perceive it differently to the permanent settlers from the same countries of origin.

Mohammad is an optimist, though. Despite his knowledge and experience of racism in this country, his need to make a living for his family has made him tolerant and accepting of his circumstances. He came from Pakistan and went to work in Germany for a couple of years before arriving Britain. He's been living with his family here for two years now, and when I asked how he feels about working in this country, his response came without hesitation: 'I love it. I love England.'

Later, I also met Mohammad's friend, a thirty-year-old man called Ali, from Pakistan, who has only been in Luton for three months. He told me that, ever since landing in the UK eight years ago, he's been working non-stop. This month is the first time he's been out of work. 'Work was everything I did,' he said. When I asked him what motivated him to come to this country, he said he liked the idea of Britain for its 'personal freedom' and 'lawfulness'. 'I can be independent here,' he said, 'while at the same time there are rules to protect you from anarchy ... and that makes you feel comfortable living here.'

However, one thing that has shocked him about life here is the level of racism he has experienced. Before coming to Luton, he had spent seven years working in a restaurant in Lincoln. He was much saddened when he found out that social attitudes towards Muslims weren't nearly as liberal as Britain's reputation. 'It was the first English town I've lived in in this country. I opened myself to everyone, from all backgrounds,' he told me. 'More than 90 per cent of my friends in Lincoln are non-Muslims. But sadly, there was a lot of racism against me as an Asian and a Muslim.'

Ali said that most of the racism came in the form of verbal abuse, which he would almost always ignore, but sometimes it was more aggressive and threatening. 'A great deal of that racism came from Polish people and sometimes Latvian and Russian people, which I found strange, them being foreigners to this country, too ...'

He shook his head, clearly feeling hurt and embittered by the experience. 'Later I realized that their racism came from the fact that they had no previous experience working or living in the same town with Asian communities ... Britain was the first time that they'd ever had any contact or even conversation with Asian people. Their narrow-mindedness really frightened me. That was the reason why I left Lincoln.'

In return, I shared with him my own experiences of racism in Britain – not only the minor mistaken assumptions based on ignorance (e.g. being remembered and addressed as a 'Thai woman' and talked down to: 'So, you must come from a big family'), but also unjust police treatment when I was searched for over an hour while the white man who grabbed and pulled me along the street, trying to mug me, was treated as a victim. Don't think if you have degrees you'll necessarily be treated fairly, I said. My experience in the world of work tells me that you need to prove yourself doubly hard because the gatekeepers of news organizations have their own agenda and can label you like anyone else.

Ali said that it has been a little better in Luton. 'There is still racism and racial conflict here ... and to be honest, it's the only thing I dislike about Luton. Anyway, now I prefer to stay closer to the Asian communities, so that I don't feel so affected by it.'

Ali feels it is a shame that there are so many misconceptions about Muslims. He clearly has a liberal attitude towards religion and always tries to befriend people from different religious and cultural backgrounds. 'I have many Thai friends who are Buddhists. One of my closest friends in Britain is Thai,' he said. 'I have even picked up some Thai phrases from them.'

Ali sees cross-cultural, cross-religious marriages as a good thing. 'For me, there's no issue of marriage with a non-Muslim. Humanity comes first; religion second. That's my belief.'

I listened and wondered about the gap between what he was saying and the stereotype of a Muslim. He carried on: 'If something bad happens to me on the street and I need help, you're not going to help me on the basis of my religion, are you? You would help me because I'm a human being. Right? Humanity comes first.'

The increase in racial harassment and abuse experienced by all sections of Luton's Muslim communities has bred a lot of anger, although that anger has not found any formal outlet of expression. Muslims of different backgrounds find their own individual explanations for, and solutions to, the situation.

Those in leading positions in the communities tend to encourage moderate politics in public life. Abdul Qadir Baksh at the Luton Islamic Centre, for instance, has written pamphlets to discourage fellow Muslims from seeking more fundamental solutions to their oppression. He says, 'Islamic radicalism is a political reaction to the oppressive policies of imperialist powers such as the US and Israel', and that a radicalized Muslim is not necessarily 'extremist'. He argues against social myths about Muslims and rightly points out that only a tiny minority of radicalized Muslims cross over to become 'violent extremists'. Abdul Qadir Baksh also writes and disseminates material that argues against the idea that violence can be justified by Islam. He argues against the minority idea that Islam places an obligation upon believers to physically fight non-Muslims. He preaches that 'justice is the basis of Islam; we must be just to all Muslims and non-Muslims'.

However, some are so angry with the way Muslims are being targeted in Britain that they would like to see a stronger leadership in their communities against such social prejudice and discrimination. Mohammad Faisal, a special-needs teacher from Pakistan, said that blame for the widespread scapegoating of Muslims in Britain cannot be attributed only to the growth of the far right and the negative portrayal of the community by the media, but also to the 'weak leadership of our mosques'.

Mohammad has been living and working in Britain for fifteen years. One of the things he appreciates most about this country is the justice system, unlike the one back in Pakistan. He also treasures very much the community spirit he has found in Luton's Asian communities. However, in recent years Mohammad has seen a decline in this spirit and a deterioration in cross-community relations. 'There seems little respect between people, and communities are seeking to put blame on each other,' he said.

Many working-class British Muslim youth, like those in Bury Park, are angry at the growing social prejudices against their communities and the general lack of opportunities for them to progress in life. I noticed the echoes between their sense of disenfranchisement and disengagement and the feelings expressed among the white working-class youth in Farley Hill.

I met a man in his late twenties named Abdul. He was chatting with a friend on a street corner not far from the mosque. 'We have nowhere else to go, nowhere to hang out, except on the street,' he told me. 'You see, the local government doesn't put in money in our area. To be honest, I think it is because they don't want anything better to happen with us ... They don't actually want us to do better. Don't they see that we need more community centres, more places for young people to go to?'

At this point, his friend, with a scarf wrapped around his forehead, who later introduced himself as Yusif, raised his voice to a woman in a headscarf across the street. 'Please don't wear the scarf! You're not Muslim,' he said.

The woman, who looked to be in her late forties, smiled and carried on walking down the street.

Yusif went over to her and said: 'Why are you wearing a scarf and pretending to be Muslim when you are begging? You're not Muslim.'

Abdul turned and explained to me that the woman is from Romania and she sometimes begs on the street around here. He said that she puts on a scarf so as to be identified as a Muslim, hoping that Muslim residents in the neighbourhood will feel sympathy for her.

Yusif also explained to me: 'There are several Romanian women in headscarves begging for money outside the mosque. They are Romanian Gypsies and they are good people. But they're not Muslims. When they beg wearing headscarves, it gives Muslims a bad name. It makes people think all Muslims are beggars.'

He continued to dissuade the woman, even though many Romanian Roma women wear headscarves, too. 'Please don't act like you're a Muslim when you're not. Please don't give us a bad reputation,' he said to her.

The woman still smiled, murmuring a few words and trying to make a joke of it, but Yusif wouldn't give up. He searched in his jeans pocket and found a five-pound note. He walked up to her and handed her the money. 'Please take that scarf away now. Please don't act like you're Muslim.'

The woman looked at him in amazement.

'Give the scarf to me, please,' Yusif insisted.

The woman decided to accept the cash. She took it from Yusif's hand and took off her headscarf and gave it to him.

His friend Abdul shook his head in disbelief. Who would give £5 just for a stranger to remove her headscarf?

Yusif sauntered back to us, waving the headscarf, a smile on his face. He looked to be in his late twenties, and wore an intense frown for our entire conversation. I assumed he must be a strong believer to go to such lengths to defend his community's reputation. Someone loyal to his faith.

But Yusif informed me that he used to be one of Bury Park's best-known drug dealers. Abdul shook his head again, and smiled out of embarrassment. 'I got involved in dealing drugs seven years ago ... when I was introduced into taking drugs by a white man who's a dealer from Milton Keynes,' Yusif said.

'Really?' I found it difficult to believe, given the exchange I had just witnessed.

'In those days, I used to gamble a lot. I got into the habit, like some Asian young people around here, because we didn't have anywhere else to go. So we stayed in the casino a lot of the time, and gradually we became acquainted with people who wanted to use us ... I used to gamble a lot in a casino with this white man from Milton Keynes.'

He told me he regretted the six months he spent dealing. 'I say Allah forgive me,' he said, his expression sorrowful; 'if I didn't meet the people from this country who taught me this game, I wouldn't have done it ... The guy from Milton Keynes knew I'm Muslim ... When we gambled together, I started to lose money and started to have to sell stuff for him bit by bit.'

'Sounds like you couldn't get out at the time,' I said.

'He made me beg ...' Yusif shook his head again, recalling the vicious circle he was trapped in. 'I used the money I made from selling drugs to gamble more ...'

Yusif said that the majority of people who bought drugs from him were Muslims. 'And there were some white guys from the ranks of the EDL ... and some of them deal drugs, too.'

This seemed to confirm stories I had heard from others, in both Farley Hill and Bury Park. More than one source had told me that Tommy Robinson used to deal drugs and got involved in a turf war with several British Pakistani drug dealers that led him to start a smear campaign to damage the name of Muslims. I have been unable to find any evidence to corroborate this claim, however.

Yusif has never met Robinson himself, but many of today's EDL activists and supporters used to be part of his social circle.

As I heard from several Muslim men in Bury Park as well as white residents on Farley Hill, back in the 1990s many local Muslim men used to either go to the same school or grew up in the same working-class neighbourhoods with the white Lutonians who now make up the rank and file of the EDL. 'I used to drink with those white youth around Farley Hill and even play football with them ... Those young ones in the EDL are just kids. Misguided kids, like I was, but in a different way.'

I was surprised by the toleration with which he described the young people who had been targeting his community for years. Yusif carried on, without any sense of resentment:

They [the EDL youth] didn't know where to go. No direction in life. Lost. Some are ordinary people. It's just that no one was there to guide them properly. They were lured into the EDL by drug and alcohol and sometimes quick cash. 'Come with us, bro, you'll have this and that,' that's how they got hooked. Cocaine, heroin and alcohol are the three main things that shape them. If you have the chance to talk to them, you'll see the look on their faces ... Yellowish colour on their faces. That's because they're on hard drug all the time.

The local drug problems were backed up by a general gang culture, and that has fed into the culture of those involved in far-right activities. Lenos Wilson of The Non Violence Alliance (TNVA) has also confirmed this, telling me there is an overlap between EDL's support base and local gangs.

Yusif sighed. 'They've been used ... These kids needed to feel they belong somewhere and the EDL leaders offered them that [group identity]. What they need is someone to bring them to the right way ...'

Yusif said he understands how they have got themselves into this situation because he's been there himself. 'I used to use more drugs than I ever sold ... in those dark days. Now I feel sorry for what I had done. I regret it deeply. If it had not been for Islam, I would have been turned into the biggest mafia around here.'

'Drugs are a massive problem in Luton,' Yusif said, reiterating what I heard time and time again from people in Farley Hill. He also drew his own conclusions: 'You see, they want people to be heroin addicts. They don't want people to follow religions. Don't go to church, mosque or synagogue. Go and take heroin and smoke shit, be in your own world and look after your bank account, how much is coming in and out ... Your mortgage ... your this and that and then you die. You finish. Drugs keeps everyone on his own.'

Yusif suddenly pointed at a passer-by. 'Look at this man! He's Muslim and yet he buys drugs ... from English people. I told him to quit. I know what it's like. The EDL people are all drug users ... May Allah forgive them and bring them to the right way. They're our brothers, too.'

Abdul stood there listening and nodding.

Yusif continued: 'Prophet Mohammad never threw stones back at the non-Muslims who threw stones at him ... One day they will be Muslims and they may even be better than us as Muslims. Go to the mosque and you'll see English people teaching Islam inside – people who were born in this country. And they'll be more clever and better Muslims. You know why? Because when they came to Islam, Allah gave them a gift.

Because they're from non-Muslim backgrounds, unlike us. Most of us are born Muslims.'

Yusif told me his new-found religious faith came because he was moved by the non-Muslims who were converted to the religion. 'I only started to practise Islam and started to pray when I came to England from Palestine. Because I saw these people here and I thought to myself: even people who were not born into Islam are teaching Islam!'

Without exception, all the British Muslim residents I talked to in Bury Park, faced with the injustice inflicted upon their communities, nevertheless have a moderate political outlook and have distanced themselves from any politics that resemble 'extremism' in any form. Unanimously, they believe that they are trying to make a positive contribution to British society through their religion and culture, and see themselves as part of a multi-cultural country.

In response to racism, the majority of Muslim residents I talked to tend to want to ignore, as much as they can, the effect or impact of the propagation of far-right interpretations of their faith and communities. While recognizing it as racism, the majority of them simply want to get on with their lives and prefer not to see the far-right influence as too much of a problem in their daily life. Even in the face of increasing incidents of racial abuse, they want to believe they have the strength to carry on life as normal.

Maintaining normality seems a way to cope with adversity, for many. Similarly, Sayeeda Warsi described the way many Muslims, all over Britain, have responded to the injustice of becoming targeted and victimized:

For me, this was a heartening act of defiance: people who came under attack opening up their doors to the wider community. The Zainabia Islamic Centre in Milton Keynes was firebombed in May and only two months later they were reaching out and hosting a fantastic Big Iftar. Just over a month after a bomb went off nearby, the Aisha mosque in Walsall hosted dozens of people at their community iftar.'

And when the Muswell Hill Somali community had nowhere to hold their Big Iftar – their centre was burnt down in June – they linked up with their Shia neighbours, the Al-Khoei Foundation, and held their event at their centre in Brent ... So many people from all walks of life are coming together this Ramadan, and so many Muslims are doing what is so very British: keeping calm and carrying on.

I wanted to provoke a reaction from Tommy Robinson about his self-image. 'How do you feel about being called a racist?'

He looked down, smiling awkwardly.

'I'm not a racist,' he said, giving the expected answer, and then added: 'That's so weak. So embarrassing.'

'What do you mean?'

'If I talk out against scientology ... is anyone going to call me a racist? Scientology is an ideology the same as Islam. I've not said one racist thing in my life.'

'Your group claims that it's not racist. But if you scroll down your Facebook web page, you see a lot of racist comments from your members and supporters.'

'What sort of comments?'

'Comments like describing Muslim people as goat fuckers.'

'Yeah? That's not racist, though.' He shrugged.

Robinson wanted to talk about how he speaks for the 'English working class'. He said the EDL is 'the biggest phenomenon to have swept this country'.

'How is the English working class different from the British working class, or British Asian working class?' I asked.

'The English working class is being abused and isolated ... and forgotten and purposely pushed into silence,' he answered, frowning. 'People who live in working-class communities like council estates ... who've lived a life like what we lived ... and then we are told about this multiculturalism ... that we should be happy about this diversity ... All these people who told us haven't lived it. So they don't know what they're talking about ... Why are you telling us how good it is, when you don't know what it's like?'

'I know what it's like. I live in the East End of London,' I said, looking straight at him, 'close to the East London Mosque.'

He went quiet.

'So what has your group done for the English working class?' I continued.

'We gave them a voice,' he said.

'But all you do is target Muslim communities.'

'Our focus is on what has affected us,' he said, 'what we see as the biggest threat to this country.'

'Do you really think Muslim communities are the biggest problem and the most important issue affecting people in this country?'

'Yes,' he said confidently. 'The biggest threat to our safety and security is Islam. The biggest threat to our children growing up in this town is the Islamic community ... We say stop building the mosques because you're just adding to the problem ... Islam isn't gonna sort itself out. It's causing massive problems. If you look at the demographics and the birth rate and how big it's gonna get, you'll just add to the problem ... 98 per cent of imams can't speak English ... We should have a points system similar to Australia. End all Muslim immigration. Complete stop.'

Robinson's anti-immigration stance isn't limited to Muslims. He also sees migration from Romania and Bulgaria as a serious problem. Prior to the lifting of work restrictions on Romanians and Bulgarians in January 2014, he had already told me how concerned he was about the 'rising crime' which he was happy to attribute to Romanians in London. He is also angered by 'Romanian and Bulgarian migrants coming to claim benefits'. 'Our country has been destroyed,' he told me.

Robinson's future blueprint for the EDL was a racist fantasy centred around the rejection of Britain's multiculturalism and the incitement of hatred. 'In the short term, we want to wake the British public up to what will be happening in twenty or thirty years if the Islamic communities continue to rise the way they are ... We want to make sure people know the truth about Islam ... to educate people about Islam ... Wherever Islam is, there is a military operation to implement sharia law. This country will be exactly the same. Five per cent of the population is Muslim. When it becomes 20 per cent, that's when there will be a war.'

To combat the 'spread of Islamic culture' and the 'threat of Islamic influence', the EDL has gone so far as to even attempt to change the eating habits of British people and has launched protests against the use of halal meat. It has been dressed up as 'concern for animals'. But having talked to Robinson, it is apparent that his rejection of halal meat comes from his anti-Islamic, anti-immigration feelings. As he said: 'Five thousand Pakistani butchers were imported into our country last year to keep up with the growing halal demand. I think we should be training 5,000 British people to be butchers, not importing Pakistani butchers ... The only people who can prepare halal meat are Muslims. So if our country starts to eat halal meat, the only people working in the abattoirs and preparing it will be Muslims. It's an unfair advantage in the meat market for Muslims.'

Given such deep resentment against Islam and Muslims, I wondered how someone like him personally rejects the influence of a globalized culture from day to day. 'I saw a debate on your Facebook web page about curry,' I couldn't help saying. 'Your activists were arguing whether it's contradictory to be in the EDL and eat curry at the same time.'

He looked puzzled, probably wondering where my question was leading.

'Do you eat curry?' I asked, trying to look serious.

'Yeah,' he said quite confidently. 'We created curry. It's English.'

'It's an English dish, is it?' I repeated his words.

'Yeah,' he said, smiling. 'Chicken korma for me.'

'But didn't you say you are against halal meat?' I carried on.

'I'll get curry from Morrisons or Waitrose,' he said. 'They don't do halal there.'

Considering how uncomfortable Darren claims to have been in the EDL, it puzzled me why it took two years for him to leave the group. He said that at the time he still maintained the idea that he was involved in fighting against extremism at both ends of the spectrum: the skinheads and the 'Islamicists', as he called them. Back then, he didn't want to let go.

'Over time, I suppose I got older and wiser. My discomfort with the group and my disgust with some of the people in it finally pushed me to make the decision to leave it all behind. I said to Steve [Tommy Robinson], "To be honest with you, I'm too old for that." I said to him, "You're younger, you're half my age. I'm tired with it." He listened and understood.'

Darren doesn't believe Robinson is responsible for the influence of the neo-fascist elements within the EDL, although others in the EDL claim it was Robinson himself who brought them on board, to give strength to the movement. Those activists suggest doing so has turned the movement into a 'monster' increasingly difficult to control. The simple question remains, if he was opposed to neo-fascists, why didn't Robinson do anything about it when he was leading the group? As Darren himself admitted, he spent three years consistently trying to warn and persuade Robinson to quit the EDL because of the rise of the neo-fascist elements in the movement. But Darren's words fell on deaf ears.

I said to Steve [Tommy Robinson], 'Why don't you get out?' I wasn't having it and that was why I left ... I made a strong decision and I know I'm right to have left ... It would have been easy to stay and submit to peer pressure but it's wrong. People [neo-fascists] attaching themselves to the demos, that was the last straw. I could read them like a book ... They work on your psyche and they love getting their kicks. They became more and more involved and they turned up at bigger demos. You confront them verbally, but they come in bigger numbers.

Steve [Tommy Robinson] was in the thick of fighting ... He nearly got killed ... The Northwest Infidels, the splinter group, were on the Bradford demo. Hateful blokes. White supremacists. And I kept thinking that Steve [Tommy Robinson] was gonna get stabbed or murdered somewhere along the line. After that demo, I just thought it wasn't for me.

When Steve [Tommy Robinson] was in prison for visa fraud during early 2013, Kevin Carroll was in charge of the EDL. Kev couldn't run a bath. But his ego tells him he could run the world. When he was running the EDL, he just messed everything up. He was talking with loads of lunatics. Great time for more of those [neo-fascist] groups to come. What allowed it to happen was Kev not being the sharpest tool in the box, not being a good judge of character ... He couldn't even work out they were Nazis he was talking to ... As long as you give him praise.

Darren said that when Robinson got out of jail, he rejoined the EDL's activities and started trying to fight the neo-fascist groups again. He fell out with a lot of them. 'He openly said they're extremists. He's received so many threats from these groups,' Darren said. 'They said openly that they're gonna kill him. He's a dead man walking. I said to him, "What's in it for you?

Get out of it, get out. You've got three lovely children." But he was stubborn.'

By this time, Darren himself had long seen through the nationalism and racism that the EDL and the rest of the far right were propagating. 'They talk about the English way of life. "My own country." When you ask them what they mean, you realize you feel sorry for them. Because they can't articulate it. They're just shouting it out, feeling something that they don't understand ... You will see that in defeated working-class mining communities that were broken up. Just like half of the lads [in the EDL] can't think it through.'

This is, as Darren came to see it, a tactic of divide and rule used by the ruling elite. 'In the 1980s all blacks were murderers; all whites are racists now and all Asians are terrorists. It's a very clever way of making sure we're kept in our place ... I've learned all that in the past five years, and you have to rethink and reshape your own way.'

Darren's departure from the street movement, as it turned out, did not prevent him from being associated with it. He could not just shake off the past so easily. One evening, just before the murder of Lee Rigby, Darren received a call. It was his elder son on the end of the line. 'I've been followed,' he said.

Twenty to thirty men allegedly associated with Anjem Choudary had recognized his son leaving a swimming pool in town. They tailed him as he drove home to the outskirts of Luton. In a panic for his son's safety, Darren went outside and broke one of the men's car windows, for which he was arrested and jailed for two weeks.

A similar incident happened during his grandson's birthday party in Marsh Farm. Several men allegedly associated with Choudary broke into the party, and Darren called the police immediately. He said he spoke with a couple of the Muslim men who came to the party. 'I talked to them about Islam. One of them said to me, "You're actually all right." He knows I'm not like one of the EDL guys.'

Nevertheless, Darren recognizes that it's no longer easy to live in Luton, as a result of his previous involvement with the EDL and his association with Kevin Carroll and Tommy Robinson, something he wishes he could erase, for his family and his children as well as for himself.

4

'THE EDL CANNOT
SURVIVE HERE'

When Darren talks about his town and expresses fiercely localist feelings, I can understand and empathize, because I, too, have developed a strong emotional connection with the place where I've chosen to live and build my life. My East End. Many times I walk the streets and feel like embracing what I've got here – its past and present of multicultural communities living alongside one another. You can be who you want to be here.

I can certainly relate to those East Enders who feel they must protect their home against those who intend to change its history and way of being. When the EDL attempted to enter Tower Hamlets on three occasions, in 2010, 2011 and 2013, East Enders of all cultural backgrounds stood together and fought back. I'm deeply proud of their resistance.

When I started researching this book, local friends gave me ideas about possible places to look and trace support for the EDL and the far right in general. During my earliest meanderings in the East End, my boyfriend Dave suggested a list of local pubs to visit, for a sense of local feelings. His family originally lived in east London but later moved out to Essex, as many did, in the late 1950s. He chose to move back here in 1991, and quite by accident ended up living close to where his grandmother was born a hundred years ago in 1901, next to a Lithuanian church. The East End is where he feels at home.

Back in the late 1970s and early 1980s, Dave told me, white supremacist groups used to play Screwdriver, known as the world's most influential 'white power' rock music, in a grotty pub at the top of Brick Lane, along Bethnal Green Road. A shop on the opposite corner to Brick Lane on the same road used to sell knives and secretly sold racist memorabilia. In the early 1990s, you would see the BNP selling their papers and handing out leaflets at the top of Brick Lane on a Sunday morning. 'In those days, you could still find one or two local pubs where if a non-white person walked in, the whole pub went quiet,' Dave recalled.

Now that's all gone. Things have changed from the days when many local residents responded to the diversification of the East End's population by leaving. Dave told me about the people who used to live in the estates but moved out to Dagenham and Essex as they saw their corner of London becoming more ethnically mixed. In an exodus popularly known as 'white flight', 600,000 white Britons left London and relocated elsewhere in a decade. Although London is still a majority white, British-born city, many feel that it is 'no longer home', owing to the growing visibility of the non-white population.

Bearing the change in mind, I wondered about the current local feelings towards the East End's transformation. Openly hostile places are a thing of the past, I gathered from Dave's description. I wanted to take a look at those old East End gathering places, the estate pubs such as the Coborn Arms, the Cavendish Arms, the

Little Driver, the Half Moon and the like, where you can still get cheap beer and a conversation with old-time residents. Some of them might have something to say about the far right.

So that was how I ended up in the Half Moon, now part of the Wetherspoon franchise, in Stepney Green. The pub is situated opposite a row of council housing known as Ocean Estate, inhabited by people from a mixture of ethnic backgrounds. The pub's clientele is mainly white British, consisting mostly of people living nearby. Sometimes you see police officers dropping by, and fights break out now and then outside the pub, sometimes between local white and British Asian youths.

I got myself a drink from the bar and looked around to see whom I could talk to. A man and a woman were sitting at the table next to me. They both had shaved heads and were chatting in standard Cockney. The man's arms were covered in elaborate tattoos. They seemed to fit my preconceived image of far-right supporters. I waited for a pause in their conversation to make my approach.

I introduced myself and tried to talk to them about the nearby estates. But as soon as I mentioned the EDL marches in Tower Hamlets, I realized how wrong I was to assume their political inclinations. The thirty-something woman, named Angela, gave a firm reply: 'We are both members of CWU [the Communications Workers Union] and I am a trade union rep; we fight against the far right in work and in our union.' She and her friend, both postal workers, are committed anti-fascists and anti-racists.

The growth of groups like the EDL is the result of our government and media misdirecting people's anger and scapegoating ... The reality is that we all are a product of immigration and many of the white British around here are in fact second-generation immigrants, like myself, coming from an Irish family. We used to live in East India Dock Road, near the old Chinatown, and grew up with people of a variety of cultural backgrounds ... The East End's history is a history of immigration; we are all immigrants. Groups like the EDL cannot survive here; they'd be smashed up. We wouldn't allow it.

The last time they attempted to make their presence in Tower Hamlets was in 2011, when they planned to march through the East London Mosque but failed to.

Tower Hamlets, described as the 'lion's den' by the EDL, was a big target for the group, as it aimed to create maximum disturbance among British Muslim communities. At the time, there were joint efforts from local communities, trade unionists and socialists to come together to oppose the march. Unite Against Fascism (UAF) and United East End (UEE), in particular, came together to help unite the resistance.

The majority of local people, of all ethnic backgrounds, felt threatened by the planned EDL march. They were so accustomed to living alongside a variety of different communities that the racist views propagated by the EDL seemed alien to them. When members of the EDL visited pubs in Tower Hamlets, hoping to secure a venue for the day of the planned march, they were refused, one pub after another. A former manager of the Urban Bar, a popular pub previously known as the London Hospital Tavern on Whitechapel Road, told me about the visit by EDL organizers in 2011. 'They came in and asked for a venue without telling me who they were. But I could tell who they were. I said to them, "You're the EDL, aren't you?" One of them nodded. So I said to him, "The man who owns the pub is an anti-racist and the man who manages the pub is black and anti-racist. So the answer is NO." They left and went to try other pubs, and everyone said no to them.'

On 3 September, the day of the planned march, people of all ethnic groups and religions stood together in opposing the EDL. The day was remembered as a day of victory for the anti-racist movement, and activists and trade unionists like Angela recall it with indignation and pride.

When Angela said 'We drove them out', she meant collectively. Workers' unions played a significant part in stopping the EDL from marching into Tower Hamlets. When it became known that the police were to allow the EDL to use Liverpool Street as a rallying point, RMT, the rail union, threatened to shut down the station on health and safety grounds and make it impossible for the EDL to use the station as their starting point.

UAF organizers said that this was one of the most significant moments in Tower Hamlets' resistance to the far right. 'All these acts [e.g. rail workers shutting the Tube stations to keep out the EDL] paved the way for the major victories. RMT members, always good UAF supporters, as with unions like PCS, NUT, CWU, NASUWT, Unite, played a key role that day. Indeed, such unions have been critical in so many ways, alongside alliances, such as the Griffin Must Go campaign UAF held in the North West.'

UAF believes that the victory in 2011 was only possible owing to the broad anti-EDL coalition that had been built up over weeks and months. 'UAF worked alongside trade unions, LGBT activists, the mayor of Tower Hamlets, faith groups and anti-racist groups ...The brilliant show of solidarity made that happen and the march was, as the *Morning Star* put it, "a victory for the anti-fascist and labour movement".'

Angela told me that members of far-right groups have no place within Britain's trade unions. Members of the CWU had expelled an EDL activist known as Leppard, she recalled. 'If they're stupid enough to be identified, they get kicked out of the union straight away. They're never allowed in.'

Since then, throughout my research, I've continued to hear the same anti-racist views among working-class people in the East End. There is a deeply rooted tradition of anti-racist, anti-fascist activism here.

Peter, a fifty-four-year-old Hackney-born Englishman who works at the Royal London Hospital as a porter and has been living in the East End all his life, told me about that history of which he's so proud. 'Dad was born in Hatfield Passage, just down the road here ... My dad's family has been here since 1816. My grandad was a cap-maker ... They were all immigrants, Dutch Jewish. My dad's mum was Portuguese Jewish. My mum's Scottish.'

I asked how he sees his ethnic identity. He said without a moment of hesitation: 'If anyone asks me who I am, I'd say I'm a British-born Jew. But I'm English first and foremost. I'm an English of Jewish descent.' Then he smiled and added a Cockney phrase: 'But my mum's a Sweaty' ('Sweaty socks' in Cockney rhyme means Scots).

I went to Stepney Jewish school till the age of nine, where most the kids were of Jewish background ... I was self-taught most of my life. Diplomas and degrees mean little to me whereas common sense means everything ...

These days, a lot of white people around here support groups like the EDL ... because they direct their anger the wrong way ... I met these two blokes in the Salmon & Ball down in Bethnal Green the other day and they said they belong to the EDL. They are from up north, Lancashire. One of them told me he was in the steel industry for twenty-five years and then lost his job and has been on the dole for a year. He's got five kids. There's no work, he said.

If you look around here, you'll see everyone's angry ... A lot of people I know have been on the dole since they left school ... and they all support the BNP. And not just the unemployed white people but the Asians are getting angry, too.

Peter started working as a hospital porter in 1988, earning £97 a week. His salary was so meagre that he couldn't afford to get married and start a family.

I'm earning a few quid an hour when my boss is living in a fifteen-bedroom house ... If I leave my job, I'll get one month's pay and I'll be out of the door. My manager and those directors who sit on their arses all day ... if they leave the job they'll get £100,000 or half a million pounds pay-off ... But my anger ain't directed at people coming into this country. My anger is directed at those at the top who brought us into this situation ... Those like Thatcher, whose policies brought us to where we are now today. It is all about class. And they are splitting the working class down the line ... time and time again ... When we working-class are against each other, the rich and powerful are laughing ... Cameron and Osborne are laughing ... They're laughing that we working-class people are killing our own ... The working class has got to stop looking at each other's colour and religion. We should be directing our anger against the banking system, the politicians and so on ... not against each other.

Life was tough for Peter's parents in the 1930s. His dad worked as a fishmonger, but there wasn't always enough work to keep his family properly fed. So he resorted to burglary between jobs. 'He usually worked up Mayfair, Park Lane, Chelsea ... He got done twice for burglary. The first time was when he climbed down the chimney when a police officer was waiting for him at the bottom ... and he got eighteen months for that. The second time he got two years ... But still, if you ask what he's most proud of, he'd tell you it was stealing from the rich!'

Peter talked with pride about his family history and particularly his dad, who took part in the Cable Street fight against the Blackshirts. When I asked him how his dad got involved, he was clearly proud of the answer: 'Everyone got involved. The whole of east London got involved! No one wanted Mosley in the area. The working-class were different in them days ... Regardless of religion and background, you looked after your neighbours. You looked after each other.'

On 4 October 1936, nearly 2,000 supporters of Osward Mosley's British Union of Fascists planned to march from the City of London into the East End. To their surprise, they were confronted by more than 100,000 anti-fascists at Gardiner's Corner. The fascists were aided by around 6,000 police officers who used violence against the anti-fascist protesters.

This was not the first time a fascist rally had been aided by the establishment. Mosley was strongly backed by press baron Lord Rothermere of the *Daily Mail*, who ensured the Blackshirts received good write-ups and helped with their recruitment drive (the British Union of Fascists reached a membership of 50,000 by summer 1934). The newspaper also initially backed Mosley's violent rally in Olympia in 1934 before he began to lose support as a result of the violence. After that, Mosley turned to the working class in the East End and targeted manual workers in local declining industries.

'The working class in the East End couldn't let that happen …' said Peter. 'The fascists at that time were mostly middle-class or upper-middle-class, and working-class people didn't want those values imposed on them … The working-class people wanted to keep their freedoms, freedom of speech, freedom of movement, freedom of worship, freedom from want … It was our tradition.'

When the police officers tried to force a way through for the Blackshirts, they were blocked by residents of the East End. When the police found a route through residential streets to avoid the anti-fascist blockade, they were confronted by yet more barricades set up by locals.

Peter's father took part in the anti-fascist fight. He described his father as someone 'who didn't like anything with an "ism" in it' but had a strong sense of social justice.

> My old man wasn't a member of the Communist Party, but he knew of people in the Party ... When Mosley was coming and the police escorted them, the Communist Party members got kids to buy marbles to use as weapons ... When the fascists and police were arriving through, they threw marbles on the ground ... My dad was among those throwing marbles. The horses split up ... My dad and his mates got hold of the police and the fascists, and kicked the shit out of them. My cousin was involved in the anti-fascist league back in the 1950s and all my family were fighting against the fascists. I despise the fascists. They are as cold as death. They don't want life. To live life is too hard for them.

Mosley was eventually beaten off the streets of east London. At the time, he was told by the Metropolitan Police Commissioner, Sir Philip Game, that he must call off the march. Mosley had to lead his thugs and retreat out of east London. But the working class were punished for fighting the fascists in the aftermath of the Cable Street incident. 'My dad was arrested for the Cable Street fight ... They gave him two choices: to serve in the British army or to do five years [prison sentence]. So he chose to be in the army ... for eight long years.'

However, this page of history remains alive in the minds of many in the East End. Many locals are just as proud of their anti-fascist, anti-racist history as Peter and his family.

Phil Piratin, Cable Street fighter and author of *Our Flag Stays Red*, said at the time that solidarity among working-class people was the key to success at Cable Street. It set a precedent for working-class solidarity across ethnic backgrounds, from Orthodox to more secular Jewish people (like Peter's family) to Irish Catholic dockers. This unity has been repeated, in the tradition of Cable Street, in the anti-racist, anti-fascist fights of twenty-first-century Britain.

The East End consists of a huge variety of communities, living alongside each other. The identity of an 'East Ender' is no longer confined to someone of 'English' or British origin. An East Ender can be of British Bengali, Polish, Lithuanian, Spanish or Colombian background.

Juan Camilo is one such East Ender. He's known as an activist and has worked with migrant communities in Britain for years. I asked what brought him to the East End of London. 'I've always loved the big-city experience, and I'm fascinated by the history of the East End,' he said, then added, 'and especially the canals here.'

Juan was in born in Cali, the third-largest city in Colombia. His father is English and his mother Colombian. This mixed parentage encouraged him to explore the world around him from a young age. At university, he wrote his dissertation on racism against black people and the black movement in Cali. That interest later led him to London to study migration. Ironically, he was never subjected to the immigration restrictions that are the day-to-day experience of many Colombian migrants because of his father's nationality.

Juan is very aware of his relatively privileged background, compared to others of the same generation from Colombia who are widely disenchanted with politics, a privilege which in turn enables him to contribute to working and campaigning for migrants' rights in London. Juan rejected 'big politics' and chose to work 'on the ground':

> We have a country dominated by two parties that were very similar to each other. We had the left that adopted a strategy of 'the ends justifying the means', so there were a lot of atrocities … There wasn't really a political alternative that was attractive to anyone … I believe more in how to work with the community and improve one's own situation rather than being involved in big politics. That applies to the UK, in the sense that big politics are just a game of blaming the migrants for everything and it was very difficult to achieve anything by engaging with them … So it's more productive to work with groups of migrants, to see how they can help each other and improve their own lives. I believe in working together rather than getting involved in the big political struggle.

During the late 1990s and early 2000s there was large-scale migration of around two million people out of Colombia. Juan became interested in how migrants settle, adapt to a new life and develop their identities. Through his studies at Queen Mary's and his work at the Indoamerican Refugee and Migrant Organisation (an organization originally set up by Chileans following the Pinochet coup, but expanded to provide services for other South American migrants), he began to work closely with many undocumented Colombian migrants, including those in political exile or those who had come here for economic reasons. Most of the people he works with have low-paid jobs, mostly concentrated in the cleaning industry.

In the 1970s, some came with work permits and worked as cleaners in schools and hospitals, restaurants, etc., and later people came, following friends and families already in this trade. It's long and antisocial working hours; you always have to get up at four or five in the morning … and have to work late in the evening. Sixteen hours a day. Sometimes I got personally involved in their lives. I would write letters for them, to the Home Office, or to the council, or employers, to demand their wages back.'

The Colombian migrants I worked with experienced racism, but most understood it as 'a fear for the different' … In the East End, people generally get on fine together. We have a lot of local friends through our daughter's school … and we have good relations with our British Bangladeshi neighbours … The only time I witnessed racism was in a local pub during a football match. An English guy was bantering with several Asian youths when watching the match. He would sometimes turn to me and say, these places are run by the 'Pakis' now. He saw me as OK and one of them because I'm Catholic. But not the Asians, even though they're born and grew up here.

Juan went on to work for Praxis, providing services to new migrants in the East End. He has organized a local New Voices festival, attended by people from all communities. From what he can see, people experience racial prejudice mainly through government policies, which affect lives on a large scale. For instance, he said, immigration practices such as immigration vans (the Go Home campaign), spot checks and raids under the coalition government impact negatively on Colombian migrant communities and have created a great deal of fear. The impact of such policies over the years has led him into more campaigning work, such as for the Migrants' Rights Network, which has campaigned for over two years on behalf of cross-cultural families that have been torn apart by the government's family migration rules.

To get a glimpse of the impact of these draconian state policies, I visited Rita Chalta of RAMFEL (Refugee and Migrant Forum of Essex and London), known for their work against the government's Go Home campaign. Rita looked overworked and drained when I arrived. As she led me upstairs to talk in quiet, she kept looking back down the corridor, at a Lithuanian man sitting on the floor. Rita told me he'd been homeless and waiting for accommodation. Her resources exhausted and having to share work with other migrant support organizations, she was very anxious about how to provide help – support and advice services – to an average of 200 migrants who come through her door every week.

In the midst of hostile government policies and social environment, Rita's organization works tirelessly across five east London boroughs: Barking, Dagenham, Newham, Redbridge and Waltham Forest. Rita said one in three of the migrants they are in contact with are undocumented. Among them are eastern European migrants who have lost their papers and face destitution because they can't prove who they are and therefore can't work (or access benefits). Rita sighed, telling me how many migrants can fall into destitution:

> Most of the eastern Europeans we see these days are street hangers. The man you saw in the corridor had been eight months homeless before he contacted us ... It happens quite easily. When they lose their jobs, they end up on the streets [because their accommodation is often provided with their work] ... While they are on the streets, they lose their documents or documents get stolen ... Then they can't work, because they have no IDs.
>
> If you want a replacement document ... the police will only issue you a lost property sheet if you confirm your passport number, name and address, etc. Even if you have your passport number, they give you a form where you have to go to the embassy or the high commission, get that stamped from them and then go back to the police station to report it. You have to do all of that before you can get a replacement passport and then you still have to find at least £100 to pay for the passport ... Polish and Lithuanian migrants are the biggest groups we see at the moment ...

Rita's organization provides homeless migrants with food services – currently 150 people in all. In 2013, RAMFEL housed sixty-eight people who were destitute on the streets. It provided support for them to be able to sustain a tenancy. Most of them were construction workers, hotel cleaners or other manual workers who were made redundant. When that happens, they have nowhere to turn.

'Campaigning against immigration vans is just part of what we do. A couple of years ago a local council used the word "Paki" in a document. We challenged them about that … And then there was Operation Sleeping Bag … The police locally took migrants' sleeping bags and food parcels and we objected to that … We are not paid to be puppets; we are paid to provide the service which we do to our clients, and to challenge things.'

When Rita was having a tense dialogue with the Home Office about the immigration vans, two migrants who used to be homeless came forward to express their anger against the government's Go Home campaign. One of them, an Irish national, has been in Britain for twenty years. Although he wasn't the target of the Go Home campaign, he felt it personally. He was a foreman on a building site and saw workers being told to go home when there was a work dispute, and he hated it. It was as if the phrase 'go home' had a particular resonance to him. He was on the streets for nearly nine months before he met Rita in December 2012. He lost his Irish passport and was all over the place. All he wanted to do was work. RAMFEL found him accommodation and he gradually got his life back together again. Through his experience, he has self-identified as an ethnic minority. When he was homeless, all the other people with him on the streets were migrants. Even though he has now left the streets, he has always had empathy for the difficulties with which migrants are confronted.

Rita believes that things are getting worse for migrants under the current government, and the policies simply fuel racism against 'outsiders'.

> Everything that this government does is around the prism of enforcement ... So if you look at the health bill, the landlord bill, etc., everything is with the view to enforcement. If you talk to Home Office officials, they used to have a rhetoric of integration ... They don't even talk about integration any more. It's now more and more about enforcement of immigration rules. You've got Operation Nexus, etc. ... You've got operations where mainstream policing is now critically looking at immigration. That means migrants aren't going to afford the same safety and the same access to justice ... We are slipping down a very dodgy slope.

On 29 June 2013, in the midst of heightened tensions over the death of Lee Rigby, Tommy Robinson and Kevin Carroll entered Tower Hamlets on their planned walk to Woolwich via the East London Mosque, calling the borough 'a shariah-controlled area' and 'an Islamic no-gone zone in Britain'. Instead of following the two alternative routes set up by the police, the pair arrived in Aldgate East and were arrested and subsequently charged with obstructing police officers.

But being on bail did not seem to deter the EDL leaders from attempting to enter Tower Hamlets and incite hatred. Robinson vowed to lead the group into the borough on 7 September. Prior to that demonstration, Robinson said to me:

'I'm not allowed to go to east London or Tower Hamlets. What was all that about? I'm angry because the speakers that I keep seeing at that mosque are all extremists. So why can't I protest against it? Muslims protested outside Westminster Cathedral with loads of scruffy tramps blockading St Paul's for months ... If all that can be facilitated as legitimate protest, why can't I as an individual hold a silent protest outside East London Mosque? Why am I going to be arrested for doing that?' (And he tweeted: 'I can't wait till my bail conditions are gone so I can enter Tower Hamlets! I'm going straight to the East London Mosque # fact.')

Robinson's persistence in targeting the East London Mosque didn't come from nowhere. In the aftermath of 9/11, sections of Britain's popular media targeted political Islam as responsible for the terrorist attack in New York without distinguishing between different variants of political Islam. East London Mosque, the oldest mosque in Britain, built in 1910, was suddenly portrayed as harbouring 'extremist' clerics and promoting terrorism. When the London Muslim Centre was opened in 2005, some media warned that 'a terrorist centre [has been] opened in London'. Since then, far-right propaganda has never ceased to utilize that manufactured image.

The communities in Tower Hamlets had a lot of experience in organizing against the far right by the time of the EDL comeback in autumn 2013. The first time the EDL attempted to enter the borough was in June 2010, when they protested against an Islamic conference at the Troxy Centre, which subsequently led to the cancelling of the conference. EDL abandoned its march while Unite Against Fascism (UAF) and United East End

(UEE) mobilized an anti-racist demo attended by thousands. At the time, Musaddiq Ahmed, secretary general of the Tower Hamlets Council of Mosques, said that 'it is vital to defend the multiracial and multi-faith tradition' in Tower Hamlets where 'the East London Mosque sits side by side with a synagogue'.

The EDL suffered a huge defeat in its second attempt to enter the borough in 2011. Six hundred EDL members, led by Robinson dressed up as a rabbi, were blocked along the way by pub, shop and railway workers and were only able to make it to Aldgate, officially outside the borough boundary.

In response to the EDL march in autumn 2013, UEE and UAF mobilized a cross-community anti-EDL demonstration, backed by major trade unions. The assembly point was Altab Ali Park on Whitechapel Road, a park named after Altab Ali, a twenty-five-year-old Bangladeshi clothing worker who was murdered in a racially motivated attack by three white youths as he walked home from work in 1978 in Adler Street. There were numerous racial attacks in the following two decades, and they remain in the memories of local residents. The number of racist attacks increased particularly following the BNP Isle of Dogs council win in 1993. The most serious attacks were on young Bangladeshi students. Quddus Ali, a seventeen-year-old Bangladeshi student from Tower Hamlets College, was attacked in September 1993; Muktar Ahmed, a nineteen-year-old Bangladeshi student, was brutally attacked by a group of twenty white youths in Bethnal Green in February 1994. The next day, several Bangladeshi students from the same college were attacked in a park by white youths armed with iron bars. This was followed by another attack on a fourteen-year-old

Bangladeshi boy, stabbed in the face by four white men on Bethnal Green Road. Dave also recalled hearing about a horrific racist attack in the 1990s when a young Bangladeshi man was badly attacked and suffered permanent brain damage. 'When you live in your own protected bubble, you don't realize these things can happen ... We were drinking in our local pub and a group of anti-racist protesters marched past us. Then we heard about the terrible attack.'

Abdullah Faliq's activism came out of this context. He is an outspoken and committed anti-racist activist and a founding member of UEE. He is also a prolific researcher and academic: he is Head of Research at the Cordoba Foundation, a think tank that promotes dialogue between cultures, and Director of Training at the Centre for the Study of Terrorism and assistant editor of the Centre's monthly journal, *Islamism Digest*, as well as head of media and research at the Islamic Forum of Europe and a trustee of the East London Mosque and London Muslim Centre. I wanted to know how he came to do what he does and got in touch with him.

We met across the road from the East London Mosque at Abdullah's favourite lunch venue, the Pie Factory, a relaxed dining place where you can find steak and kidney pie and chicken biriyani on the same menu. He told me he came to the UK from Bangladesh at the age of four, and has had experienced and witnessed racism all his life. 'In the 1980s and 1990s, almost every Asian person suffered some form of racism, verbal and physical,' he said.

At the age of eleven, in the 1980s, as I was walking towards the mosque, two BNP guys came up and punched me ...

I was shocked as this is a fairly safe area and yet the attack happened just opposite the mosque. And in the old days, there was always racist violence following every football match ...

In response to all this, the Youth Connection was formed by local Bangladeshi youth, which was supported by the Bangladeshi Youth Movement and the Progressive Youth Organization and the Young Muslim Organisation UK [YMOUK]. The former two groups were more cultural in nature, organizing trips and operating in a way similar to youth clubs ... All these three groups provided educational forums and facilities for Bangladeshi Muslims, and YMOUK gives it an Islamic framework. It offers protection and defence against racism.

Since the formation of YMOUK in 1976, it's been the most popular national Muslim youth organization. I've been very active in the group. It was like a refuge for many Bangladeshi youth, especially when they faced racist attacks. With the Youth Connection formed, we had the confidence to fight back [against racism] physically. We didn't feel the police were protecting us. They didn't take us seriously. The Muslim community then wasn't very organized ... They were scattered everywhere and there was no political voice. We had to defend ourselves. So when racists came to Whitechapel, we put up a fight. We showed them that they couldn't pass through here. Then, it was mainly the BNP. What we did was empower the youth and protect our community. That lasted from the early 1980s through to 1992, 1993.

At the time, the wider community, involving both black and white people, was also contributing to the anti-racist defence. Abdullah said that it made Bangladeshi youth see that they are not alienated and alone and there's a wider anti-racist struggle out there on their side.

That struggle had politicized and transformed many white youths, some of whom might have otherwise joined the other side. Paul Sillett, UAF organizer, told me that his life changed when he became involved in anti-fascist activity at the age of fifteen.

The Anti-Nazi League [ANL] and RAR [Rock Against Racism] back then helped turn a generation away from the neo-Nazis and to anti-racist and left politics. I was one such kid; so were several pals.

I grew up in east London. I was aware of the NF from about twelve. You couldn't not be aware of them back then. They, of course, were very active all over east London, e.g. Brick Lane, and had regular stalls in Hoxton, Shoreditch, Newham, Barking, Ilford ... I came close to joining the National Front. One of my good mates joined the NF when I was fourteen and I nearly followed. Some of my mates joined the Young National Front ... Where I lived in east London, quite a few were attracted to the NF and their appalling 'Paki bashing' ...

At the time, I and some of my mates conveniently ignored the fact that our favourite music bands like the Clash and Sex Pistols (punk meant a lot to me) were anti-fascist. Johnny Rotten criticized the Front, and this was amazing. We loved the Pistols, and what he said about the Front being 'despicable' rang true – they were despicable! People like that speaking out was important ... Meeting people like the Clash at gigs and talking about things helped change me. The music was anti-authoritarian, anti-everything that me and my friends hated. Partly through that and the influence of RAR gigs, I veered away from the NF.

Also, only after an older mate pointed out that if the Front ever got anywhere, 'hooligans like us would be locked up', did I start to question some of the racism. Ska and Dub was something we loved too, and though we used to get grief sometimes from Brixton dreads, they soon accepted us skinheads. That too turned us away from the goon squad.

I was just over fourteen when I realized that I was going to make a break with the NF/British Movement ... A lot of the Front were bullies, and this had an impact, too ... All-round horrible people. I knew people in the NF who knifed another [fellow friend] because he had criticized their filth. I was at gigs where NF skins would attack people for any number of reasons, not just racism. One night me and some mates (punks and skinheads; I was a skin) decided we'd seen enough. This was at a Sham 69 gig in central London. There was a horrible atmosphere before the gig with NF goons picking on an Irish bloke. We steamed in and done some of them. Later on, some of their pals came back. It was very nasty, but we just about held our own ... That was a night we'd crossed a line, and I'm glad we did ... But after that we were marked out by the NF on other occasions at Sham gigs, or on the streets ... Things were very violent back then.

ANL-supporting teachers made an impression, though I never told them back then. Their ANL propaganda was stark and effective. I was a horrible, violent kid, but the ANL material cut through some of that. My teachers were amazed one time, when they recognized us on an ANL demo! ... By now, I was a convinced anti-fascist. Working for Unite Against Fascism, I often think back to how things might have been, had I gone down darker avenues ...

As a result of growing cross-community activism, UEE was formed in 2009, as a multi-faith organization. By this time, British racism had shifted from a focus on race and racial differences to culture, cultural practices (such as religion) and cultural differences. EDL ideologies are part of this development. As some of these ideologies have been acceptable in mainstream society and incorporated into mainstream politics, it means that their development might pose much more of a threat than the traditional far right. In response, communities of all cultures resisted in unity. Abdullah said: 'The first time we knew of the EDL's plans to enter Tower Hamlets, we had our first meeting in Bethnal Green and tried to work out what we should do. We have a history of fighting against fascism and racism in the East End. The racists cannot come into this area without being challenged. Racism and racist attacks do not just affect Muslims. They affect everyone in the community.'

Abdullah's activism has put him at risk. He has received three hate mails, two of them death threats from the EDL, saying they will slit his throat. One of the letters was sent to his office at the Cordoba Foundation. Their aggression, however, only made him determined to continue with his work.

Since the Woolwich murder, there's been a sharp increase in the level of racist abuse and attacks in Tower Hamlets. 'Women have had their hijabs pulled off and attacked at bus stops,' Abdullah said. 'One night six months ago, one of the mosque volunteers was attacked by four EDL guys. They jumped on him and badly injured him.

'Attacks on Muslims have increased by threefold across the country. Our mosque is big and protected here; but smaller mosques in other places are more isolated and vulnerable. People have become reluctant to go to the mosque, especially at night-time.'

Across Britain, hundreds of anti-Muslim offences were carried out, with the Metropolitan Police recording 500 Islamophobic crimes since the Woolwich murder. The far right was fired with outrage over Lee Rigby, as if racist attacks and abuse could be morally justified. Even in multicultural London, UAF reported a frightening 69 per cent increase in reported anti-Muslim hate crimes from April 2013 to April 2014.

Clearly, this level of racial hatred has created fear in the Muslim communities. The fear factor had, in the past, prevented some Muslim residents in Tower Hamlets from taking part in anti-EDL resistance. 'Two years ago when the EDL wanted to come into this area, our local politicians were divided,' said Abdullah.

The mayor [of Tower Hamlets] said we must all come out, demonstrate and show our unity. But some of the other parts of the Labour Party and the Tories said, 'Don't come out', 'stay home'. That mixed message from the politicians affected many Muslims and many parents ... It was a confused message. But this time round, everyone's saying we must come out. This borough has a very large youth population. When the EDL comes, there'll be thousands and thousands of young people standing in front of the mosque. Many of them aren't even Muslims, but they're coming to defend the mosque.

That strength of unity that Abdullah talks about was evident in the first UEE–UAF organizing meeting, which took place in the London Muslim Centre in autumn 2013, attended by over a hundred anti-racist activists from a variety of campaigning organizations and faith groups, local residents and members of Unite, PCS and the NUT. I saw that everyone was eager to defend the East End against the far right.

UAF organizer Paul Sillett said: 'Once more, UAF worked well with key actors from the mosque, e.g. Dilawar Khan, United East End, in the run-up to the demo. UAF and others spent nearly three months working up to the day of the demo. Countless meetings, leafleting and a huge host of trade union and community groups united in activity ...'

The police proposed three options to UEE for how to handle the EDL march: Option 1, the EDL to be allowed to march through the borough (which was the police's preferred option until they saw the strength of the opposition to the EDL); Option 2, the EDL to be told they could not come to the borough and must hold their demonstration in central London; Option 3, the EDL to be allowed to hold a 'static demonstration' in the borough. UEE responded that the vast majority of people in Tower Hamlets would find only Option 2 acceptable. Eventually, the campaigners reached a compromise with the police, who allowed the EDL to march into Aldgate, just outside the border of Tower Hamlets.

The EDL's failure to enter the borough was a victory for the campaigners. UAF said:

> We are political and tactical in our approach, and when we use direct action we must have a huge number of people with us – as we did with great effect in Waltham Forest, in 2012, and in the victory in Tower Hamlets, in 2013 ... The latter came when we stopped the EDL from marching on their route in the borough and curtailed their rally. This was not simply a symbolic gesture; for the locals it was a real victory – the EDL were stopped from marching on mosques. The eighteen trade union banners on the march showed the social forces crucial to undermining EDL ... Bringing on board important parts of the labour movement helped quantitatively and qualitatively on the day.

Back in 2010 and 2011 when EDL entered the borough, some businesses such as shops and pubs refused to serve the racist demonstrators. In autumn 2013, I was interested to see how local businesses would respond. I visited the well-known Blind Beggar pub, on Whitechapel Road. The French barman wasn't aware of the EDL as he had only just arrived, but he pointed to the pub owner, David Dobson, who was having a break at a nearby table. Dobson, originally from Birmingham, told me he'd been running the pub for fifteen years. 'The last time I heard about the EDL was when they were doing their planned march down this way, in 2011,' he said.

> It was all new to us at the time and we didn't really know the good or bad about it ... It was relatively unknown. But then you heard about the violence that came with it ... The first thing I heard about it was the disruption and the conflict with the police and the various different communities in Whitechapel.
>
> The individual members [of the EDL] have been to this pub a few times before, over the years, and my manager has refused to serve them. The last time [2011] they met down in Aldgate, and then they made their way, going by the [East London] Mosque, and then by the backstreets and all came down here ... There were police vans outside. We decided to close the pub for five minutes. Then there were about thirty guys all wanting to come in. I said to them, the pub's closed for a while ... They were all looking aggressive. The police had to get them to all go in the White Hart across the road and contain them in there for a while.
>
> Later, there was a campaign against hate which all the local pubs in this area supported ... Pubs put up leaflets in their windows saying that the EDL and the like aren't welcome ...

Like many who have lived in Tower Hamlets for a long time, Dobson said that the far right would find it very difficult to grow in this area.

'The thing is, the area is a melting pot of cultures ... and we all want to live together and we all live together very well. Everyone's welcome here as far as I'm concerned. I don't know anyone who feels sympathy for racist views. Nobody wants hate ... We're living in a city where more than 300 languages are spoken. Groups like the EDL want to return to the Middle Ages. They're not in this world. Where we are, everyone's working hard to make it a blended community here.'

I went to the Indo pub just opposite the mosque, to enquire about their approach to the far right. A staff member replied: 'Our manager is anti-racist and we wouldn't serve drinks to members of the EDL. My colleagues came across the EDL several times and always refused to serve them. Once, one of them got aggressive and tried to start a fight. He even threatened to get a knife from the kitchen. But even after that incident, we still absolutely say no to them coming in to try to use the pub as their venue.'

I went back to the Half Moon in Stepney Green, where I started my initial conversations with local residents. I expected the manager there would be more 'relaxed' about the EDL presence because of their white-majority clientele. But he surprised me by saying that he has made it a rule that they don't serve drinks to members of the EDL. The definite local response I witnessed in autumn 2013 was a clear indication that multiculturalism has become the norm and is here to stay.

That day, I watched the 300-strong EDL crowd marching into Aldgate from the City. They were singing loudly, chanting, while Tommy Robinson and Kevin Carroll gave speeches. An armoured van was parked by the side of the road. I approached the cautious-looking drivers, Daz and Michael, who'd come down from Leicester. They told me that they knew no one here on the march and their job was to bring equipment for the rally. They've done this for several EDL marches.

I asked them what they did for a living. Daz said he was a lorry driver; Michael worked as a builder. They told me life was tough in their communities and there was little employment for young people.

They were both of English Roma origin. I wondered how they perceived racism and prejudice against minorities. Michael said the travellers are much discriminated against in this country and he himself felt part of that victimized community. He'd had few opportunities in the early years of his adult life, and could not read or write. He was the first illiterate person I have ever met in Britain.

Michael told me he'd joined the EDL two years earlier. Given his ethnic background, how did he come to choose such an allegiance? His response was to repeat the party line: 'Muslims are taking over,' he said, 'faith schools are teaching Islamicist ideas ... Women aren't being respected ...'

I looked behind him and saw the chanting mob of alienated, hate-filled males. Women have always been the minority within the EDL. Among these 300 demonstrators, I could see no more than a dozen. When I asked Michael about the unbalanced gender ratio, he didn't know how to answer me and simply shrugged his shoulders.

Women were rare, and are thus referred to as 'EDL angels'. But they were no 'angels'. The EDL Angels, now with 150 members, was set up by a woman called Lady England, who was involved in police liaison for the EDL's activities. The offshoot group was originally named the Female Footsloggers Division. Then the regional organizer for Yorkshire, known as Gail Speight, and her then partner John Sheridan (aka Chris Renton), changed the name to EDL Angels. It became a forum for female activists who felt the EDL didn't take them seriously. When Gail Speight became the only female regional organizer on the committee, she started to argue for women's demos apart from the main demos, but so far, except for the one women's demo in the early days of the EDL, there have been no more. Many male activists see them more as 'trouble' than real activists as they had to tag along at the end of the women's demos for protection.

Gail Speight was later featured favourably on a BBC3 documentary, *EDL Angels*, and has since been nicknamed 'Miss EDL' by many in the movement. However, she's no angel herself and was in fact called a 'tramp' by Tommy Robinson and is known by many to be 'thuggish'. She is one of the regional organizers who is 'relaxed' about the role of the neo-fascists within the EDL. Robinson said: 'She has caused a lot of trouble. There've always been problems around her. All her associates were racist pricks. She's one of those organizers who don't mind the idiots [neo-fascists] ... The leader of the Northwest Infidels, a scumbag ['Diddyman', real name Shane Calvert, a neo-fascist who was convicted for violent disorder in September 2013], was very close to Gail. He was always around at her house. She didn't care; she let them [neo-fascists] in.'

Robinson revealed another side to BBC3's version of the attack on Gail Speight by local Asian youth. 'She did get her jaw broken and no one deserved that, but she got it because all the men she hung out with were arseholes, Nazis, and were probably provoking [the attack]. If you associate with Nazis, even if you're not one yourself, wouldn't you be seen as a Nazi?'

Back then, Robinson had had problems removing the neo-fascists from the group, as I will discuss in the next chapter. 'You won't get rid of them, because if you get rid of a regional organizer, they'll just bring their mates and set up another group. It's a circle; it won't end.'

It puzzles me why the media, including the BBC, has portrayed the 'EDL Angels' so positively, while there has been no coverage of British Muslim women campaigning against racism.

During the mobilization for the anti-EDL march, a new group was set up by local Muslim and non-Muslim women, named 'Sisters Against the EDL'. Their existence has effectively challenged prejudices against Muslim women in Britain. Contrary to popular myths that Muslim women are home-bound and passive receivers of male domination, many British Muslim women take an active part in mobilizing against racism. 'A woman's place is in the streets,' they said.

I met a nineteen-year-old British Muslim woman, Tahsin, who's been active in the anti-racist movement in the East End for years. She stood out during Sisters Against EDL meetings owing to her confident manner. I asked to meet her again.

We met in a Bangladeshi café on Whitechapel Road. Tahsin was relaxed and open, and was willing to share her thoughts on anything I asked. She described her family as working class, although she said the family was middle class back in Bangladesh. Her father graduated from South Bank University and was a housing officer for the council. Her forty-seven-year-old mum holds a degree in child psychology and used to work for a nursery. Their relatives back home see them as very 'British', as her grandad fought in the British Indian Army and in the Second World War, and he was also a footballer.

Tahsin told me she comes from an activist family. Both her parents were involved in the Socialist Workers Party and were active supporters of the Respect Party.

The war in Iraq changed everything ... It affected everyone, even conservative Muslim families. They found that they had to speak up for the first time. Many Muslims who would be scared of demos were out demonstrating for the first time ... There you meet many socialists ... From then on, my dad got involved. Many British Bengalis are probably socialist-oriented but they don't mix with formal socialist crowds ... so they never get recruited into socialist organizations ...

In those days, my dad was a strong socialist. George Galloway was often in our house ... but later when Galloway left, it fell apart ... They [local Bengali activists] were so disappointed with Galloway ... and felt they were stabbed in the back. They did so much for him ... through the election. But after that, he invited us to one dinner and that was it. We never heard from him again. They invested so much in him and so when he left, it symbolized the loss of hope. My parents phased out of it around 2010, 2011 ... disillusioned after ten years of activism and felt nothing has changed – and they just felt that nothing's gonna change. It's a shame that they've given up their socialist morals and ideals ... They used to like to speak up.

As Tahsin spoke, I couldn't help but remember those years when the Stop the War Coalition gathered support and Respect drew in so many in the local communities. My ex-partner and many activists like him devoted their time to campaigning for the anti-war cause, and yet, sadly, they were let down by the dissolution of Respect, leaving many totally demoralized, just like Tahsin's father.

'Nowadays they've mellowed and just want to live comfortably … I wouldn't call my dad a socialist now. They've switched from Respect back to Labour. They became disillusioned. They are much more nervous now about things.'

Tahsin is a fun-loving young woman, and at the same time incredibly emotionally mature for her age. She told me she's addicted to cinema, particularly American horror films. But she's also a very logical reader of history. 'I'm interested in finding out how religions progressed,' she said. 'I enjoy studying the history of religion.'

But she told me there are other reasons behind her regular visits to the mosque. For many British Muslims, mosques aren't there only for religious practices. For young people, in particular, they function like social venues. 'We can just socialize and talk to people. It's like a youth club,' Tahsin said. 'There are no youth centres around here. There used to be a youth club near our house funded by the council but it was shut down … That was a shame. For Muslims in the area, the mosque is like the community centre. They organized a lot of funfairs near Altab Ali Park and it's open to everyone. That's the side of things about the mosque that other people don't see.'

At the time of our meetings, there was an ongoing debate in the media about the use of the Muslim veil (of all types). It's one of the ways by which British Muslims are put under social surveillance. I cannot think of another group of people whose clothing habits are monitored in this way. I wanted to know what Tahsin thought about this, as she wears a hijab.

She told me that, contrary to popular misconceptions about women being forced into wearing a veil, it has always been her own choice. And in fact, for her it was an act of rebellion, as her family doesn't want her to wear one. 'My family don't adopt an Islamic way of life as much,' she said.

> My brother is like a typical teenager, and my older sister only began to wear Islamic dress recently as she got bored wearing jeans and wants to have the freedom of not allowing men to watch her ... and then she began to study Islam. I'm the only one in the family who follows Islam more actively.
>
> I started wearing the headscarf a few years ago and it was quite a difficult step. When I got home from school, I had to quickly take it off and put it in my bag so my dad couldn't see it. It's not that my parents didn't like the headscarf, but they were scared for me and how other people would see it ... My mum wears a headscarf now but she didn't wear it when she was younger. She was fine wearing it only when she was about thirty. When I first started to dress like this [wearing a hijab], my parents were very nervous. I feel more pressure to *not* wear it than to wear it.

Tahsin's parents are very concerned about the implications of her participation in religious or political activities, and how it would impact on her future.

185

I bought a book about Moazzam Begg; I was reading it and my parents were so shocked. They said to me, if you're reading this, they might put you in Guantanamo Bay! The fear is that we're constantly being watched ... Every conversation we have, everything we look at on the internet and everything we speak about is being recorded by the government and secret services somehow ... and they're just working on evidence to lock us up. That is a genuine fear among Muslims. Everyone feels like that, particularly the older generation. When they hear stories of Muslims being arrested because of certain things, they feel everyone is under threat and they are very easily scared by what they see on the media. For instance, they are more scared of the EDL than they should be. They are more scared of the government than they should be. I think it's because even though they've lived in this country for a long time, they are not really familiar with it in some ways ... And for those who don't speak the language, they are even more scared. It's a genuine fear.

Despite opposition from her parents, Tahsin insisted on wearing a headscarf, which for her is choosing what fashion to follow.

I really enjoy wearing it. I went to a Bengali school and there were about five or six non-Bengali people in my class ... There, I fitted in completely. A lot of girls there didn't wear the headscarf. It's our own choice whether to wear it. It was mixed – some people wore it, some didn't. Some liked it, some didn't. Those who wore it chose to wear it. The peer pressure was to not wear it and to look nice ... The girls who didn't wear it did their hair nice and had their make-up nice ... They were always the most popular kids. That was the norm [not to wear a headscarf]. The girls who chose to wear it weren't as popular ... or as liked. But I liked it.

The same as anyone who dresses differently. Why do some people do facial tattoos? I wanted to rebel, to make decisions for myself. I was young and it was quite a spontaneous decision. I didn't put a lot of thought into it ... In Islam, there's encouragement to wear it; if a woman decides to wear it, obviously it's completely up to her. Chapter two, verse 256 in the Quran says there's no compulsion in religion and you can't force anyone to do anything in the name of religion. The verse says: 'There is no compulsion in Deen (no one can be forced to enter the fold of Islam).' I didn't understand why it had to be an issue in Britain. To me it was like wearing anything ... It was just a piece of clothing. I didn't see why it had to cause offence.

During the first year Tahsin started to wear the headscarf, she and her friend, who wasn't wearing a headscarf, were harassed by a group of local white men on the street. They looked to be in their mid-thirties to forties. They stopped the two women and shouted at Tahsin's friend, 'Where's your rug?' Tahsin said it was her first encounter with ignorance. 'They had never heard anything about Islam. All they heard was from the media,' she said.

My friend shouted back at him, 'Where's your wig?' It was always white people who asked Muslim girls who weren't wearing the headscarf why they weren't wearing it.

My dad was worried about me ... because of experience of racist attacks. In the 1990s, one of my uncles was attacked by a large group of white men. He was beaten by baseball bats and other weapons, and was in hospital for three weeks. He was walking home from work ... They saw him, brown skin, definitely Asian, so they attacked him. It was completely unprovoked. After that, my parents became very, very worried ... My dad was always very, very nervous about us dressing too differently ... It's a shame. At school we were always encouraged to choose to do what we want ... I want to be the way I want to be.

When I go out with my friends, they don't dress like me, which is fine. They can dress the way they want. I see how men heckle them ... and it just seems really, really unfair. It's just because they aren't wearing the headscarf. They should be able to wear what they want without having men heckle them. I don't want to be in that position ever. So I decided that I would wear it. In that way I get a lot less attention ...

I was the vice-president of the Islamic Society at college. A girl came to me one day, crying. I asked her what's wrong and she just hugged me. She said she wanted to dress the way I do and her parents wouldn't let her. I found that so upsetting. Her parents wouldn't let her because they worried about abuse ... A lot of young people are in this situation. The younger generation, like me, my cousins and my friends, choose to wear headscarves whereas my parents and aunts don't. More and more young people are choosing to dress like this ... A bit of rebellion. Just like youths of other communities. There's something very universal about this.

I've got a friend who's now the head of the Islamic Society and she's one of my closest friends. Her dad banned her from the East London Mosque. In college, she started to dress like me, and her dad said that the East London Mosque was having a negative impact on her ... The ideas of the EDL are corrupting everyone, even Muslims. The EDL hates the East London Mosque, and now many Muslim parents dislike the East London Mosque and it's quite common that they don't want their children to go to the mosque. They even believe that the mosque is extremist ... It's crazy! How can the mosque be extremist? All we do is go there and pray and we leave.

One of my uncles told his wife to not let his kids, i.e. my cousins, stay with me. I found that really sad. Because when they came over, most of time we just played games or read ... We just do what normal people do ... Everyone's taking on the EDL mentality and thinks anyone who dresses like this is an extremist. Once I was walking out of college to get myself a drink, a group of about ten Muslim boys aged between twenty-five and thirty, they just shouted, 'Oi, you ninja come here'. They were referring to the full veil. And I wasn't even wearing it ... I was getting that much hate! Obviously they thought that I must be really quiet, an oppressed lady, so when I turned round and asked, 'What did you say?' they were just completely shaken up.

Tahsin said she has acquired a good understanding of Islam through her own study. 'The older generation don't really have much teaching of Islam themselves. People here learn about Islam

later on, in their late teens … and they decide for themselves …
My parents tried to teach me the basics, but I learned everything
myself later on. Now I know a lot more about Islam than my dad
but he would never admit it. Sometimes in a debate, I quote the
Quran, leaving him shocked.'

Tahsin said her decision to wear a headscarf was not only
about religion but about society as well. She wants to be identified
as Muslim while her parents want her to 'fit in'.

She said:

> I want to fit in as well, but I don't want to change the
> way I look, and I don't want to lose my identity. Are we
> all going to look the same, have the same hair colour and
> wear contact lenses? It's nice to have a mix of people. It's
> nice to come across people with crazy hair or facial tattoos
> … I didn't think about the political meaning of wearing a
> headscarf at the time, but I think about it more now. When
> I started wearing it at the age of thirteen, I didn't think it
> would make me different or have any consequences … It
> was just a piece of clothing then and now I never go out
> without this on. It means a lot more now … more social
> … and more about rebellion … I want to show people that
> even when I wear the headscarf, we can get along fine. This
> is not a barrier.

However, Tahsin has met with prejudice everywhere she goes,
even in the university, where she has experienced racial stereotyping of Muslims. 'At uni, I find it very hard to fit in, unlike
in college and school in east London where there was a good

mix of people – a lot of Muslims, Christians and atheists. But at uni there are hardly any Muslims. There are lots of overseas students and students from up north. The places they have come from don't have many Muslims ... so it's the first time I feel like an outsider.'

The way Tahsin chooses to dress has marked her out, which upsets her deeply.

Often, I want to have a conversation with the girls and boys about things, but they don't want to have that conversation back ... Once, we were doing group work, and when we were talking about history, I thought it was going really well. But when I started speaking, they all stopped listening ... It was really rude ... I tried to get their attention and make conversation. If they were talking about TV, I would talk about the same characters ... to make them see that we do have a lot in common. I like scary movies and I tell them that ... I do hope things will get better. It's been difficult for two or three months now.

Experiencing racism first-hand triggered Tahsin's activism. But she isn't interested only in resisting racism. She also adopts a class analysis for understanding racism systematically. When I asked her how she identifies herself politically, she said: 'I'm a British Muslim and I'm a socialist. My experience tells me that Islam and socialism go well together ... I went to a Marxism festival where I attended a meeting, among others, on the EDL and history of Cable Street ... I'm also very interested in international politics. People I've met on the left support personal freedom and I've never seen a contradiction between being what I want to be religiously and my involvement with political activities ...' Tahsin has also taken part in TUC marches and mobilized people to travel from Tower Hamlets schools to the Embankment to take part in marches. She has also worked with the UAF.

'We were getting everyone familiar with the UAF and going into assemblies to speak against the far right. We were leafleting around Bethnal Green in 2011 and that was my most active time ...'

Tahsin is critical of the conservative reactions to government policies among Britain's Muslim communities. 'Things have got a lot worse since the coalition government got into power. Immigration has become much tougher ... What I find so disgusting is that some immigrants themselves have started to argue against immigration ... It's all part of the idea of trying to fit in. Those people are giving up on Islamic dress and their culture, giving up on their morals and beliefs ... outwardly they are trying to hide away their religion and they are quite ashamed of it ... and they want to see more controls on immigration. What really bothers me is the immigration debate.'

She explained why she's out on the street protesting and why she will remain an activist: 'There are different types of people. There are people who see injustice happening and they try to stop it even if they get hurt in the crossfire. And there are people who want to push this aside and get on with their lives. They want their lives to be comfortable. I'm on the side where if something's wrong, I'll speak out against it. I don't think we should be comfortable when other people aren't.'

5

THE CHANGING FACES
OF THE RADICAL RIGHT

G iven our last conversation, I was more than surprised to
hear about Tommy Robinson's departure from the EDL
in October 2013. He decided to quit his leadership position and
leave the group altogether. The most sensational part of the story
was that his announcement was made during a press conference
held by Maajid Nawaz* from the Quilliam Foundation, the previously government-funded counter-extremism think tank.

Robinson looked concerned as he spoke to the press: 'We
[Robinson and Kevin Carroll] have decided to leave the EDL
because we feel we can no longer keep extremists away.' He
then said that he was to work with Quilliam, to 'combat Islamic
extremism'. He said he opposed extremism at both ends of
the spectrum. 'I have been considering this move for a long
time because I recognize that, though street demonstrations
have brought us to this point, they are no longer productive. I
acknowledge the dangers of far-right extremism and the ongoing

---

* For Nawaz and Quilliam's detailed background, see www.middleeasteye.
net/ columns/circus-how-british-intelligence-primed-both-sides-terror-
war-55293733.

need to counter Islamist ideology not with violence but with better, democratic ideas.'

Robinson made a statement to the EDL about his resignation: 'I need to make it clear that I left the EDL because I was spending too much time trying to keep goose-stepping white-pride morons away from our demos and not enough time actually doing anything to stop the advance of Islamic extremism. I wanted to make sure our legitimate concerns were not ignored because Nazi morons destroyed our voice in mainstream politics and media.'

The EDL website responded: 'End of the party for EDL? No, it's only the beginning.'

I was surprised because, only two months prior to these statements, Robinson told me, 'The EDL has created the biggest street movement Britain has ever seen.' He never expressed any opposition to the neo-fascist elements of that movement, nor any wish to leave the group. Similarly surprising was that Quilliam came out supporting Robinson and legitimizing his anti-Muslim politics by publicizing their plans to work with him. Eagerly, Maajid Nawaz equates radical Islam with neo-fascism: 'We hope to help Tommy invest his energy and commitment in countering extremism of all kinds, supporting the efforts to bring along his former followers and encouraging his critique of Islamism as well as his concern with far-right extremism.'

The former leader of a far-right movement was suddenly a liberal who believes 'Islamic fundamentalism' deserves the same social condemnation as fascist skinheads.

Arun Kundnani, author of *The Muslims Are Coming!: Islamophobia, Extremism, and the Domestic War on Terror*, was not surprised about Quilliam. The founders of Quilliam have embraced the government's anti-extremism initiatives under the Preventing Violent Extremism programme (nicknamed the government's 'Islam policy'). It was one of the 'Muslim organizations' to be integrated into the government's surveillance apparatus. It supports the official line that 'ideology [i.e. religion] is driving radicalization' and foreign policy is of little relevance, said Kundnani.

In order to get funding, Quilliam once drew up a document that argued for tackling 'a broader Islamicist ideology' and featured a list of groups to be banned from public funding and government engagement, which included the majority of Muslim organizations in the UK. But the draft was leaked, and the plan had to be dropped. As a result of that mess-up, by the end of 2010 Quilliam had lost credibility with the government and its funding shrank drastically.

Clearly, Maajid Nawaz intends to benefit from events as much as Robinson does. According to the Political Scrapbook, figures released by the Home Office reveal that its funding for Quilliam shrank from £674,708 in the year 2008/09 to just £26,993 in 2011/12, since drying up completely. The Foreign and Commonwealth Office's funding also ended in 2011. The Political Scrapbook suspects that, given its loss of major funding from the state, the organization has cynically resorted to adopting Robinson as a 'trophy convert from extremism', in order to win funding. This suspicion was soon proved well justified by the revelation that Quilliam's Maajid Nawaz (a Liberal Democrat parliamentary candidate for Hampstead and Kilburn; he came third in the 2015 general election) had written to the Department for Communities and Local Government to apply for funding on the day Robinson left the EDL.

Meanwhile, Robinson decided that reshaping his brand and moving into the mainstream was his only way forward. The EDL had become a synonym for street thuggery and bigotry, and there was nothing for Robinson to gain by remaining in the group. Having taken part in the BBC documentary *When Tommy Met Mo*, Robinson had got a taste of the possible gains of going mainstream. With potential new projects in mind, such as working with various think tanks like Quilliam and being involved in TV documentaries, why would he want to cling to the old-fashioned street fights of the far right? Furthermore, he had a court case pending, and some suspected this was his underlying reason for quitting the EDL.

Arun Kundnani said of the episode: 'Rather than converting Tommy Robinson, they seem to be providing him with a more mainstream platform for his views, which have not substantially changed … The key point is that Quilliam don't have any kind of independent agenda and are mainly a vehicle for getting government funding and pushing agendas coming from neo-cons and from government agencies.' Indeed, and in May 2015 Maajid Nawaz called on David Cameron to appoint a so-called 'counter-extremism czar' in order to 'combat terrorism'.[*]

Regarding Maajid Nawaz's equating radical Islam with neo-fascism, Kundnani said:

> There is a long tradition in Britain of community organizing against the far right, which always connected anti-fascism to wider issues to do with race and class. But over the last

---

* See report at www.ibtimes.co.uk/maajid-nawaz-calls-david-cameron-create-counter-extremism-czar-1501116.

decade we've seen a government 'anti-extremism' agenda that tries to equate the far right, the far left and Islamists as essentially similar forms of 'extremism' and that superficially appropriates this history for a very different purpose, while suppressing anti-fascist activists as themselves 'extremists'. This official anti-extremism agenda – embodied by Quilliam – takes a top-down, managerial approach that enables much of the far right's narrative to continue circulating in the mainstream.

Meanwhile, as Europe prepared for elections to the EU Parliament in May 2014, far-right ideologies were growing all over Europe. Anti-Muslim and anti-Semitic sentiments ran high and ethnic minority and migrant communities were constantly under attack. Racist and neo-fascist parties in Europe were exploiting fear common during economic bad times. In Britain, the BNP was seeking the re-election of Nick Griffin in the North West and Andrew Brons in Yorkshire and the Humber, while UKIP was gaining influence and the coalition government was bringing in the ever harsher Immigration Bill in an ongoing competition for electoral gains.

After Tommy Robinson left the EDL, there was a period of several months during which people expected the collapse of the movement. But that didn't happen. Instead, the group changed direction and consolidated its politics of race. The neo-fascist section of the EDL has further diversified into splinter groups, some of which moved closer to seek 'unity' with the rest of the far right, as I will go into in more depth later in this chapter.

On the streets and in public spaces, British Muslims are facing ever greater difficulties. With the growth of racism and media complicity, British Muslims have become the day-to-day objects of surveillance and monitoring. Anti-Muslim racism has been dressed up as a debate on cultural practices, putting Muslims' lives under intense public gaze.

British Muslim youth like Tahsin have witnessed an increase in racial stereotyping, abuse and attacks over the years, at their peak in 2013. It has angered many like her, compelling them to take part in anti-racist activities. Tahsin recalled: 'Three or four EDL members came to this area and tried to damage the [East London] mosque, kicking the doors and chanting racist abuse … At the time, the mosque had informed people not to come near as the EDL was coming.' Young Muslims were becoming politicized. Tahsin's brother, for instance, wasn't really interested in religion, but on hearing the news about the EDL attack, he went there to defend the mosque.

Many British Muslim women have become more aware of being the objects of public scrutiny and are ever more fearful for their safety. Tahsin told me that a friend of hers was assaulted while sitting at a bus stop. 'It happened when she was on her way to college … All of a sudden a man under the age of thirty came up and pulled off her veil. Then he shouted abuse at her. She was so fearful and upset by the experience that she vomited … She ran back home and was consequently late for her exams.'

In the following months, Tahsin said, many Muslim women had their veils pulled off or were otherwise harassed on the street. 'I have a friend who was spat on for wearing the face veil. I was there with her walking home from college, and a group of white men tried to spit on us and they missed me. They got her. I asked them, "What's your problem?" They were shocked that we responded, so they walked away.'

Meanwhile, we continue to see the debate in the popular media against the niqab, despite the fact that only a couple of hundred women in the entire British Muslim population of 1.5 million actually wear one and there has never been any evidence of any women being 'forced' to wear it. Racism disguised as the defence of women's rights. Tahsin sighed and asked why it's always women who are targeted. 'It's funny how it was always women. Muslim men have very distinct Islamic dress like women do … They wear white clothes just above their ankles. They're dressing completely different to the norm as well, but they never get harassed. Why is no one saying that Muslim men are oppressed?'

The politics of race propagated by the EDL have their resonances in wider society, with the popular media endorsing and reproducing them. The daily drip-feed of hate in the tabloids, in particular, provides ideological and moral justification for racism preached by the far right – the two are constantly interacting and reinforcing each other.

Many young British Muslims have seen through this process. In Tower Hamlets, the EDL and UKIP have taken their turns at disseminating this politics of race, in the name of 'integration', an important part of the mainstream discourse on the topic. When UKIP's Nicholas McQueen – a celebrity florist, cousin of the late fashion designer Alexander McQueen, and a self-claimed 'real East Ender' – ran for mayor in Tower Hamlets, he talked about 'integration' (claiming Muslims are unwilling to integrate), echoing David Cameron's comments on 5 February 2011, on the day of the EDL's largest demonstration. In defence of his so-called 'muscular liberalism', Cameron launched an attack on Britain's multiculturalism, warning that it is contributing to a 'home-grown Islamic terrorism'. He urged Britain's Muslims to 'integrate', and said that government funding would be granted only to Muslim organizations that promote integration.

But young British Muslims, well educated and well integrated, see through the lies and how far-right ideologies reflect racial prejudices in mainstream British society and political discourse. On a day-to-day level, British Muslims experience a hostile public gaze. Listening to Tahsin reminds me of what I witnessed in the case of Uighur Muslims in China, who are also subjected to intrusive public scrutiny and social monitoring of their basic cultural practices. Recently, the Muslim veil and beards have been banned in Karamay, a city in northern Xinjiang (East Turkestan), with pictures of all types of banned veils and beards on display in public places.

Tahsin said:

Social attitudes towards Muslims have gone from bad to worse ... People in this area are more used to the way I dress ... whereas people in the city or farther up, they react differently ... They just look at you and stare. That's the worst.

I don't mind if on the Tube people come up to me and say 'By the way, why do you wear this?' I prefer that than them thinking, 'Oh, she's oppressed.' This is one of the reasons why I want to wear the headscarf. I want to communicate with people and talk to them about difficult issues. I want people to ask me questions, so they understand more about it. A lot of people have stereotypes ... and I'd love to talk to them about it.

'Appropriate dress' for Muslims became a public debate about the niqab, which involved the tabloids as well as broadsheets. This is an unprecedented intrusion into personal lifestyles. Tahsin said: 'If you want to wear the niqab, why should anyone tell you not to wear it? ... A white British commentator said in a Channel 4 debate at the mosque that women shouldn't wear it because he feels uncomfortable with it. He said women should consider how other people feel. That's just rubbish. People can tell you they're not comfortable with leggings or tattoos; do you have to cover it up?'

Contrary to popular myth, there is no authority in British Muslim communities dictating what Muslim women should wear. Tahsin told me that even elders don't have the say in this. 'East London Mosque's position is that if you want to wear it, wear it; if you don't, don't. That's what Islam says. There are Muslims who argue for the ban as they are influenced by the media ... My uncle said that the veil should be banned; so do my friends' parents who ban her from the mosque ... My dad said that women shouldn't wear the niqab ... because he, like many others, wants to fit in. He's changed a lot over the years. He just wants to fit in, simple as that ... They want to adopt a way of dressing like everyone else because they don't want problems.'

This prevalent control of how Muslims should live, down to the level of how they should dress and look, has angered many young in the community, who in turn insist on adopting practices of their own choice. Tahsin and some of her friends are among this increasingly politically aware youth. 'Given all the attacks in the media, I was thinking about wearing the face veil, as a political statement. It's originally an optional piece of clothing you can wear, meaning modesty. A lot of women feel more secure and liberated that way ... They can pick who sees their faces. For them, that's freedom.'

A friend of Tahsin's wears the niqab only inside college, as her way of protesting against the mainstream attitudes against the practice. 'This is what I want to do too,' said Tahsin, 'and this is because a lot of people say it should be banned in educational institutions. If more people wear it, then they can't just ban it ... This is in support of women who actually wear the face veil.'

Again, Tahsin's parents are concerned. 'Last year I wanted to wear it [the niqab] and my parents said no. Now I feel even stronger about it. This is the right of women to do so, and I feel I would be oppressed if I'm forced to show my face to everybody.' Tahsin then bought three face veils, and put one on to show her mother.

'She was quite scared to see me wearing it,' Tahsin said, shaking her head.

Then I asked her: 'Mum, do you think it suits me? Can I wear it?' She didn't answer me. She thought I was messing around with the face veil. I asked her again, and then she got worried. 'What? Do you actually want to wear it?' she asked me. My sister was there and she said, 'If you wear it, no one's gonna speak to you.' Everyone has the idea that if you wear it, you are disconnected from society. And then my mum started telling me about people she knows: 'Look, this and that person wears it and look what happened to them.' 'Now you're going to uni in the city, it's going be too difficult for you,' she said. 'Too many people will be looking at you and you're going to have to deal with it.' Eventually, she said, 'Your dad is not going to let you wear it.' I couldn't face my dad. I couldn't ask him. He would say he's too scared for me to wear it.

I asked her what she's going to do about it. She's a strong young woman and I knew she wouldn't just follow the rules. 'I think I'm to keep having that conversation until Mum says yes,' Tahsin said.

And this time, even if my dad says no, I'm going wear it. I hope that when I go to seminars and classes, people will start asking me, why are you wearing it? So it is a statement I'm making by wearing it ... If there had not been the debate, I wouldn't decide to wear it. I feel I need to stand up more now, to make sure that women wearing the face veil are supported ... I'm not the only person who feels like that. A friend of mine is also doing it, and she's my age.

Young people between seventeen and twenty-five appreciate this way of dressing more now ... because they don't see it as often as before [as they're discouraged from wearing it by wider society] and it becomes more appealing to them ... When something's under attack, you value it more. They see it as a sign of struggle.

Tommy Robinson's departure from the EDL was seen as a victory by anti-racist campaigners, while his cooperation with the Quilliam Foundation was treated with suspicion. Quilliam isn't an organization much trusted by the majority of the British Muslim community owing to its close ties with the neoliberal establishment.

Tahsin, for example, doesn't trust Quilliam because of its conformist and assimilationist approach to culture. 'The Quilliam Foundation was set up by one of the presidents of the Islamic Society at my college ten to fifteen years ago. He's one of the Muslims who would like to conform ... He changed his name from Mohammed to Ed. You can keep your culture and identity and still fit in, can't you? That's why I don't like Quilliam. Any sort of religious institution that follows the religion fully, they would call them extremist.'

I asked Tahsin what she thinks can be done to challenge racism against Muslims in this country and what she aspires to do to achieve that change. In contrast to Quilliam's approach, she believes in communication and the exchange of ideas.

> British Muslims don't really have a platform to challenge the far right ... We don't have a platform to challenge misconceptions, a platform where we can reach out to those people. This was something I wanted to do through the Islamic Society ... for people to come and speak to us ... so if they have any questions, they will get answers from Muslims and not the wrong sources.
>
> We had people of all faiths in our society. We need to get out there more ... If I could, I would wear a sign saying

'If you have questions about Islam, ask me'. So people on the street can come and ask me. We also need a large media platform, to communicate to a large number of people a lot easier ... I'm organizing a programme for the Islamic Education and Research Academy. We go out in the streets and present people with material about Islam. If people have questions, they ask us. We're holding training courses soon, to teach people how to go out in the streets to talk to non-Muslims about Islam. Every Sunday at Hyde Park Corner, volunteers from Islamic Education and Research Academy are already doing that. We want it on a larger scale ... The volunteers sometimes get heckled, but that's part of it ... We need communication.

Those who work for Quilliam are also talking about 'dialogue', although on a flawed basis that treats radical Muslims the same as far-right extremists. I talked to Usama Hasan (also mentioned in Chapter 2), senior researcher at Quilliam, to find out more. He comes from Tottenham, north London, and used to be an active preacher in mosques all over the country. He moved away from radical Islam a long time ago as he started his own family, and now wants only to combat 'extremism' and promote 'integration'.

For Hasan, combating 'extremism' also involves challenging racist myths, although this hasn't been highlighted in Quilliam's work. Despite his weariness and slight suspicion of me, I did agree with him when he talked about the role of the media in polarizing communities since 9/11, thus encouraging 'extremism'. 'That polarization [between British Muslim and white communities, often both economically marginalized] was made worse by the media … ' he said. 'Today, there are daily headlines about British jihadists … Ordinary people don't know where they're coming from, and with the media going on about it, they start to believe that all Muslims are terrorists … The Irish were treated the same way in the 1970s and 1980s.'

Hasan sees a working future with Tommy Robinson. I asked what common ground he has with Robinson that can form the basis of a working relationship. He paused for a few seconds, and said: 'We are both British. And we're both human. That's a lot in common.'

Tommy Robinson has also seemed to advocate a dialogue about Islam, although it was unclear what the nature of that dialogue would be. The news about Robinson's contact with his anti-Islamic friends Pamela Geller and Robert Spencer in the USA in November 2013 raised suspicions that he hasn't really changed his views. In a joint blog post, Geller and Spencer said Robinson wrote to them confirming this.

I wanted to meet with Robinson to find out about this. But on the phone I felt his guard was up again. He didn't have time to meet, he said, so we talked on the phone instead.

Robinson told me he had become 'the most wanted man on either side'.

My departure has let a lot of them down in the EDL. A lot of people feel that hope was stolen from them … People [in the EDL] called me Judas and said I've sold out … Some people thought I'd taken money … A hell of a lot of anger in the first few weeks [of my departure]. I think that has died down a little bit now. People are starting to listen to what I'm saying and trying to look at it from my point of view. When people do certain things on demos, it is my face ... It's me who has to answer the questions. If there's anyone to blame, it should be the regional organizers when they had the opportunities [to change] ... But despite their anger, I haven't been confronted by EDL followers directly since I left ...

The disruption to his family life was also a background consideration for his departure from the EDL. 'My family wanted me to leave for so long. They'd prefer if I just dropped out of politics and went back to work. I had a successful business before this.' However, leaving the EDL seems to have created more problems for Robinson's family. He said his wife has been threatened. 'Straight after I left, Scotland Yard came to see me 'cos they think my family is now a target for the far right ... I've had problems with them for years, even people like Nick Griffin ... all those sorts of people I've had problems with for years.

'At the end of *When Tommy Met Mo*, I decided I was gonna leave. I needed to sort my family life out. I had all this crazy shit for four years. I needed to sort my finances out; I need to go back to work ...' Meanwhile, Robinson insisted that the making of the documentary with Mohammed Ansar did not make the decision for him, although he said, 'It helped me to clear my head.' He'd been reading about Quilliam for years, and was introduced to them during the making of the documentary. 'They're vocally opposed to things I'm opposed to. I realized then that our views are similar ... I thought this is the right way forward.'

Since then, Robinson has cooperated with Quilliam in organizing a meeting in Luton, in December 2013, where twenty EDL activists and ten local Muslims took part and engaged in a dialogue for six hours. Usama Hasan told me: 'They [EDL followers] were very keen. Both sides learned and became friendly and shared jokes … Since then, two Muslim groups from Bradford contacted us and asked if they could establish the same sort of dialogue, too.'

At the time of his departure, I questioned Robinson about his officially stated reason for leaving the EDL, his frustration with 'far-right extremism'. He was no doubt the first on the far right to make such a statement. 'What is the far-right extremism you are talking about?' I asked. 'When did you come to the realization that you could deal with it no longer?'

Robinson couldn't quite define the meaning of his terms. But I understood later that he was referring to the same categorization used by the National Domestic Extremism Unit. The Unit doesn't categorize the EDL (or its counterparts in Scotland and Wales) as part of the 'far right'. These groups are placed under 'defence leagues', a specific category different from 'far right' which comprises groups like the BNP, Britain First and the National Front. According to the Unit, 'far-right extremists' refers to groups such as Combat 18, Blood & Honour, Aryan Strike Force and the Infidels. Like the authorities, Robinson doesn't see himself as being on the 'far right' at all.

'For years within the EDL, you could always find someone with completely racist ideas …' he said.

Over four years, that created about ten different groups around the EDL, such as the Southeast Alliance, the Northwest Infidels, the Northeast Infidels … All these different groups got their own little groups because I said they're not welcome [within the EDL] ... At a Blackburn demo, we had a massive fight with the Northeast Infidels. A full-on fight, with bottles, glasses and bricks going ... and that was the start of us basically battling out of Luton ... During that confrontation, a female activist from Luton was injured.

When I went to jail for immigration offences in January 2013 [he was arrested in October 2012 for using someone else's visa to board a Virgin Atlantic flight from Heathrow to New York, to attend an event organized by Pamela Geller and Robert Spencer, his US allies] and when I came out, those [neo-fascist] people had been invited back. They were invited back by the northern regional organizers, such as in Manchester ... in a demo in March [2013]. The Racial Volunteer Force was there ... When I was in jail, they were all invited back, along with Northwest Infidels. There was another demo in Yorkshire, where the Yorkshire Infidels was also allowed to come, when I wasn't there. When I came out of prison and saw the videos of the demos, it did my head in ... I can't go to each demo. And on the next demo I didn't go to, in Portsmouth, they were there again. When I wasn't there, they would come in.

I wondered to what extent Robinson was actually concerned about these groups and the overall neo-fascist elements within the street movement. After all, it was the intention of the EDL leadership to involve a bigger crowd, including neo-Nazis, from the beginning, as the 'muscle' of the movement.

'I'm the public face,' said Robinson.

The fact that they've been invited back by the people who're in a position to organize in the area ... I felt betrayed. These groups are radical far right and they hate everything. They want a violent solution to problems. The EDL wants to get thousands on demos, so it's perfect for these groups to come and hide their identities and use it as a march for their racism. That's what they're trying to do. The Northwest Infidels has something like sixty to seventy people. But if you get sixty to seventy hardcore, complete morons on a march of one to two thousand, you'll get problems. And that's been going on all the time, for four and a half years.

He continued to tell me about the pressure he'd had from some in Luton: 'I hate Nazis. When I confronted them, I could walk around with my head held high ... When I was in Luton, I could still look at my mates in the same way ... whereas if I was in an organization and people know these people are here and are being allowed to be here, I can't do that.'

The neo-fascists have been working within the EDL for the entire lifespan of the group. They have always been part of the EDL, as Robinson admitted. The question is, if Robinson really didn't want them in the movement and had the support of the regional organizers about that, as he claimed to have had before his prison sentence, why didn't he manage to keep them out?

And does his departure mean that his views have changed? I asked whether he still believes there should be an end to building more mosques. Yes, he said, sounding slightly exasperated.

I still do believe that until we regulate and moderate mosques in this country, there should be no more. There should be no religious institutions built until they're moderated and regulated ... It's quite simple. We don't know who's preaching or funding them ... 90 per cent of imams can't speak English. They're creating problems. We need to bring them under control. They talk about British Islam, but we're not going to get that if we have an imam from Afghanistan! Until mosques are regulated, they shouldn't be building more! Why are we allowing imams from outside to polarize the country?

I felt that I had to talk to Robinson face-to-face, to get a better sense of what he's thinking and where the EDL's going. We arranged to meet in his favourite meeting place, the Icon Hotel in Luton, at eleven that morning. He appeared more trusting this time, and, as we sat down to coffee, he seemed to open up much more than in our last meeting before he had quit the EDL. He showed me his new tattoo, done the previous day. 'It's my kid's name,' he said.

'What do these words mean?' I pointed to a line of Latin.

'"Under the sun will be victorious". It's from Churchill,' he explained. 'There's a forgotten, almost forbidden word, a word that means to me more than any other word; that word is England.'

He told me he was awaiting sentence on 21 January (2014), for mortgage fraud. This could be our last meeting for a while if he was found guilty. By now I've lost count of the number of arrests and convictions Robinson has. He truly lives on the edge. He insisted that the authorities have 'stitched him up'.

'In 2010, the police came in and arrested me, my wife, my brother-in-law, my cousin … all my family. They went through all my family stuff to see what they could find … I pleaded guilty to two mortgage frauds. They're not even my mortgage. I had to plead guilty to my brother-in-law and my cousin's mortgage … because the police sat me down and said if I pleaded guilty, they would drop charges against them. So I pleaded guilty, so they would leave my family out of the case.'

'How long will you be in there?' I asked.

'I could get twelve months this time. It's so unfair … My brother-in-law got a mortgage in 2008. He earned 12K a year and on the form he said 20K. That's it. That's the crime. It's bullshit. I had to plead guilty because I don't want my wife or my family's face all over the press.'

Robinson's marriage took second place in his life after he joined the EDL, and his wife has been opposed to his involvement from the beginning. He admitted to having abused alcohol since the beginning of his EDL days. 'I was drinking a lot … I thought I dealt with the stress quite well, but in hindsight I'd just been drinking a lot. It didn't used to be like that. I was neglecting my family, my wife during my time in the EDL …'

In a way, Robinson saw it as a relief to be arrested, in October 2012, and then jailed in January 2013, although in public he complained about the injustice. 'The Americans let me through [with a false visa]. I got through. It was only six weeks later when I was back here that I got arrested. The Americans didn't want to prosecute me. But the British did,' he said. 'I spent three months on remand, and when I finally went to court in January, they said if I didn't plead guilty, I'm not going have the trial till

July. So that means I would have to spend the next six months in solitary confinement ... If you plead guilty, you're out in ten weeks. So I pleaded guilty.

'But in hindsight, that was the best thing that happened to me. I needed to go to jail. I needed it ... at that stage of my life.' By the way he shook his head and sighed, I knew he meant it.

'In there, I had the chance to reflect on the person I've become.' He shook his head once again, looking regretful. 'It's not recognizable to the person I was. During those eighteen weeks in social confinement, I was alone in my room, thinking about it all ...'

After Lee Rigby's murder, it seemed that the neo-fascist part of the EDL became louder and even more visible. Some of the regional organizers were in favour of joining forces with the BNP, whose members had infiltrated the EDL from the beginning, their influence going all the way to the top. Robinson claimed that it was Rigby's murder which stopped him from quitting the EDL. The incident provided the key momentum for the EDL's rapid growth, and he wanted to lead that. He stayed. 'Rigby's death changed everything for me. When I came out of jail, I was trying to work out how to leave ... I didn't go to demos. I stayed away and I told people that I was on a break with my family. So that was me buying time to work out how I'll leave and what I'll do with it ... A big problem for me was to work out what to do. I don't want to fall into the hands of the wrong people. Rigby's murder changed my whole perception and I knew that people were angry and we had to protest ...'

Robinson said he tried to take on the neo-fascist organizers. 'When Lee Rigby was killed, I kept out the organizers that allowed the Nazis to come. I expelled four organizers in the North West who let them in … Two of these organizers are women.'

It seems that a lot of the fallout between Robinson and the neo-fascists was over the battle for influence and leadership in a permanent power struggle which manifested itself as endless personal disagreements rather than contending political ideologies. A section of the EDL has always been ex-military, and splinter groups like Combined Ex-Forces (CxF), for instance, has been a very visible presence, despite its small membership of twenty to thirty. They have strong links with the Northwest Infidels and Northeast Infidels, and used violence as their preferred method of intimidation. Their members are often found wearing the Nazi swastika. But they were always part of the EDL-led street movement. They attended demonstrations outside court cases involving Asian men accused of paedophilia, a major anti-Muslim item on EDL's menu of racialization (while according to *EDL News*, 10 per cent of CxF members have a history of involvement with child pornography. Their Deeside Division leader Raymond Woodward was charged with fifteen counts of level-one child pornography offences and one level-four child pornography offence). One of their main activists, Michael Rafferty, was a senior leader in the EDL, and became marginalized only following his critique of Robinson.

Robinson said of CxF: 'It's a mixture. Some of them are good lads … They were part of the [Northwest Infidels], so a lot of them called me Zionist … A lot of these groups call me that because I said I support Israel. I was also called a race traitor by a lot of them because they say I promote multiculturalism.'

'You promote multiculturalism?' I was truly surprised, remembering what he said in our last meeting about defending the English way of life and Luton being flooded by other cultures. He replied:

I don't say that multiculturalism has failed; I say religion has failed. Because in this town in Luton it is as multicultural as you'll get and it works. There's been no racial tensions in this town, just religious tensions. All ethnic groups get along great; it is just Islam that's stopping integration. The more extreme people in the EDL would oppose multiculturalism full stop ... A lot of splinter groups like this [CxF] were formed because they were pissed off with me and what I was saying.

They [CxF] didn't like it at all when I said I don't want violence. One of their leaders called himself a fucking commander and said he was bringing a gun to London a year ago when we went to London on Armistice Day.

'Was it Michael Rafferty?' I asked.

'Yes, that's him!' Robinson confirmed, and then paused and whispered: 'Could you turn off the recorder for a second?'

I did as told.

'Let me tell you, Michael Rafferty talked about bombing the Muslim protesters in London.' While Robinson asked me to turn off the recorder, he did not tell me that this was off the record or request that I not divulge this information.

I was shocked, speechless, thinking, 'And you allowed him to come to London?'

He carried on, whispering: 'And I was thinking, if he did carry that out [carrying a bomb with him] and I already had prior knowledge that he was saying this ... then it will put me in a bad position ...' Robinson considered dismissing Rafferty.

'Later I kicked him out of the EDL because he's fucking mad,' Robinson said. 'Then he threatened me by phone, saying he's going to come and kill me ... and then he did a picture of me with bullet holes in me.'

Then Robinson bent forward to show me a YouTube video on his mobile phone. 'Look at this,' he said. 'This is the Racial Volunteer Force with the English Volunteer Force burning an EDL flag ... You see, in the early days they went on our demos. They told people on rallies not to stand with the EDL because EDL are a bunch of race traitors and Zionists ... They're a small group but you don't need a big group to cause terror, do you?'

And then there's the Casuals, also known as the EDL Casuals. They were set up in 2009 by football hooligan Jeff Marsh, former leader of the neo-fascist Welsh Defence League. The Casuals are basically an aggregate of football hooligans and at their height claimed membership of around 200. But in autumn 2013, Robinson said the Casuals had been reduced to just three women and one man running the show, with twenty to thirty members and a blog. He sneered: 'They just sit around, bitch and moan, that's all they do. They create the name for themselves but if they held a demo on their own, there'd be no one there. They always try to play off the EDL.'

Robinson called Jeff Marsh a 'nightmare' and said they had a big falling out. 'Then I expelled him. They all tried to get rid of me. So I said to them, if you want to lead the EDL, show me your face. All they do is set up these little groups with no names. Attack online, spread rumours and lies. I said to them, show me who you are. Stand up and say that's what you're going do ... I kicked out the Casuals after I came out of jail because they were part of the unity thing [with the rest of the far right].'

Robinson also fell out with the neo-fascist Welsh Defence League,* 'all Nazis', he said. 'Jeff Marsh's just a bitch,' said Robinson. 'They threatened to kill me. When we first started, they came to demos and dressed normally. But as the demo went on, they started to dress in bomber jackets, Doc Martens ... By the end of it, we saw they're all Nazis. We fought with them loads of times ... We don't want them there. They're finished now. Without our support, they didn't last ... As to the Scottish Defence League, they'll never be as successful as the EDL. They had Northwest Infidels people at their demo and let them talk ... so I didn't want to ally with them after that.'

One of Robinson's biggest opponents was Paul Ray, who was in a leading position in the early days of the EDL but gradually found it too 'tolerant'. His resentment towards Robinson and his leadership was first revealed when he exposed Robinson's real name to the public. Paul Ray was seen as an extremist within the mainstream EDL. He branded the Robinson-led EDL as 'false

---

* Unite Against Fascism (UAF) said: 'In Cardiff, some football supporters from the Soul Crew helped run the Welsh version of the EDL out of town, in 2010. The Welsh Defence League [WDL] never recovered. The WDL had become notorious for their neo-Nazism ... Welsh anti-fascists, often led by Wales UAF, including long-time anti-fascist Peter Hain (a key UAF ally), mobilised significantly each time the WDL appeared. The broad nature of UAF again was central and our turnouts humiliated and isolated the other side. From skinhead band The Oppressed, to Welsh Assembly members, there was never any welcome in the valleys by big numbers of anti-fascists.'

patriotism' on the basis that 'none of the EDL core leadership is a professing Christian'. Ray called them 'wolves in sheep's clothing', and said: 'Second-generation Irish Tommy and Kevin are wedding, funeral and confirmation Catholics ... meaning they do not attend church every Sunday or on a regular basis, so do not sit under the word of God nor subject their lives to the word of God.'

Paul Ray hated Robinson so much that he once fabricated a story that Robinson was holding his mother hostage and put it on YouTube. 'My mum didn't know I was in the EDL at the time,' Robinson recalled. 'She heard from someone else about Paul Ray's online video. She called me in a panic, asking me, "Did you kidnap someone's mum?!" She was very scared of my involvement in the EDL ... When Paul Ray exposed my real name, it was my mum's address that could be found on Google.'

And there was Nick Gregor, nicknamed Nazi Nick, from Germany.

In the early days, the EDL had a big fallout with him ... One day, Paul Ray called me with Nick Gregor, and threatened me: 'Hand over the website, the password and everything, hand it all over, by midnight.' I didn't know who Nick was at the time. He was just with Paul Ray. So I just said online, 'Fuck off, you German prick. I'm not gonna listen to you, German mug and your muggy mate, trying to dictate and run the world from your laptop!' It was only later that someone told me it was Nick, the well-known Nazi Nick. Nazi Nick wants to start a holy war, Christians against Muslims. They want to take control of the EDL. They haven't managed yet but they are there. Time will tell whether it will happen. They always had followers in the EDL but they have all now ended up in the Northwest Infidels and Northeast Infidels, and all these splinter groups would support Nazi Nick. They may become part of the unity.

The neo-fascist section of the EDL has wanted to take over for a long time. The power struggle seemed out of control, particularly during Robinson's jail sentence in spring 2013. During his time in the EDL, Robinson claims to have expelled up to fifty people, some of them organizers.

Each time I kicked someone out, splinter groups were formed ... The Northwest Infidels, for instance, was formed after I kicked out the man who became the leader, some racist little prick. You got the Yorkshire Infidels; I kicked out their leader. You've got Paul Pitt of the Southeast Alliance; I kicked him out. They're opposed to supporting Israel. Just like the BNP and Britain First.

Then an agreement of unity was reached with these splinter groups at a demo in Manchester. I missed the demo, but by then I had already made the decision to leave.

Robinson realized that the far-right street movement wouldn't benefit him in the long term.

The EDL has made a lot of noise but there's no end goal. All through summer 2013, people were asking to have a demo in Luton again. I didn't want a demo in my town ...

I don't think it will do good. The first two [demos in Luton] had to happen. The council had to see people were fed up with what is going on. But to continue doing it would only have a negative impact. So I started to weigh it up and think what we're asking for … I came to the conclusion that the only way to achieve what we want is to work with Muslims. That's the only way. You're never going get there with the brand EDL. There's no option really. I can say what I want, and people can turn up and shout Mohammed was a paedophile. But no Muslim would ever have dialogue with you.

Clearly, reshaping his brand seemed the way forward for Robinson. However, how 'committed' he was to ridding the EDL of neo-fascists is questionable. Despite his talk following his departure in October, there is footage of him marching with Northwest Infidels neo-fascists only two months before. According to the group's Facebook page, Robinson led a march in Luton on 26 August 2013. The caption in their anti-Muslim photo album, filled with open, racial hatred, said: 'Great day, great company, great food, and great result.'

But Robinson insisted that the influence of these splinter groups was the main reason for his departure. 'There will be more and more groups like this forming … Some of the main organizers up north would allow groups like this to be involved … not in Luton or Birmingham, though.'

In the first two months after leaving, Robinson believed that the EDL had more or less dissolved. 'Most of them are my friends … So since I left, they're gone … although the support for the EDL is still there in Farley Hill.'

But my experience was somewhat different. Back in Farley Hill, the mood had changed and few were confident about the future of the far-right movement. Alfredo, the barber who expressed significant anti-Muslim sentiment, had softened his tone and no longer laid blame on local Muslims and migrants. 'It is all economic circumstances that push people to resort to far-right extremism,' he said to me. 'When times are hard, people think in less logical ways ... I know that people [migrants] generally come to this country to better themselves. It is economic situations that make them be seen as a problem ... It is always the people at the bottom who end up blaming each other, isn't it?'

The EDL itself was in a disoriented state. Many had tried to ask Robinson to return to the group. 'Like the Sikhs, they talked to me last night. We have a Sikh Division. They said to me, "Tommy, in all honesty, is there any chance you're going to come back? We're going to leave if you're not coming back." They're probably already seeing the change [the group turning even more extreme] and are not happy with it. Trust me, the Jews will all leave the EDL, too. The group is going have a real struggle in the next twelve months.'

Since Robinson's departure, the EDL has been run by a committee of fifteen regional organizers (known as ROs) from across the country. In autumn 2013, there were talks about drastically changing the mission statement and drafting a clearer position opposing all immigration. Robinson believed the group would turn more hardline. He said:

My mission statement said 'stand up for human rights'. They want to get rid of all that. They are turning against

Irish Republicans and all immigrants. There are fifteen of them on the committee; half of them want to do that [adopt an end-all-immigration position]. Those organizers from Yorkshire, for instance. The Yorkshire people are organizing a demo against Irish Republicans in February. The minute they change and turn more far right, they'll lose numbers and they'll finish. They'll have just one to two hundred hardcore members. That's all.

People who're leaving are calling me, asking me what they can do. They say they don't want to be part of a far-right organization ... No one in the EDL actually sees themselves as being on the far right. They're just pissed off. When the EDL changes its mission statement and direction, all those people who swell the numbers will leave. Guaranteed.

The new mission statement, however, as it turned out in spring 2014, hasn't been changed much. It follows the EDL's original ultra-nationalist and racist ideas (mainly in the form of cultural racism), with no added demands for 'an end to all immigration'. They have clarified that 'mass immigration' is a major concern for many in the group and is central to their campaigns. The EDL's statement of cultural assimilationism remains: '... If people migrate to this country then they should be expected to respect our culture, its laws, and its traditions, and not expect their own cultures to be promoted by agencies of the state. The best of their cultures will be absorbed naturally and we will all be united by the enhanced culture that results. The onus should always be on foreign cultures to adapt and integrate.'

Meanwhile, EDL's strength and ability to mobilize proved to be have been weakened in the last quarter of 2013 and the beginning of 2014. The size of demos shrank following Robinson's departure. On 1 February 2014, there were fewer than 200 people on the EDL's demo in Slough.

Robinson said: 'A lot of people in the EDL are leaving already. The East Anglian Division is about to pull out. Kent members have left the EDL and joined Britain First ... Britain First is trying to capitalize and get people from the EDL.'

The neo-fascist splinter groups have continued to call for unity with the rest of the far right. On the same day as the Slough demo, there was also a Unite the Right meeting. Robinson said: 'The unity meeting in February consisted of reps from all those groups, sitting together on the committee and saying we're all united. All the groups are coming together. They want the EDL to be part of that. They'll be working together. When there's a demo, all those groups will come together.'

Before the unity meeting in February 2014, Robinson said:

Tony Curtis, from Nottingham, from the BNP and who works directly with Nick Griffin, might end up being the leader of this unity thing ... He'll probably be the public face. I don't know how long the EDL will hold out. If EDL can't hold out and all these other groups take control, then Tony Curtis will be the leader ... because he had quite a good following in the EDL. I still defend the EDL now, because it's still got good people in it. But once it's taken over by these groups, it'll become the NF and BNP ... They've been trying to take over for four and a half years. Now it will be likely for them, because there's no leadership.

The Nazis aren't big within the EDL ... They're actually a small minority ... But when they all get together, which they are all starting to do, they keep calling for unity. When I was leaving, they were already saying, Unite the right. I was opposing that, I was saying no unity with any of those groups. I'd never do that; ... 'cos what EDL stands for is different to what everyone else stands for. As soon as they do that, they won't appeal to the mainstream ...

As it turned out, there has been no takeover by Tony Curtis. Instead, after Robinson, Tim Ablitt became the EDL chairman. He lasted until January 2014, when the group announced that he had resigned as a result of ill health, to be replaced by the forty-eight-year-old Steve Eddowes, nicknamed 'Edders', regional organizer for the West Midlands and Head of Security.

When Steve Eddowes became chair, the majority of activists I talked to said that there was no current leader and the group didn't need one. Activists seemed more concerned about their local divisions, particularly those in the South. They don't seem concerned about the leadership or who it is, as the core of power seems more concentrated in the North. Activists in the South have adopted a less structured way of working, with individual activists engaged in their own separate, local activities. Those who became frustrated with the loose organization and unclear position towards the rest of the far right might choose to leave the group.

I was introduced to Steve Eddowes, the new chair, by Robinson. Eddowes comes from Wolverhampton, and had worked as Robinson's bodyguard for some time. They clearly trusted each other. He told me that his daytime job is transport logistics. He committed most of his time outside of work to the EDL.

Eddowes said the EDL went through a few months of crisis after Robinson left, but he believes that it has now 'settled down' and is growing. There are currently five to six thousand activists, he said. Wolverhampton itself has several hundred. Eddowes insisted that nothing much has changed since Robinson's departure, apart from the fact that the group no longer has a 'TV face'. He himself is not interested in coming into the limelight. 'I'm just a bloke in the Black Country ... Even in my personal life, I'm not fond of cameras.'

I went to visit Eddowes in Wolverhampton. The West Midlands has grown to become the heartland of EDL support and far-right groups as a result of a rapid decline in major manufacturing industries in the past decade, leading to job losses and a deterioration in living conditions. The unemployment rate, which in 2014 was at 8.3 per cent with 226,000 out of work, according to the Office for National Statistics, has always been well above the national average.

On arrival, the first thing that confronted me was three local young men, standing idly around, repeatedly shouting racist abuse at me, calling me a 'mail order bride'. Incidents such as this always sadden me. But worse than that, I felt fear as I walked along the dark pathway to get to the hotel. I felt an instant chill as I remembered the brutal murder of a Chinese man in Wigan a few years ago. Racism has become the aggressive expression of the hopelessness the young here feel.

The next day, Eddowes and his wife came to pick me up from Wolverhampton station after work. Their house on the outskirts of town looked semi-empty. Eddowes said they're doing some building work. The hallway had nothing but concrete walls with two large EDL flags on them.

Like Robinson, Eddowes disagreed with my lumping of his group under the label of 'far right'. 'It is a patriotic organization,' he said. 'The truth is the far right hates us ... I've had as many threats from the far right as I've had from radical Muslims.' (By 'far right', he meant the neo-Nazis.)

Eddowes had never been politically engaged before joining the EDL. He comes from a Labour family and had always supported Labour. He browsed the Forum, the online discussion group prior to the formation of the EDL, and felt that he could relate to the concerns of the people posting there. When he first got involved, Eddowes didn't like the chaotic way the demos were organized, and contacted the media team to advise them on how to engage stewards. Soon enough, he was given the task of forming the media security team. This was how he got to know Robinson, and eventually he was asked to work as his bodyguard.

Eddowes was cautious around me. He said that he had to seek 'permission' from the committee to talk to me, and had to record our conversation. Throughout, he answered each question very carefully and never gave more than asked. The committee consists of fifteen regional organizers (ROs) representing fifty divisions across the country. The RO structure was set up at the end of 2010 by Tommy Robinson and Kevin Carroll for the purposes of best controlling EDL activities. Robinson and Kevin Carroll hand-picked all the ROs, most of whom still remain after their departure. It was obvious that Eddowes followed this structure much more strictly than Robinson ever did.

Unlike Robinson, Eddowes seems optimistic about the influence of those farther right in the EDL. He doesn't want to admit that the neo-fascist influence is still a problem within his group, and said that it has been making an effort to 'remove' this element. But when asked how this had been achieved, he couldn't comment, but simply said that 'they've been made unwelcome'. 'I don't think there was ever any serious challenge to the EDL from the far-right extremists [referring to neo-Nazis]. There was never any threat of any takeover ... We can't actually control who comes to our demos ... but I don't think there was ever a big number [of them] ...'

Eddowes adopts a more relaxed attitude towards the splinter groups. He does not even include them in his understanding of the 'far right'. 'The splinter groups don't bother me,' he said, disagreeing that these were part of the reason for Robinson's departure and that they remain a major problem for the EDL. 'What made him leave was more the huge pressure that he was under.' Also, Eddowes was confident that there was no tendency within the EDL to move towards working closely with the BNP. Both the BNP and Britain First had approached Robinson in the past about working together, but their invitations were rejected.

The committee, according to Eddowes, has maintained the basics of the previous mission statement, with a little simplification, to suit the majority of their followers. The only change of direction, he said, will be for the group to look into covering a wider agenda instead of focusing on a single issue ('Islamification'). As for immigration, Eddowes expressed a similar line to Nigel Farage: 'We want more controlled immigration. But we don't argue for an end to immigration. We are not against immigration.

We are in favour of a system similar to a points-based system like in Australia.'

Although the number of people attending demos isn't growing, Eddowes said that the EDL's message is already out there in society. 'And that's not something you can take away.'

R obinson reiterated that he wants to go mainstream.

Because it's too important to ignore. What we want to do is to give a credible platform ... If you continue to live out at the fringes and continue to alienate people, then you're going to create big problems. What we are trying to do is to create a credible working-class voice that doesn't do street protests and isn't causing problems and intimidating ... but still saying what needs to be said in a more constructive and democratic way ... These issues have to be spoken about in a wider arena and a wider platform, and that arena is not on the side streets of Tower Hamlets or Luton. It's not. It needs to be spoken about on a mainstream level. I do want to reach a wider audience.

It seems that there is much common ground between Robinson's politics of race and UKIP's. He talked about the need to limit migration from Bulgaria and Romania, in the same way as Nigel Farage, and at times in much the same way as most of the British establishment. 'This Bulgarian who lives here for two years and lives above my shop ... a hard-working great guy ... Even on St George's Day he's out with the English, he's already integrated and knows everyone. So I'm not against individuals coming to earn a few quid,' he said. 'But uncontrolled numbers, which is what's happening, too fast too quick, you're breaking our communities ... You're alienating us.'

In the same way as UKIP, Robinson talked about local jobs for English people.

I get all these messages all the time from people, English people who can't get jobs ... So many kids are out of work. They can't get work. And yet our council gives contracts to people from outside of Luton. We got lots of Welsh men coming in and building in Luton town centre ... for a company called Wates, which is based in Wales. What about kids in Luton? We're developing Luton. This is how people feel ... on building sites and at schools ... They feel they've become the minority. EasyJet ... We're going approach them for a cleaning contract ... and say, give it to us, we will employ only young kids from Luton. Any profits made will go back to Luton.

But surely 'young kids from Luton' should also include British Asian Muslim kids, who were also born and bred here?

Robinson, like Farage, intends to tap into the anger and frustration felt by disadvantaged white working-class people trapped in permanent unemployment and a life of little future prospects. That anger and frustration came from economic degradation resulting from the gradual decline of major industries in Britain under successive governments that confined many working-class men and women to a life of permanent poverty. As Owen

Jones describes in *Chavs: The Demonization of the Working Class*, when New Labour came into power in 1997, manufacturing made up more than a fifth of the economy. Twelve per cent was all that remained by the time Blair left office in 2007. 'Back in 1979, there were nearly seven million people working in factories, but today's number is just over 2.5 million,' says Jones. 'Already embittered sectors suffered yet more crippling blows at the hands of the Great Recession of 2008. The crisis may have been caused by the greed of bankers, but manufacturing paid the price. It lost well over twice the proportion of jobs as finance and business services in the first years of the crisis.' When the political elite created the myth that 'we are all middle-class now', as Jones pointed out, industrial jobs continued to steadily disappear, which led to much anger and bitterness among the manual working class. The far right, thus, finds its breeding ground: they point to migration and migrants as the cause of the problem, when in fact migrants themselves have also found themselves victims of a restructured economy and job market in which one of the most pronounced features has been the casualization of labour and downward pressure on wages.

Robinson wanted to find a new platform from which to tap into the discontent he saw among the manual working class. Despite having left the EDL, he kept in contact with its followers and supporters and has maintained a dialogue with them. 'I do feel a bit of a traitor, a coward, to take that voice away from them [EDL followers] ... I knew how upset and hurt they'd be. But my wife said I don't owe anyone anything.'

That desire to have a platform led Robinson to accept an invitation to speak about 'tolerance' at Duchess's Community High School in Alnwick, Northumberland. The school contacted

Quilliam to invite him to give a talk because apparently many white British pupils there would like to hear him speak. 'These are predominantly white working-class areas,' Robinson said.

Quilliam said that there's a lot of support for the EDL among the kids, in the schools in the North East ... one in Peterlee and one in Sunderland ... The twenty to thirty Muslim kids at that school are probably getting a hard time ... because of what's going on in the country such as issues like terrorism. They [Quilliam] wanted me to address youth anger. Because a lot of the kids look up to me, so they'd like me to address the kids and tell them that they can't just lay blame on individual Muslims.

Most English kids do support groups like the EDL. They probably listen to me more than they do to the teachers ... They were petitioning the teachers to say they want to listen to me. I receive twenty tweets from them each day ... Kids message me every day. But the school cancelled the talk after pressure ...

I speak to them and I hear their stories. They've got no one talking for them. Asian kids convert to Islam because they need that identity. But an English kid doesn't know what being English means. The real far-right groups ... these kids would be easy pickings for them.

Robinson said many young people write to him, every day, telling him about their grievances. It seems that a general lack of opportunities, growing up in isolated, depressed communities, has driven them to despair – and eventually to racism.

As Robinson spoke, he seemed to detect my disbelief, and immediately showed me his tweets on his mobile phone. 'Look.' He pointed to long streams of messages. One of the messages came from a fourteen-year-old schoolkid in Luton. He wrote: 'Most of the students in my school are Muslims and they go out mugging white kids ...' Robinson said to me: 'This kid feels he's in a minority and he's only fourteen. I wrote to him every day. Do you call him a racist, a fourteen-year-old boy? I say, no, he's not. He's just scared. Kids like him feel under attack. That's the reality.'

Robinson said he always tried to reply to desperate, lonely youngsters like this. Having nowhere to turn, they put their trust in him. And, predictably, the messages of scapegoating and resentment he passes on to them will help to keep them in their desperate, marginalized positions.

He carried on: 'This kid said schools aren't helping. He lives up in Farley Hill ... The police, the government, everything's in favour of the Muslim community. Everything.' This was Robinson's response, to blame the Muslim population for the teenager's misery.

I asked him how he sees himself politically in the next couple of years. He told me that he is thinking of a new future, a new organization. 'I want to set up a new group. Something that represents the working class, a working-class think tank, something based in the grass roots ... The new group will work with a few organizations, and Quilliam will be one of them. We'll be organizing debates and talks. People need to talk about issues.'

He said Britain needs more meetings like the one he held with Quilliam in Luton in December 2013. 'They [the local Muslims] need to understand why we're angry and we need to understand why they're angry. A lot of them are misconceptions.

But there were things we agreed on. Seminars like that break down barriers. One meeting like that has done more than anything else that we've done in the last four and a half years.'

Meanwhile, Robinson believes that national pride needs to be instilled in working-class youth and that this has to come before any 'dialogue' with the Muslims.

White working-class children are now the biggest under-achievers at school. There's a reason for that, because they are neglected ... They have not got their identity and they are lost. So the first thing we need to do ... is to move away from Islam and Muslims ... The first thing we need to do is to install pride in working-class kids. They should be proud of who they are and where they come from. If you solve that issue, you solve a lot of other issues ... Many English lads are lost ... If you want to tackle extremism, you need to put hope back into their lives. If you take away their identity, they'll be the next generation of extremists. You really need to change that. I'd like to concentrate on politicizing the next generation. They need to vote. People just don't feel like they have a say. When you have that massive disengagement, that is quite dangerous ...

Robinson now avoids saying he wants to 'tackle Islam' as he used to in demos and in public. Now he wants to 'tackle extremism'. This puts him closer to the mainstream, which often equates radical Islam with far-right extremism. He told me: 'I want to start to tackle extremism. Whether you like it or not, what we're saying has resonances among masses of people. If you watched Sunday morning TV the other week, 95 per cent of viewers agree with what we're saying. So it's about giving people a voice which is not there.'

At one point, I thought I detected a slight tone of regret – or you could call it remorse – over what he has spent the past four and a half years doing, inciting hatred against Muslims and causing much harm to their communities. 'I'm spending time with Quilliam and am learning. I also want to spend time with a couple of other top-ten political think tanks ... I've never done anything like this. I need help in this. I'm hoping when the next programme [he was making] goes on TV, people will say, "We should help him." Labour and other parties, your fuck-ups and your experiments have created millions like me. So you have the responsibility to solve it, to support it.'

But I also saw that his politics of race has not fundamentally changed. His views on Islam remained essentially as they were, as does his conviction that Muslims benefit from the poverty, unemployment and lack of opportunities among manual white working-class British. 'There's a poll that says that 60 per cent of British people think that there's going to be a bloody civil war between Muslims and non-Muslims ... I think that. I do think that ... If that is the case, at which point do those 60 per cent start preparing for that war? Unless we start changing things, you'll get sectarian conflict. It's not going to go away. If that does happen, where is it going to burn? Farley Hill, not Westminster!'

Meanwhile, Robinson reasserts that he will not be returning to the far-right street movement. 'Marching through the streets ... is going to create a sectarian-style conflict and that's not what any of us wants ... It's not going to be beneficial. Now we've created the platform, we'll take the opportunity ... to have a voice.'

6

THE COLOURS OF
BRITISH RACISM

The post-Robinson era of the EDL has been characterized by a fundamental tension. Outwardly, the group has been attempting to popularize itself by reshaping its racist image in the public sphere. But internally, the reaction has been negative, and the group has become mired in infighting.

I came across someone who has been witnessing the entire situation unfold and is willing to talk to me about it – Hel Gower, originally from Bow in east London. She was Tommy Robinson's PA but remained in the EDL after his departure until she was dismissed by the EDL committee at the end of May 2014. I visited her in a village near Dover where she resides alone. In her conservatory, overlooking a well-maintained garden, she told me about her political history.

In well-spoken English, Gower, a degree holder, told me she was one of the few middle-class activists in the EDL. Prior to 2009, she was already involved in anti-jihadist activities around the anti-Muslim blog Gates of Vienna and the Anti-Muslim League, which merged with the EDL. In between the United People of Luton and the EDL, she joined the Forum, a discussion and information platform set up by Robinson and those involved, for a select like-minded few, including BNP activist John Sheridan (aka Chris Renton).

Gower got to know Robinson via 'Nemesis', a man centrally involved as a 'strategist' in the administration of the EDL but who never wanted to make his real name known online. Everyone refers to him by his onscreen name. Gower agreed to register EDL with Companies House under her name as managing director, practically making her the 'owner' of the group (and later the managing director of EDL Angels). Together with Nemesis and another activist, Steve Simmons, she formed the Support Group for the EDL. The Support Group was subsequently divided into three sections: administrative, editorial and visual departments. Gower soon became Robinson's PA, acting almost as publicist and adviser. In many activists' eyes, she was the 'mother figure' behind Robinson's public image. She also brought in the ideological back-up that she felt the 'ordinary EDL activists' lacked, and had writers from Gates of Vienna contributing to the group's website.

Gower has witnessed problems with the neo-fascist elements (whom she refers to as extremists) within the EDL through the years, and told me that it is only getting worse, and that they are 'creeping back in'.

> The so-called measures they've taken are just token gestures … such as removing people if they're doing Nazi salutes on demos. But actually the National Front people were allowed in on the Grantham demo … And on other demos since, people who were kicked out by Tommy were back in, such as Diddyman from the Northwest Infidels. And I should

imagine that the splinter groups have been invited back on demos ... Eddowes would want to look good on the committee, so he'd let those people back.

Also, they'd find offensive comments [about Jews, Muslims and gays and lesbians] online funny and would do nothing about it. When I complained about that, I'd get all sorts of abuse.

These abusive comments have been saved and archived by Gower as screen shots. She has maintained the practice of recording Skype conversations since Robinson's era as a way of dealing with changeable and difficult regional organizers.

Gower told me that, as soon as Tim Ablitt was appointed chair, he set out to 'get rid of the extremists [neo-fascists]'. Ablitt himself claims that his steps to clear out extremists from the ranks led to up to fifty 'Hitler-loving, Nazi boot lickers' being driven out. He said his first role as the chairman was removing seven White Pride Nazi banners from a Bradford demo. However, according to Gower, this was the reason for Ablitt's short-lived time on top: he was soon critiqued by the committee and a decision was made to dismiss him while he was in hospital, in January 2014. 'The committee didn't like him because he was basically doing the same thing as Tommy ... They replaced Tim with Steve Eddowes, who's only interested in getting numbers on the street. He doesn't care who comes.'

For more than six months, Gower began feeling increasingly uncomfortable in the group and considered leaving in April. Steve Eddowes then invited her to go to Wolverhampton. There, he told her that she was needed and asked her to stay. However, three weeks later she was dismissed anyway, under Eddowes' chairmanship. He has been acting the dictator since he became the group's official leader, she says. Gower believes she was dismissed for arguing for the inclusion of LGBT and Jewish members. She also believes that the EDL leadership is moving closer to unity with the rest of the far right. Her dislike of the splinter groups, which have been growing and becoming increasingly more active, she said, also contributed. She believes Eddowes had 'done a deal' with the splinter groups in return for her dismissal.

When asked about the EDL's current position on Jewish and LGBT groups, Eddowes looked irritated. 'If I found anyone who holds homophobic or anti-Semitic views, I would take them out … But we are fed up with being apologists. We've had to prove we're not far-right Nazi scumbags … We've spent a lot of time trying to shed that image.'

Nevertheless, Gower said that many in the Support Group have left since Robinson quit, including Nemesis. 'Eight of the regional organizers, mostly in the South, left the EDL since Eddowes was selected as the chair. They've come to join Team Tommy, a collective of people that support Tommy and what he stands for. There's around a thousand to twelve hundred people in there. Team Tommy would follow Tommy whatever he does – including the think tank he wants to set up. We're all biding our time at the moment and waiting … to see when Tommy's ready for what he wants to do next.'

Gower believes there is no 'credible' or even recognizable leadership any more. For her, Team Tommy's the future. 'Now the EDL hasn't got a public face any more. They're trying to put forward a man called the Boss Man, but all he can do is swear on YouTube.'

Apart from the ongoing infighting and smear campaigns within the EDL, which Gower said has always been a feature of the organization, there is also an increasing North–South divide. As the leadership is more concentrated in the North, where there are bigger regional divisions and more members than in the South, the organizers and activists in the North tend to push for more demos and activities up north. The EDL as a whole is weaker in the South, and is more divided by splinter groups. This North–South tension became such a problem that there was even a period when northern members wouldn't travel south to take part in demos.

Some of the infighting is caused by ideological differences. Several of the northern regional organizers, such as Gail Speight of Yorkshire and Alan Spence of Newcastle, want to drastically change the mission statement to include a clear opposition to all immigration and the IRA. This is not a position shared by all activists of other regions. As a result, some have chosen to quit the group altogether. The infighting and departure of regional organizers have led to the growing number and strength of splinter groups, as these organizers bring their supporters with them when they leave the EDL. In early 2015, Gail Speight was thrown out of her role as a regional organizer by the EDL for her theft of charity money, and is working with the splinter group Northwest Infidels.

Despite the allegations that the committee has tended to ally the EDL more closely with the neo-fascist far right, along with their anti-Semitic and anti-LGBT stance, the group has also tried to change its public image by openly presenting the 'ethnic' elements of its membership, which remains extremely limited.

I saw this for myself when I joined its march in Peterborough in March 2014. Peterborough City Council, Conservative-run since 2002, seemed tolerant of the demo and urged local people to 'carry on their daily lives'. Over 150 anti-racist campaigners protested in a park while a few hundred residents of the town stood watching with indifference as the agitated 300-strong EDL demo assembled in front of the magistrates' court.

As the crowd began to gather before the march, I tried to talk to a group of five supporters, two women and three men, who were staggering along with bottles of beer and seemed to be walking towards the meeting point, a local pub down the road. I started with the forty-something woman. Apart from an obvious tattoo on her arms, she wore heavy eyeshadow and looked worn out. I explained why I wanted to talk to her.

'Go away!' came her throaty response, without so much as a moment of hesitation.

I turned to the forty-something bald man clad in leather and tried to strike up a conversation. Another, younger man told me that this was the 'deputy head' of the EDL's Peterborough Division.

'Shut up.' The woman waved at me again. She then turned to her colleagues and warned them, 'Don't ever talk to a reporter!'

I walked on for another half mile to a pub where the EDL crowd was gathering. Most had been mobilized from London. Dave Bolton, organizer of the London Division and one of the EDL's leading activists, said they were expecting 300 or so people on this march. He admitted that the local division in Peterborough is small, consisting of only around thirty people.

Dave Bolton works as a bouncer in London, and has been active in the group from the beginning. He used to be close to Tommy Robinson, but since Robinson left, Dave Bolton hasn't had any further communication with him. A police officer came up and tried to listen to our conversation, and soon Bolton moved away from me. The officer told me that the EDL had kept their promise about the number of people they were bringing, and therefore the police were not expecting any trouble.

Then I got talking to a man who wore a T-shirt with the words 'South United' on it. He whispered his real name to me, but said that he didn't want everyone to know it. In the EDL he is simply known as Viking. He heads up the EDL's South United Division, based in Reading. He had just got himself a pint of beer from inside the pub, and looked in good spirits. I was welcome to record our conversation.

Viking is an optimist. He believes the EDL has been growing since Robinson's departure. There seems to be a tendency to 'reclaim' the EDL from the legacy of Robinson's leadership. Viking blamed Robinson for the 'neo-fascist' problems. 'Tommy brought the neo-Nazis and the extremists in and allowed them in ... He didn't realize what he was doing ... We had a lot of racists around at the beginning when it all started because there were a lot of football hooligans [from across the country, among whom the Bolton football fans were particularly seen as neo-fascists], people who just wanted a fight. He let them in. And then later he moaned about them,' Viking said in an agitated tone.

Since he left, we managed to gradually get rid of a lot of them – as many as we can, by making it less interesting for them. We didn't want those thugs, those who want to hurt others. We identified them in marches when they were shouting things we didn't believe in and behaved in a way that we didn't accept. They are not what we're about. The media say we're Nazis, but we're not. I'm Jewish; I can't be a Nazi. We asked those extremists to leave and they wouldn't. They started fighting us and we fought them back. Many of us hate Nazis ... The splinter groups have their own agenda. Our division wouldn't allow anyone who's fascist. Some have left the EDL because they want to join the unity movement with [the rest of] the far right, and it's up to them.

Dave Bolton saw us talking, and came over to stop it. 'You know we don't do interviews,' Bolton said to him.

Viking smiled at him, nodded, turned back and carried on talking to me.

'Since Tommy left, the EDL has doubled,' he said assuredly. 'My division now has 237 members; fifty-nine of them joined after Tommy left. Basingstoke has doubled. Derby has doubled. Sheffield has doubled. Yorkshire's got twenty-three new members ... Plymouth's got seven new members. Portsmouth's got four new members. The growth is because people started to see through the lies that have been told about us ... In my division, we got new members after the BBC3 documentary *EDL Angels*, and since then the number increased ... The TV portrayal was very positive.'

A minute later, Bolton returned, pointed his finger at Viking, and said in a heavy voice: 'I'm seriously telling you to stop this.

I told you already. You're talking to a reporter on tape, and you have a beer in your hand. I mean it, stop.'

Bolton left, annoyed. Viking looked somewhat frustrated with Bolton's instructions. 'What is the point of being in a street movement that doesn't talk to people?' he said to me.

But he had to leave. He quickly noted down his phone number, saying I could call. Then he left with the group.

I walked ahead of the crowd as they set out on the march to town. The chanting of slogans was loud, but the group kept to the set route with no disturbances. When they reached the magistrates' court, I suddenly found myself caught inside the small area surrounded and sealed in by the police. The angry crowd pushed in, chanting slogans even more loudly. I felt quite claustrophobic and intimidated as the crowd closed in on me. We were surrounded by railings and there was no exit in sight. Some men were still holding cans of beer as they chanted. I would have no chance to escape if things went wrong inside this tiny space, I realized. The thought frightened me.

The crowd started cheering the first speaker, Naomi-Anne, a member of the Skegness Division, who described herself as coming from a mixed-race background. Since her speech at a demo in Grantham, she has been put up by the EDL as evidence of the group's 'diverse' make-up, to demonstrate that the group isn't racist. Activists like Naomi-Anne are explicitly being used to show the 'inclusive' nature of the group. On its website, she smiles to the camera and tells everyone how she discovered the EDL as the place she belongs. Naomi-Anne's Peterborough speech was deeply sensationalist, filled with racist hate. 'Islamic extremists are using religious freedom to groom and rape your children! Open your eyes!' She spoke in a loud and clear voice. 'You call for multiculturalism, for Islamic extremists to live alongside you, to convert you, subjugate you, or kill you!' The crowd cheered and applauded.

I went to visit Viking in Reading. He told me to meet him at his 'Saturday job'.

When I got there, Viking was standing alone in front of John Lewis, with a placard in his hand. 'Stop female genital mutilation,' it said. Viking greeted me, and explained that the members of his division are often here on Saturdays, with the aim of spreading the group's message and recruiting more people into their ranks. 'I come here when I'm not working, at least once a week,' he said. 'Our division, with twelve core activists, works to put our message across to the public. We're not just loosely organized like some other divisions. We're like family.'

Five minutes later, four other activists arrived with placards. In fact, the main organizers of this division are basically two families, Viking and his children, and his daughter-in-law's family. Their activities are like family days out. Viking is forty-seven, a single father of seven. Apart from looking after his children and working as a songwriter, he devotes most of his time to the EDL.

Viking said they have only a few people out on the street like this because they don't want to cause alarm. 'People for some reason think we're scary,' he said. 'But if it's just a few of us, people are more likely to come up and ask questions. On average, each time we have around twenty pedestrians stopping to talk to us. Some come up and say we're racist.' Occasionally, angry local Muslim residents approach them and tell them to stop. Viking has injured several of them. 'I put them on the floor before the police got here,' he said, without any expression of shame or embarrassment.

Viking joined the EDL after talking to a friend who was already in the group. Two of his sons and his twenty-year-old daughter all joined at the same time. He said that the prominent issue that drove him to join the group was 'the treatment of women'. 'That is why I'm always talking to people about the issue of female genital mutilation ... sixty-six thousand girls have been mutilated in this country in the last three years,' he said with conviction, 'and we believe there are still twenty to twenty-four thousand girls still at risk.'

I asked him where he gets his figures from. 'Various articles in the newspapers,' he replied.

'Which newspapers?' I asked.

As expected, Viking didn't know off the top of his head. He turned to his son: 'Which newspapers did we get our statistics on female genital mutilation from?'

'Ah.' The son paused, hesitated and answered, 'The *Mirror*, and the *Daily Mail*.'

The basis of Viking's argument is that female genital mutilation is common practice among Britain's Muslim communities and is central to their religion. I asked whether he thinks the cases of female genital mutilation are exceptions rather than the norm. He said, 'Yes, but it happens within a culture that accepts the practices ... We're not against Islam, but against the culture of some parts of Islam ... like the way they treat women and the way they interpret Islam.' The EDL has pulled in women supporters with this rhetoric, and Viking said that the group has seen many more women joining in the past year.

At the same time, the embrace of English culture and identity was also the main thing that attracted Viking to the EDL. 'We are defending the culture of being English ... In this country, it's illegal to be English,' he said.

I couldn't help sneering at the idea. He quickly explained: 'It's true. It's illegal to be English. All the things that are English, for example, freedom of speech, we can't have ... And it's illegal to be intoxicated in a licensed premises ... Our culture is drinking ... and when we practise having a beer, they can arrest us.'

Viking continued trying to stop passers-by to talk to them. A couple walked past and wished him 'Good luck'.

Viking's stand on immigration is typical of the majority in the EDL, and much of UKIP. The majority of the EDL's supporters vote for UKIP as the only electoral choice on the basis of its stand on immigration, Viking told me. 'We believe that all immigration needs to stop until Britain sorts out its own problems. This is what our division says. So does the entire EDL. We welcome doctors and highly skilled people to come, but not cleaners. We want British jobs for British people ... We want all those who're here illegally to be sent home ...'

Viking described EDL's position on immigration as 'centre right' instead of far right. 'If you ask British people on the street, they understand what we're saying. If everyone's thinking what we're thinking, we're not far right. None of the members of our South United Division have ever been involved or associated with parties like the BNP. It's impossible to think of the likelihood of my Asian and black friends who grew up in this country having to leave.'

His son, who was also holding a placard, nodded at me. Viking has six sons and one daughter, and has been a single dad for twenty-four years. His eldest son is thirty-four years old and the youngest eleven. Viking said it's lucky that all his adult children are in work, in the catering trade. His son turned to me and said that he's a bar manager in a nightclub in Reading town centre. 'I joined the EDL because I'm worried about my children's future,' he said.

Viking said most of his children got their jobs through personal connections, and they wouldn't have got them otherwise. 'It's hard for people now,' he said. 'I don't believe that the English are lazy. My boys would do any work that pays enough to live on … I'm absolutely against the zero-hour contract; we need proper jobs.' At this point, I couldn't say that I disagreed with him. I can relate to the anger among many working-class men and women against the invented idea that the English are 'lazy and work-shy'. His point about zero-hour contracts and the need for jobs has been raised by many UKIP supporters and voters that I've talked to.

I tried to trace the process by which someone like Viking moves from the discontent with his economic circumstance to a race-based analysis and far-right solution. Personal events in his life must have played a part in that transformation. He seemed glad that I was taking an interest in his past – I guess few people would. He told me he was born in Forest Gate, London, and his dad used to run a pub in Aldgate East, called Elephant & Castle.

Viking looked bitter as he spoke about his father, who used to abuse his mother.

When she left him, he started to abuse me. He often hit my feet with a hammer ... and sometimes starved me. I was so scared that I tried to avoid going home, and became a street child from the age of eight to twelve. One day, on a cold January morning, I was so badly beaten by my dad that I ran away and walked all the way from the Kings Head in Barbican to Hammersmith, in a pair of shorts, without shoes. I was only nine and a half years old. At Hammersmith flyover, I was picked up by someone who tried to touch me up. Luckily I escaped. When he went to get something in the boot, I drove his car away, in first gear, without knowing how to drive, until I got to my mother in Reading. But she sent me straight back to my dad. I was then locked up in a room for a week and a half, as punishment. I thought that was normal; I thought that was how everyone was treated.

Eventually social services placed Viking in a boarding school in Rye, but there he was bullied by other children, because of his Jewish surname, Cohen (his dad is half-Jewish). So he ran away from school and found himself a bedsit, at the age of thirteen and a half. 'Then I went to social services, telling them that I would run away and never let them find me, or they should let me stay in the bedsit and I will go to school every day and do everything properly. They said yes, so I had my own bedsit at thirteen and a half ... I took myself to school until I joined the air force when I was sixteen. My childhood and those adolescent years hardened me. Since then, I've never lost a fight.'

Viking had never been back to the East End until he went on the EDL marches to Tower Hamlets, in 2011 and in 2013.

After leaving the air force, he found it difficult to cope economically and bring up his four young children. He resorted to burglary around Reading for two years. 'It was businesses, though, not private houses,' he added. 'I only stole from businesses.' He went to prison for nine months as a result. He said he realized it was wrong and 'tried to be a better person'. He got into religion.

'When I lived in Derby, I became known as a Viking there. I'm a Viking by religion. I'm an Odinite,' he told me, proudly. 'We believe in the consciousness of the world ... I fought in Derby courts for the right to carry my sword for special, ceremonial occasions in public. It is actually very British. We sometimes went sword-fighting with each other. I wanted my right to carry my sword ...'

This seemed the beginning of Viking's path to extremism. I looked at his excited expression when he talked about his religion and wondered about his desperate search for meaning in life.

Forty of us were in this group and I was the leader. I was arrested by the police and they took the sword off me and told me they were going to destroy it. I took over Derby Cathedral to protest against it, because, by determining that I couldn't carry my sword, they were not allowing me to practise my religion in this country. So I said, if you tell me I can't practise my religion, then you can't practise yours.

I went into the cathedral and said, 'Excuse me, ladies and gentlemen, please make your way to the exit and leave the church.' When they all left, I shut the door, put the lock on, and went and sat on the bishop's throne and put my feet up on the altar, had a cigarette and a Ribena, and waited. And then the police came and negotiated … And then I talked to the press, which was the only way to fight my cause. Eventually I appealed and the judge said I had the right to carry my sword to religious meetings as long as other people were.

In the meetings, Viking and other members of the group, whom he described as 'mostly middle-class people', engaged in sword-fighting, had a few drinks and food, and talked about armour. But for him, it was more than a hobby. I asked him how his religion fits in the EDL as almost everyone is Church of England. He said there are around twenty people in the EDL who call themselves Odinites. 'This is obviously not the mainstream belief in the group, and so we are quite secretive about it, because we get attacked for our views. But generally I haven't had a problem with it in the EDL. We Odinites are always trying to fit in.'

At the moment, Viking is trying to make a living songwriting because it's his passion. When I asked him what type of music he writes, he started singing loudly in public. 'All sorts,' he said, 'all sorts.'

His division's street presence went on, week after week. However, when asked, other core members didn't seem able to explain their reasons for doing it. A twenty-six-year-old colleague of Viking said he works as a labourer on building sites and has known Viking since he was a child. When asked what drives him to be active in the EDL, he couldn't really put it into words. 'Just don't like people doing horrible stuff.'

But Viking is convinced that the EDL is slowly growing and drawing in 'better people', people who 'have a better understanding of what we're about'. At least it is so in the South East, he said. 'People in the region are more aware of the mission statement. Tommy Robinson wasn't upholding some of it, and he let it go off the rails. We're trying to get it back on the rails.' He said the size of marches these days has shrunk slightly to around 500 or so, as neo-fascists are leaving. 'But this is a good thing. At least we have less idiots now.'

When I talked to him in early May, Viking said he had stepped up his activism by staging a public 'performance': one afternoon, he wore a niqab on top of his EDL T-shirt, and walked around shops in Reading, to provoke responses from people. He said no shop tried to ask him to leave or even warned him about his behaviour. The only reaction came from a few Muslim youngsters, who looked at him with anger. Viking said he has performed this public stunt many times. Despite his previous attempts to demonstrate to me that his dislike of Islam comes from his distaste for the 'treatment of women', I could see that was only a disguise for his deep-seated hatred of Muslims. That hatred isn't silent. It's confidently expressed and dangerously manifested – and, in this instance, in an old-fashioned, Combat-18 style.

I remained calm and asked him what he wanted to achieve by this action. He put on an even more serious tone of voice: 'I just wanted to know how they'd react to transgender people wearing a niqab. I could have been a man changing sex to be a woman and then wearing a niqab.'

Another time, having returned to Reading from a Rotherham demo along with seventeen activists from his division, Viking seemed much encouraged and became even more active in his recruitment activities. Not only does he continue to talk to people on the streets every week, he also managed to get a few students from Reading Technical College interested. They want to listen to what he has to say, and are now organizing a meeting for him to talk to students on behalf of the EDL. A Christian group in town was also keen to organize a street Q&A for him. This seems an indication that his group is gradually winning the confidence of the public, especially in the context of May 2014's anti-immigration discourse during the European and local elections.

Viking told me that he voted UKIP after he heard Cameron calling them 'fruitcakes and loonies'. 'I'll vote for anything that the main parties disapprove of,' he said with pride. 'But I'm not a protest voter. I do believe UKIP says the right things.'

During the march in Peterborough, a man from the EDL came up and asked me where I came from and who I was. His name was Andrew, from the Southend Division. We agreed to meet for a proper talk in Willesden Junction, where he lives, the following week. I wondered why Andrew volunteered to meet me. This was the first time it had happened in my time researching the EDL.

The forty-year-old Andrew was friendly, approachable, and seemed to talk freely. He led me through the streets of Willesden Junction, pointing out the boarded-up takeaways and pubs along the way. He works as a bus maintenance supervisor nearby and does night shifts. He hates the job, he told me repeatedly. 'The EDL is all I do outside of work,' he said. He had the whole afternoon free, but in the evening he would be busy watching Chelsea. I looked at the large, colourful tattoos on both his arms, and thought he fitted exactly the stereotype of a Chelsea fan and football hooligan. And I wondered how our meeting would turn out.

Andrew took me to his local pub, the one with the cheapest beers, he said. The pub owner didn't seem to like the look of him, and watched as we entered. I felt particularly self-conscious in Andrew's company, as he stood out with his shaved head, tattoos and intimidatingly large arm muscles.

But as soon as I sat down to a beer with him, the first thing Andrew wanted to talk about was his daughter by his Japanese ex-wife. 'She's nine years old now.' He showed me her picture on his mobile phone. 'Isn't she beautiful?'

'You were married to a Japanese woman?' I couldn't quite believe an EDL man committed to the politics of race would choose a partner from outside his own culture.

'What's strange about that?' he responded. 'I met her in 1998 when I was twenty-eight. She was reading a book during her break time at an English school in Soho Square ... I was having my sandwich on the bench during my break – I was working as a builder on a site nearby. I sat next to her and said hi.' They got married in 2004, but were divorced a year later. They didn't get along. Now he sees his daughter only once a year.

'I don't want her to come to study in the UK because schools are shit here,' he said, downing his beer, 'because of the influence of Islam.'

I took the opportunity to return to the subject of his involvement in the EDL. He felt angry with the lack of media coverage of the EDL's Peterborough march, which he believed was 700 strong. 'There were no good press reports, but we were actually so happy after the demo because the police treated us like human beings and the public came out ... There was clapping for us. The change came because there have been hardly any arrests during our demos in the past six months.' Like many in the group, Andrew believes the EDL is growing in size and strength.

I was surprised to hear the main thing motivating him to join the street movement was his resentment of the left. 'I hate the left – more than I dislike the Muslims. During the Falklands War, I was disgusted with the position of the left wing. And then their attitude towards the Muslim protest in Luton.' The trigger for him came with stories of gangs grooming young women and how the left 'lied about it', he said. 'I watched RT [Russian TV] and they tell you things that your country won't. They reported grooming gangs.'

Andrew isn't actually a Londoner although you can't tell that from his mixed accent. He grew up in Grimsby, a depressed, old industrial town scarred by unemployment that has its roots in the Great Depression. Andrew worked as a fisherman when he was a young man. It was tough, he said, but was his only means of livelihood. As the fishing industry declined and the beer refinery and other factories closed down one by one, many left town to look for work elsewhere. In the 1980s, four million were unemployed in Britain and there were simply no jobs for the young in Grimsby. Andrew didn't want to leave home but to stay felt pointless. He began to feel a deep sense of marginalization, and it became easy to lay blame on any new faces in town, despite the fact that the migrant population has always been extremely small. 'Unfortunately, being poor and being the same colour as this government is not a good thing in this country,' he said. Andrew's race politics thrived in circumstances of material scarcity and a lack of future prospects. 'The government just can't see farther than London.'

Andrew went with four of his jobless friends to Paris and lived by shoplifting for a while. As former fishermen, they didn't have the skills to get jobs in the cities. Later, in 1984, Andrew decided to come to London, and found work in the building trade. He's lived there ever since.

His home town has a long history of anti-immigrant, anti-outsider responses to economic decline. I remember the Lindsey oil refinery dispute in 2009, when migrant workers were the focus of a hostile campaign and had to be given accommodation on a barge at Grimsby Docks, completely isolated from the local community. I spoke at the time with Italian workers Francesco and Gianluca, who were among the 100 Italians on four-month contracts to work at the oil giant Total. The building of a sulphurization facility at Total sparked a series of nationwide wildcat strikes involving more than 6,000 workers. Despite the well-justified anger against the Posted Workers Directive and the need to ensure service providers follow national labour agreements across the EU, the divisive, nationalist slogan 'British jobs for British workers', an invention under New Labour, was used by some trade unions, when they should have been arguing for equal pay and conditions for all workers. When I mentioned the oil refinery dispute to Andrew, he immediately said he was 'disgusted' with the Italian workers. 'They had to stay on the boat because otherwise it would be unsafe for them. That shows you the power of the majority,' he said. Andrew's sentiment echoes not just those on the far right, but many of the local workers in general. Although the leadership of the oil refinery strikes didn't have a racist agenda, they should have challenged the racism prevalent among their rank and file and mobilized a non-nationalist, non-racist campaign against the Posted Workers Directive.

'It's a white town and I like it like that,' Andrew said about Grimsby. 'It has only a hundred thousand people, but they have over one thousand members in the EDL. They have the biggest EDL turnouts anywhere.'

Far-right groups have built a stronghold in his home town. The bizarre thing is that the focus of EDL activities in Grimsby – 'Islamic extremism' – is completely irrelevant to the town. The Muslim population, who've become the imaginary enemy, is hardly visible there.

Andrew sometimes goes back to visit for a few days. Despite the brevity of his stays, he is always saddened and angered to see the degradation blighting his home town. His brother is a heroin addict, and remains unemployed.

I was lucky because I left before the drugs hit Grimsby. There wasn't a drug problem when I was there. Now it's horrendous. And the place stinks with piss, covered in graffiti and crumbling. It's heartbreaking to see how things have just been left to deteriorate.

Labour is disgusting. Problem is, UKIP is splitting the right-wing vote, and we'll be stuck with Labour again. Our family always voted and supported Labour, but like many others, they'll be voting UKIP now. I'm definitely voting

UKIP. They're no different from us. UKIP's just EDL with briefcases.

In the 2015 general election, Andrew voted UKIP again, but was angry that despite winning nearly four million votes, the party has won only one seat in Parliament.

Most of Andrew's family have emigrated to Spain and live in an English area in Malaga. Interestingly, despite his claim that 'Muslims don't integrate', he doesn't find it odd that the English want to be among themselves in Spain and do not welcome Spanish people into their area. He didn't want to talk about English integration in Spain. But, instead, he showed me long, elaborate tattoos of Grimsby and England on his arms. 'My country, my home town,' he said, looking at the tattoos.

We met a second time, around lunchtime, and I asked him to take me to an affordable dining place in Willesden Junction. But he couldn't find any restaurants or cafés in town. 'This is not a place you come to do lunch,' he said. 'There's nothing in this area.' Eventually, we ended up in a fast-food place not far from his local pub. Over greasy, overcooked fish and chips, Andrew wanted to talk about the history of his relationships.

He showed me a small tattoo written in Japanese characters on his right shoulder. 'This is the name of my first wife.' He was working in a plastics factory assembling sex toys and oxygen masks in Japan when he met her. 'She was coming to England, first time she'd ever been to England. So excited. She worked hard and saved £7,000 in two years to come to England. But she'd spent that money within two months. We had a good time together, and then we went back to Japan together and lived in her mum's house in Kyoto ... I lived in Japan for three years in all.'

I interrupted and asked why he chose to go to Japan.

'Ah, because I like oriental women,' he said, shrugging his shoulders. 'And, of course, I was also interested in Japan as a country.'

Then he added, laughing, 'But most of all, I like Japanese legs.'

I could now understand why his relationships with Japanese women do not contradict his politics of race.

He recalled another factor that affected his relationship with his first wife. He was sent to prison for being involved in football hooliganism in Scotland during a match with England. No England fans were allowed to go, but Andrew and his mates were determined to be there.

> Our national anthem was playing and they started booing it. So we took our England flag out, and started fighting ... A policeman grabbed hold of me. I didn't know it was a policeman, and I used my elbow and broke his eye socket. I didn't mean to do any harm. I didn't mean to hurt him in the eye. They gave me five years for that.
>
> My actual prison time was three years and four months. I started in Wandsworth prison, then Leicester ... That was the worst time of my life. When you're in prison, you're on your own ... I went in when I was twenty-seven and came out at the age of thirty.

I asked whether his football mates ever visited him while he was in prison.

'Never,' he said, looking down and flipping his chips.

From 1993 to 1996, my grandma visited me every two weeks. She died two months after I came out of prison. I was heartbroken. I was so close to her. She was like a mum to me. When I was growing up, every time after school, I went to her house, instead of my mum's.

My first wife, twenty-two at the time, waited three years for me ... She came all the way from Japan, having fallen out with her family and given up her job and everything there, just to be with me. She was in love with me. She used to send me money when I was in prison, because the food was bad in there. With her money, I was able to visit the prison shop twice a week ... Two weeks before I came out, she went to my town, Grimsby, and stayed with my mum. My mum, who usually had no time for anyone, was taking her everywhere, obsessed with her. When other people tried to talk with her, my mum would say she's with me. None of her friends understood what the hell she was doing with me. She was waiting for some working-class guy coming out of prison! She's beautiful; her hair was black and shiny ...

Andrew didn't finish his lunch. He sat there, looking saddened by the memory of the past.

Unfortunately, after three years in prison, I changed ... It was like losing her and getting over it. It was like it was over and I was heartbroken for a long time. And after three years I saw her again; it's just not the same any more. I got over it. I wasn't in love with her any more. But I couldn't tell her. How could I? She'd given up everything for me.

It was very strange coming out of prison after such a long time. Everything became so loud! And you have to make your personality quite hard in prison. When you come out, you can't just change back to normal. It takes a while. You become less sensitive. My first wife made me a jumper and it was really poorly made. She spent a long time, something like a year, making it … and I just said to her, 'What the fuck is this? It's shit.' It must have hurt her so much … I didn't think at the time. Now when I think back, I cried to myself, why did I do that? I should have been more sensitive. And I was a disloyal bastard. I couldn't say no to other women. We were together for two years after we got married, and during that time I was unfaithful about sixty times.

His first wife was working in an upmarket handbag shop in central London while Andrew worked as a labourer on the building site in Shepherd's Bush where he earned £5.15 an hour. Andrew smiled and said the cheapest handbag in that shop cost a thousand pounds. 'I went to visit her once, just after my work, because I lost my key to the flat and I had to get the key from her. This female pop star was in there, and I got talking to her. The manager was shocked and panicked, saying, "My God, he's talking to her," and started shouting at my ex-wife. Because he thought I was a working-class piece of scum, with my tattoos and bits of paint in my clothes, talking to his customer who spent 30,000 a week in his shop …'

Andrew seemed to keep his personal life separate from his political involvement on the far right. He never discussed the EDL with his wives. He went on a couple of BNP marches in the late 1980s, but felt uncomfortable with its white supremacist stance, although he openly admitted to having racist views himself. Because of his personal and social connections with non-white people – such as his two marriages with Japanese women – he felt it would be hypocritical to be involved in BNP activities.

Andrew was introduced and recruited into the EDL by Donna, a thirty-one-year-old single mother from Bexley, whom he met in a pub on Shepherd's Bush Road. According to Andrew, she had been checking him out for a couple of weeks in the same pub before trying to pick him up. 'Can I hold it for you?' she asked him when he was drunk as he came out of the men's toilet. They had a drink and became friends on Facebook, where she suggested he had a look at the EDL online. She then took him on his first march, in Luton, in 2009. There were 6,000 men and women on the streets that day. Since then, Andrew has been on numerous marches across the country, from Birmingham, Newcastle, Chichester, Lincoln, Liverpool and Manchester, to London's Tower Hamlets, Slough, Peterborough and Stevenage.

He grew close to Donna, who is now one of his best friends. And on marches, he would look after her two young daughters while she worked as security for the EDL. Donna is now one of the leaders of the neo-fascist English Volunteer Force (EVF). She's one of the few women active in the EVF, because women aren't encouraged on EVF's marches. Yet she is always recruiting and encouraging Andrew to join them. Through her, Andrew has become friendly with people in the EVF. Donna was also involved in the BNP. Andrew said that many EDL activists, like him, also take part in these activities, including the far-right unity marches. This situation reflects the EDL's lasting relationship with the neo-fascists. While the current leadership is not openly working with splinter groups or other sections of the far right, their activities and their loose membership often overlap.

I asked Andrew where his views diverge from Donna's. The only difference is a question of realism: 'Donna wants a White Britain. But White Britain is not durable any more ... It can't be done any more. Chasing that ideal is not possible. It's just a waste of time.'

Andrew introduced me to another close friend of his, also named Donna. She was using a fake name. Like many in the EDL, she fears any possible exposure. That was when I realized Andrew wasn't using his real name, either. 'I've got to be careful,' he explained. 'I don't know who you really are.'

Donna told me it was Andrew who recruited her into the EDL. Two months before that, he showed her a video of Naomi-Anne speaking for the EDL. The video convinced her that the EDL welcomes people from all ethnic backgrounds.

Donna is a forty-one-year-old single mother from Hackney. With a strong Cockney accent, she told me that she comes from mixed parentage: her English mother comes from Tottenham, north London, and her father is from Jamaica. Her mother is Church of England, Donna emphasized, and works in a handbag factory in the East End. Her dad is Catholic and was once a lorry driver.

Donna sees herself as 'English' and identifies totally with her mother. When faced with ethnic minority forms, 'White Other' is the box she ticks. But deep down she feels English.

Donna left Hackney fifteen years ago and moved to Plaistow, east London. 'There, I started to see the build-up of all the immigrants ...' She struggled to find words. 'I saw this Muslim community ... even down to my twelve-year-old daughter's school ten years ago, where they were doing a project on Muslims. What is that about? This ain't what we're used to. The past ten to fifteen years it's got worse. Muslims seem to be taking over.'

She was agitated, and I listened to her undisguised racism, wondering what the elderly West Indian customers sitting next to us in the pub would make of this. Donna didn't even look straight at me. She just carried on: 'I dislike the way they [Muslims] treat our country and the way they treat women. All the Muslim boys behaving rude and I just thought, what is going on? It's not choices any more, it's like we have to accept them ... We should have the right to stand up and say, look, we don't want this any more.'

Apart from the young Muslim boys in the neighbourhood with whom she has had problems, Donna couldn't tell me what has driven her to such a deep hatred of the entire British Muslim population.

'How has it really affected you personally, the fact that you had Muslim residents around?' I asked.

'Er,' she still struggled to explain, 'it just got a bit domineering around you, you know, and you just build up a hatred ... Seeing all these changes in this country made me join the EDL.'

Once again, I asked her to justify her feelings of 'danger' and 'threat'. She had no answer beyond repeating the usual tabloid messages that 'they're rapists, terrorists and criminals'.

Andrew became more vocally racist in her company. As I sat with them, I began to wonder about the way mobs form. These were two deeply alienated individuals confidently expressing the crudest form of racial prejudice. There appeared to be no self-awareness. Then they got up and ordered a couple of pints and sandwiches. 'Tonight we'll be back to watch Chelsea,' Andrew said, in high spirits.

Donna is unemployed and on social benefits. Her three children, in their twenties, no longer depend on her and live away from home. She now lives in a bedsit consisting of two rooms next to Andrew. The last time she worked was in a bar three years ago in Kingston Road, Hackney. She has trained as a chef but couldn't get a job. 'I went on three job interviews in the last two months,' she said hatefully. 'I didn't get the jobs. I bet they were all given to immigrants.'

'Your dad came to Britain as one of the post-war immigrants that Britain needed,' I said.

She looked at me and slightly softened her tone: 'In those days, black people used to sit on the upstairs of the bus and white people downstairs … I know that …'

'Surely, that kind of racism and segregation in those days affected your dad and your family,' I continued. 'Your dad was once an immigrant, too.'

'Yes,' she responded. 'But he worked. He worked hard.'

'So are the immigrants today,' I said.

Andrew came back in from his cigarette break, and started talking about the next demo. Donna quickly moved on from her dad to talking about her first demo in the EDL. 'That was in Westminster six weeks ago. I felt elated. I felt part of the family.'

Andrew said he wanted to show us an EDL video. So we went to his place five minutes down the road, a bedsit in the truest sense of the word: his home consisted of a box of only three square metres, big enough only for a bed. There was no kitchen, only a sink, full of dirty dishes. No table or desk. Andrew asked us to sit on his bed while he turned on his laptop – the only item of any value – and showed us YouTube videos. He went on to Keyboard Warrior Everywhere, a Facebook forum for debates between the EDL and the rest of the far right. He enjoys the heated rows and is an active poster. I asked him whether he's ever interacted with any anti-racist campaigners. 'Yes, quite a few times,' he said, 'and the EDL guys criticized me for being too friendly with left-wing girls ... those anti-fascist women on the internet. When I felt I was wrong in a debate, I said sorry to those women, and some people in the EDL said to me, why are you saying sorry to those left-wing bitches? I said, because I was wrong! Then they called me a pussy.'

I began to feel a little claustrophobic, three of us crowded into this small space. The EDL film he showed us of the Brighton unity march on 27 April, organized by March for England, depressed me. Andrew grew agitated while watching it, and talked angrily about the 'leftists' who confronted the protesters in Brighton. Andrew agreed wholeheartedly with the call for unity among the far right. 'To be honest, most people in the EDL don't care either way. They will follow and be led whatever happens.' He went with Candy and Susie from the EDL. He'd introduced Susie to the EDL a year earlier, and she had joined him on the 4,000-strong Birmingham demo a month after the Lee Rigby murder in 2013.

I asked him what motivated him to go on the Brighton unity march. Because of the left, came the answer again. 'That's why

I have sympathy with these groups,' he went on. 'Brighton's a great location because it's a left-wing place. So we are telling the left, you don't tell us where to go.'

He said the EDL and other groups came together on the Brighton march. 'It was because we all hate the left. We go there looking for the lefties, just like the lefties will be looking for us … When it comes to a punch-up, the lefties are all cowards, because they're all middle-class students whereas we're builders and scaffolders. If it's one on one, they got no chance. Once one of us beat up someone from Black Blog; the guy just went down.'

The EDL mainstream fell out with March for England long before Tommy Robinson left. 'I saw them abusing each other on Facebook, but I get on with everyone,' Andrew said.

The disagreement is mainly about the Israeli flag. Sometimes EDL people bring it on the marches, to annoy the Muslims and left-wingers who fly Palestinian flags. But the nationalists [the BNP and the rest of the far right] hate Jews and they really don't like that. There have been big fights, and some people got stabbed … In Luton, 2011, for instance. I stayed in the pub and didn't get involved in the fight. Generally I don't get involved in all the rows between the groups, and I'm one of the few from the EDL who would be on Facebook with the splinter groups …

At this point, I didn't feel like asking any more questions. I felt I'd had enough for the day. Andrew noticed my silence. He switched off the EDL film and started showing us a video of his home town, Grimsby. Then he found his parents' home on

Google Maps. 'Look, this is where I grew up,' he said to us, and then moved the arrow all the way to the seafront. 'See, I used to live near the sea. It was a good place to grow up ...'

'What are you doing down south, then?' Donna asked.

Andrew shrugged his shoulders and went quiet. It appeared that the EDL made up the bulk of his social circle in London.

He was keen to befriend me. 'Can't we go somewhere, do something, like along the Thames, and not talk about the EDL all the time?'

Before I had the chance to reply, Andrew jumped on the next big news. 'Bob Hoskins is dead! I can't believe it.' Then he showed us a video of *The Long Good Friday*. He couldn't move his eyes away from the screen, and looked genuinely saddened.

Andrew believes London is no good for the EDL. 'The London Division has only a few thousand members and is rubbish because people are frightened of going on demos ... This is because London is more politically correct ... and people can get sacked from their jobs if found out that they go on demos. Outside of London, the left doesn't have all this power.'

There are no activists in the Willesden Junction area, so Andrew joined the Southend Division, which has 100 to 150 activists. Every two to three months, they have a so-called meet-and-greet, where activists get together to have a drink and organize their events. Andrew is often responsible for organizing transport to demos. The head of the Southend Division is a man called Steve Riley, whom Andrew talks about a great deal and refers to as one of his best mates. Steve Riley is also widely known to have a Filipina wife, said Andrew, which apparently indicates that 'he isn't racist'.

Andrew doesn't think much of his fellow activists. When I asked him what they do for a living, he replied sarcastically: 'Rocket scientists, brain surgeons and politicians.' Then he put on a straight face and said: 'No, actually, most of them do menial jobs. Some are supermarket cashiers and cleaners.'

Like others, he has noted an increase in female activists in the Southend Division and across the country. 'For every ten men who're joining the EDL, there are eleven women now,' Andrew joked, pointing out that the changing gender balance is a clear tendency. 'These days, 20 to 30 per cent of the EDL are women. You remember the Peterborough demo? Twenty per cent of protesters were female.'

Andrew often describes EDL activities as his social life. He said the best time of his life was on a demo in Newcastle, just after Lee Rigby was killed. 'Two days before the demo, Rigby died. There were 7,000 on the march.'

One day, Andrew insisted on showing me a YouTube video of the Newcastle demo. I didn't want to go to his place on my own. So he took me to a local internet café. He said he often comes here and talks for hours about football with the customers. The shopkeeper is a local Muslim man, but Andrew talked loudly about EDL demos in his presence.

We went for two days to Newcastle and booked into the Royal Lodge. They didn't know we were the EDL. We came as individuals. There were 150 EDL in the car park, booking into the hotel. It was a non-smoking hotel and we were all smoking. A whole barrel of beer we drank ... We were making a big disturbance ... That was fantastic. And when we left, the woman in the hotel was so grateful as they made a lot of money from us that she made a cake with the name EDL on it. Brilliant. It was actually depressing to come back to London, to work. Depressing to come back to reality.

When the EDL was first set up, the authorities were eager to crack down on us. So we went to the football hooligans and asked for help. They were the only ones who would take the beatings and also give it back and do the prison time. Now we are established and we have evolved and got rid of most of them ... We've booted them out and moved on ... In the past, when we had 2,000 on the march, 1,000 was football hooligans and the more violent type. We're getting rid of them now. The left's laughing that we're reducing and getting smaller in size. But it's actually because we're getting rid of our worst stock.

The talk Tommy Robinson gave when he left because there are extremists in the EDL was bullshit. He was after a deal not to go to prison and the government believed that once Tommy was out the way, the EDL would collapse, therefore saving a lot of money on policing, etc. But the EDL didn't collapse and he ended up doing eighteen months in prison.

Andrew said he was almost in tears when Robinson quit. He was close to Kevin Carroll. 'Since Tommy left, the relationship between EDL and splinter groups hasn't been good a lot of the time. Sometimes there are clashes between groups, like the other day ... The Britain First guys went to Paul Pitt's house [Paul Pitt, leader of South East Alliance] with knives and everything ... Paul ran out ... They'd come to do him. Not good to have too many leaders ... Too many chiefs, not enough Indians. It's too tribalist.'

Andrew said that, after Robinson left, initially there were fewer people going on marches, as in Exeter and Slough. But the numbers have since increased again, as the group has attempted to reform its public image and to 'destroy left-wing propaganda'. 'The Grantham march started to turn things round, because Naomi-Anne came to speak and was treated like a princess by the EDL and gave the impression that EDL isn't really that racist and bad. We got her to speak because we thought it'd be a good idea to destroy the left-wing argument ... The left has made the name of the EDL have the same effect as a child molester ...

Meanwhile, despite the gradual image change of the group, Andrew himself doesn't shy away from admitting his own racism. 'Of course there are many racists in the group. I'm quite racist; I don't like Pakis near me. I don't like the way they smell and look. I don't wish them any harm but I just don't wish to associate with them.'

As to British-born Muslims, he said: 'If a dog is brought up in a stable, he's still a dog, not a horse.'

Andrew's deep-seated racial hatred also extends to the Roma communities. What contribution do they make to society? he asked me. He said the EDL leadership is thinking about campaigning against the Roma, although he thinks the current focus should continue to be on British Muslims. 'There'll be a civil war,' he said, repeating Tommy Robinson's old line.

Despite the group's image reform, even a quick look at its website tells you that the post-Robinson EDL remains what it ever was. There continues to be a stream of the most blatant racism while writing by international fascists and racists has disappeared.* In one article, it argues against the need to treat racially aggravated offences more seriously. It says: 'Why is it inherently worse to attack someone because of their race than it is to attack them because you don't like their hat, their choice of football team, or their stupid grin?'

Offline you get an even clearer picture of the EDL today: incitement of racism remains at the core of its activities. Moreover, the neo-fascist elements remain active in some regions.

On the 700-strong EDL Bradford demo in October 2013, the first following Robinson's departure, neo-fascists such as the Casuals United, March for England and Northwest Infidels were present, as ever. Elsewhere, the EDL's activities have long created a culture of violence. In Devon, according to the *EDL News*, there have been many racist attacks conducted by EDL activists and followers.

The *Exeter Express & Echo* reported on 25 October 2013 that twenty-year-old Nathan Taylor, a local EDL member, attacked a group of language students in town. The newspaper also reported, that September, a story about Mark Sleman, who kidnapped and tried to rape a ten-year-old child, and went on

---

* As Paul Sillett of Unite Against Fascism (UAF) observed: 'Islamophobes in the US, for instance, who the EDL aligned themselves with, like Pamela Geller, would once frequent EDL Facebook pages and share "Gates of Vienna", "anti-jihad" propaganda. But, in the post-Robinson era, this is largely a thing of the past. The efforts of Robinson and his UK backers proved ultimately futile in encouraging the average EDL goon on to the writings of Weston, Geller and Co. ...'

the run after fleeing his bail hostel. It was found that Sleman had set up the Church of the Templars, whose members were all from the EDL and its splinter group South East Alliance. Among them were the Exeter-based racist Bob England and the EDL Plymouth organizer (and former deputy organizer of South West EDL) Hayley Wells, who were reported to be dressed like Knights Templar preparing for 'the Crusade against Islam'.

According to the *Plymouth Herald* (23 February 2013), the twenty-eight-year-old Hayley Wells and her fellow EDL member, thirty-year-old Kelly Watterson, conducted a vicious racist attack on a Kurdish family in a takeaway shop in town after an EDL meeting during which they both got drunk. Someone threw a glass, which smashed next to a baby in a car seat outside the takeaway. Wells then scratched the boy's mother on the arm. They eventually pleaded guilty to racial and religiously aggravated assault and avoided a prison sentence.

In Torquay, Tobias Ruth and John Rodd, both Newton Abbot EDL members, styled themselves on and drew inspiration from the Norwegian fascist Breivik, as reported by *Exeter Express & Echo* in November 2013. They branded each other with hot irons to initiate themselves in Breivik's Order of the Knights Templar and went on a six-month graffiti spree, spraying the letters KT in more than seventy locations, including the Islamic Centre and vehicles all over Torquay. They also sent racist letters to mosques and prayer centres in Plymouth and Brighton, saying 'Leave this town today or there will be hell to pay'.

Exeter has been a particular target for the EDL, which resents the multi-ethnic make-up of the university town. In November 2013, the EDL announced it was coming to Exeter because the university was the home of the European Muslim Research

Centre as well as the Institute of Arab and Islamic Studies. The university has accepted funding from people and institutions in the Middle East for the purposes of teaching and research. In response to the EDL march of 16 November 2013, local communities united across faiths and cultures. Mike Gurney, of Exeter's Unite Against Fascism (UAF), said:

> The EDL tried to mobilize publicly here in Exeter, in 2011. They leafleted to argue for banning the burka. We very quickly organized a counter-protest. Twenty to thirty of them and we had 300 of us. The EDL went quiet for a while after that … until 2012 when they started campaigning around shops that do halal meat and talked about sharia law …
>
> We built a very broad coalition, Exeter Together, involving a thousand people on the march including trade unionists, plus several hundred supportive passers-by at a city centre rally that went on for four hours … We even had the dean of the cathedral involved, which is completely unprecedented. It was a fantastic and joyous celebration and completely marginalized the EDL.

Lizi, also of UAF, said: 'The confidence among the Muslim communities also grew and they took part in the organizing of the anti-EDL rally … The mosque used to keep their heads down in the past but that's changed.' Many young Muslims were involved in the organizing of the rally, and local communities were very supportive.

Some of the EDL activists came from Woolwich Strong – chaired by the twenty-one-year-old Somerset-based Joshua Bonehill Paine, a supporter of UKIP and a regular hoaxer who invented news stories about British Muslim communities on his website Daily Bale. He once created a hoax missing-person poster, claiming a six-year-old girl had been kidnapped by an 'Asian grooming gang'. Woolwich Strong was set up after the Rigby murder, as a front for the EDL.

Some of those involved in the EDL march in Exeter were ex-army, such as those in the Combined Ex-Forces, who are more active in Plymouth than in Exeter. There is much infighting between EDL groups in the South West. Lizi said: 'The march was mainly mobilized from outside ... We have a very diverse community here and the EDL has had real problems trying to build here ... The falling-out between them didn't help them to grow ... The Plymouth group had a demo in Exeter and there was a big fight between them.'

The far right are on the rise across Europe, as evidenced by results in the European elections in May 2014. From the violent Golden Dawn in Greece and the anti-Muslim Freedom Party of Geert Wilders in the Netherlands to the success of the Front National in France, these trends are occurring alongside the growth of the British far right. Mosques have been attacked, Muslim women abused and minority communities intimidated across the country.

Back in the East End of London, trouble emerged again when news broke that a so-called Christian Patrol had been founded in the area at the end of January 2014. Activist Abdullah Faliq recalled: 'When we finished prayers and our weekly election at the mosque, we heard shouting outside. We went out and saw eight or nine white men coming out of a US-style Humvee. They pulled up next to the East London

Mosque. Then they unveiled a banner with messages about Islam and women, shouting that we're against women.' But the men rushed back to their vehicle when several young Muslim men became alerted, and drove off.

Others also saw three or four similar vehicles parked in Brick Lane. Abdullah Faliq discovered later that these men belonged to the neo-fascist Britain First. Launched in May 2011 as a political party, Britain First engaged Paul Golding, a BNP councillor in Sevenoaks in 2009–11, as its chairman. Britain First was also associated with an unregistered party called National People's Party and the Protestant Coalition. Currently, their activities focus on campaigning against 'Islamification' in Britain.

The Britain First men, under the name Christian Patrol, roamed around the borough, confronting and harassing Muslim residents on the streets, particularly those who were drinking or holding hands in public. They were also distributing leaflets asking people to report any 'extremist' activities in the area. They asked pedestrians to call them if they were 'harassed by Muslims', and said they would come to defend them. These Britain First men clearly aimed to create a climate of fear, and they succeeded, among Muslim residents in the area. These men are ex-military and they could cause serious harm, especially in places such as busy mosques visited by women and children. 'Britain First is dangerous because they're raising and creating divisions between Christians and Muslims, therefore inciting religious hatred,' said Faliq. 'But they don't represent Christians.'

Looking at the origins of their organization, Britain First's intentions come as no surprise: Britain First is the creation of James Dowson, the man dubbed as 'the person who owned the BNP'. Few would need to think about what lies behind their talk of 'Islam and women': Dowson led an anti-abortion campaigning group, the UK Life League.

When Dowson made contact with the BNP in 2007, Griffin saw his anti-abortion campaigns and close relationship with Loyalist paramilitaries as assets. Griffin even moved BNP operations to Belfast, where Dowson lived. That relationship eventually ended along with the decline of the BNP after the 2010 elections. Dowson left the BNP in October 2010. Then, in May 2011, Dowson and Paul Golding announced a campaign to 'protect British and Christian morality', and Britain First was born as a critique of Griffin, with its key activities opposing immigration, Islam and abortion. Its stated aim is to 'save this country and our people from the EU, and the politically-correct, multicultural insanity that is now engulfing us'.

I talked to Paul Golding just after his Christian Patrol had been receiving attention from the police. He left his mobile number on the leaflets given out on the streets of Tower Hamlets. As a former head of publicity for the BNP, he must have been using this patrol as a publicity stunt for his group, I thought.

'The first two years [after setting up Britain First in 2011] we were struggling to build up, slowly but surely,' he said. 'We took up like a rocket since Lee Rigby was murdered.'

He told me about Christian Patrol: 'Our main focus is on Islamic extremism … You can't ignore the elephant in the room. One thing that's causing the biggest problem in this country is the rise of fundamentalist Islam.'

His organization shares the same focus of activities as the EDL. But he dismissed the idea of working with them.

'I have a lot of contempt for the EDL. Because most of their demos are characterized by drunkenness, people charging around in an undisciplined fashion. We are not like that. We are highly organized, highly professional, highly disciplined. We have 70,000 registered supporters and activists nationwide.'

'Really? I've never heard of you,' I said, trying to provoke a response.

'The reason why you haven't heard much about us is the biased agenda of the media,' he said. 'If you got two groups, one is full of drunk hooligans running around town, then the media would focus on them because they want to present a bad image of British people on the patriotic right. If you got a highly organized, disciplined, sensible organization like Britain First, even if they're probably the biggest of them all, the media would completely ignore it and not give us any coverage whatsoever. Because they don't want to present a sensible face to patriotic activism in this country.'

A sensible face? I thought to myself. Harassing Muslim residents on the streets?

He continued:

The EDL at the moment is a hostile bunch of racketeers. They have not produced any financial records since its launch. The whole thing is a shady business, with hundreds of thousands of pounds unaccounted for ... Who knows where the money's gone? They are basically an undisciplined rabble, who turned up in one town centre and go to another town centre, not achieving anything but giving everyone a bad name because of their hooliganism and drunkenness.

We absolutely despise that approach.

We actually achieve something. Not only through Christian Patrol, we also confronted Anjem Choudary … The EDL never achieved anything apart from just collecting together every dreg in this country … The EDL is a one-trick pony, they're only anti-Islam. We are completely different. We are a broad political movement with principles and policies … We don't want to live in a filthy, immoral society. We don't want to be under the EU. We don't want political correctness. We want all immigration stopped …

'So you're just like the BNP,' I said.

'We're nothing like them. We're not neo-Nazi; we're not fascists. My commanding officer in north London is black. But at the same time, we are a small, overcrowded, tiny island, and we've only got enough space and resources for our own people. We're full up. We can't take any more immigrants, whether they're black, white or people with yellow spots.'

Knowing that some in the EDL have joined the ranks of Britain First, I asked whether his members have infiltrated the EDL.

He said: 'I know of one of my officers who went to the EDL demo in Slough. He went there purely to see if the game's up. He came back to me and said it's a farce, a joke, everyone's drunk and it's a complete waste of time …'

Instead, he said, Britain First is growing.

We got units all over the country. It's a completely different approach [from the EDL's]. We're turning a lot of people away. People are coming up to us and they want to get involved. We looked at their Facebook page and saw them wearing masks. We just thought that's totally moronic. If you're not gonna show your face, then we're not interested. We are recruiting ex-military, people from the security industry, people who're sensible. We don't want anyone who's got a screw loose. There's a huge number coming out of that EDL now and we don't want them. It's just like Football Factory where they'll all get on the coach, all getting drunk, all going up to have a fight. That's what EDL is. We are organized on a military basis ... We have a strict code of conduct. No drunkenness. No hooliganism. No masks. No racism.

'Sorry,' I interrupted him. 'Did you say "no racism"? What do you mean?'

Golding was getting agitated. 'As I said, my commanding officer in north London is black, and he's got a group of ten to fifteen white activists who he's in charge of ...'

Throughout 2014, Paul Golding and his Britain First continued their racial harassment and intimidation of British Muslims by invading major mosques all over the country, such as the East London Mosque and mosques in Luton, distributing anti-Muslim material and doorstepping well-known preachers. Britain First has built up an online following of forty million via social media, with its pro-army, nationalistic propaganda such as D-Day messages and images of the royal family. Using publicity material acceptable to a mainstream audience, Britain First managed to lead many online readers to their site, some even joining the group or becoming supporters without understanding what lies behind the organization.

Andrew invited me to go with him and others to the Lee Rigby Memorial March on 24 May. It would be, he said, a unity type of march involving all the far-right groups. The police had set the route from Charlton to Woolwich. I met with Andrew in Victoria, and we travelled together to Charlton. On the train, he was particularly vocal about the 2014 European parliamentary and local elections in which he voted UKIP.

'I did, just like most others in the EDL, vote for UKIP. In fact, the whole country did, except London,' he said, laughing. 'English people are outvoted by foreigners in London.' I asked him what he thinks the differences are between the politics of UKIP and those of the BNP.

He shrugged and said: 'The BNP aren't very intelligent. They've got quite a few councillors but didn't do anything. They just sat in the office, looking out the window!' He laughed from deep within his belly, and then repeated a line straight out of a Farage speech: 'We want immigration. But we don't want Romanian drug addicts and alcoholics.' He then added: 'We got enough of our own!'

I was surprised he didn't turn up with people from his division. He explained that Steve Riley, head of the Southend Division, didn't want to join this memorial march because he didn't get along with the other groups. As it turned out, around 500 people from the EDL and splinter groups like EVF and the BPA (British Patriotic Alliance) attended the march. There were also neo-Nazi groups such as Combat 18 and the ex-military groups. Aside from these, I also spotted local families. In all, there were more than 2,000 people marching to Woolwich.

The far-right groups assembled at the White Horse in Charlton, where Andrew and I met with his EDL mates and acquaintances. As soon as he entered the pub, all Andrew was interested in was getting us drinks. He looked more relaxed with a pint in his hand, and he struck up conversation with a local blonde woman called Wendy, from east London. She said she was paying her respects to Rigby. 'I don't like Muslims,' she said. I was taken aback by such open racism. I asked whether she was a member of any of the groups in attendance. She said she wasn't interested; she doesn't like organized politics.

I then talked to two women who said they were members of the BPA, formed the previous month as a splinter group of the EDL. They have only seventy members, based in Bournemouth. They couldn't really tell me what was behind the split from the EDL, apart from the fact that they didn't like the rivalry among the leadership. There are no real ideological differences between the two groups.

I couldn't think of a more unnatural environment for me to be in. It was difficult, if not impossible, to talk to anyone. Many of the men were dressed in traditional Nazi gear, one of them with C18 embroidered on his shirt. I was intimidated. Then I saw Dave Bolton, head of the EDL London Division, talking to some people. I approached him and he greeted me. 'There're quite a few Nazis here,' Bolton said to me. I knew later that he had banned EDL people from wearing any identifiable EDL clothing, this despite the tattoo on the back of his head reading 'EDL'.

I followed Bolton and a group of other EDL activists to the Albion down the road, where they drank and waited for other marchers to arrive. I tried to talk to the EDL crowd; one of them said she was from Basildon in Essex and had moved out of the East End because 'it wasn't the same any more with all the immigrants coming in'. Meanwhile, she said, she has found it difficult to settle in the local Essex community. 'They talk down at us from the East End, you see. They've always been there and we're the incomers and we are from poorer backgrounds.'

All the EDL members that day, including her, said they voted UKIP.

Back in Luton, Darren watched the development on the far right with amazement.

The BNP, including the Young British National Party, became ever more vocal in their call for unity. 'Our struggle is burdened and fractured by the egos of many nationalists. Good nationalists ought to strive to be the next leaders of nationalism ... in this new age of multicultural darkness that has swept through our streets. What holds us back more than anything, more than the left-wing traitors and the unions, is our inability to work together towards a greater goal ... Politically, we are divided, even on the street. Various groups wish to promote their own version of nationalism ... This must stop. We must come together as one.' Racist and fascist organizations on the far right have now gone farther than ever before to attempt to achieve unity. Their aim is to take over the far-right street movement that has been dominated by the EDL over the past few years.

March for England and splinter groups of the EDL, such as the Infidels and the English Volunteer Force (EVF), attempted to join forces in 2014 and organized their actions jointly. They've set up the United British Patriots (UBP), combining anti-Muslim hatred with a traditional far-right support for Ulster Loyalism.

One of the leading figures in the UBP is Paul Prodromou, former leader of the Essex, Kent and Sussex EDL. He is now leader of the neo-fascist South East Alliance and was organizer of March for England's demo on 27 April in Brighton, which was promoted as a unity demo for the UBP.

Darren doesn't think they'll grow in real strength, although they might prosper in the short term, given the bad economic times.

Unity they'll never have. These groups will lose eventually, because they're ruled by fear ... But in a recession, they can gather support quite quickly, even though they're quite small. In a recession, people are disgruntled. Times are hard. And they're just tapping into people's emotions ... That's the unity they are calling for: of disgruntled people ...

Disgruntled people, come with us and we'll give you the answer, they say. I've seen that before at football when there were lots of them in the 1980s ... when it took a foothold. Hundreds and hundreds of grown men in the terraces ... In those days it was the NF, one group under one banner. Now you've got different groups, which is quite dangerous ... It's very hard to get a grip of who it is now.

The white working-class communities are trying to work it all out. They [working-class people] are not overnight racists ... They're good, hard-working people. It's times like these ... These splinter groups are capitalizing on the one in ten ... Working-class communities got it really hard, you know. Most people are still trying to hold on to what is right, even if they got nothing going for them in their life ...

In the middle of all this, Robinson pleaded guilty to mortgage fraud and was sent to prison. He couldn't tell his children that he was going to jail. So he lied and told them he was going away to work. Darren kept in contact with him and told me about Robinson's experiences inside. Initially, he was put in Woodhill prison, and the governor of the prison was said to have instructed the guards to put him on the same wing as Muslim inmates who'd been convicted of terrorist offences. The prison guards told Robinson that he'd be murdered within fifteen minutes of being put on the wing. 'He'll be served up,' Darren asserted.

His mother called me and asked me for help. Basically he's on his own now ... since he left the EDL. The mainstream doesn't like him, either. Supporters can just stick up for him, writing letters, but they're not gonna stand outside the prison and organize a demo for him ... That's the situation he's in. The system takes over.

If he does come out safe, I said to him, he might need a year to find himself again ... I did try to get that to him before ...

'Is he feeling regret now?' I asked, wondering how he felt about it all, now he was faced with the possibility of being harmed in prison.

'I think if he could, he would have gone about it differently,' said Darren.

A week later, on 8 February, Darren told me that Robinson was beaten up by three men in prison, and had subsequently been transferred to Winchester, where there are no class-A inmates. 'That was lucky,' Darren said to me. 'He wouldn't have survived Woodhill.'

Darren was angry about the way Kevin Carroll tried to capitalize on events as they were unfolding. He thought Carroll should keep his opinions to himself and not publicize them without considering the effect it would have on his family.

As I said, he's a narcissist. He doesn't admit defeat. Even after leaving EDL, he's still shouting about Luton – Twitter is his only forum at the moment. He needs a reality check.

He's gone mad and said on Twitter that the government is forcing sectarianism on us. He's opposed to receiving refugees from Syria. He's talking about Christians being persecuted, but as soon as we're talking about letting them into this country, he said 'We're full' ... He put up a Union Jack and said 'Fuck off' to Syrian refugees. How can you deny people entry to this country who're refugees and shout about being a Christian? When the whole of Christianity is built on a refugee family ... He's an idiot.

Darren has not talked to Kevin Carroll for a long time. 'I just wonder, how can you have learned nothing from your journey? How can you be five years down the road and have not learned nothing? Not changed on the way!'

I asked him how he would summarize Robinson's role and activities in the EDL in the past five years. He paused and sighed. It was as if he was refreshing his memory all over again.

'He was wrong,' Darren said firmly.

The biggest mistake he made was the generalizing about Islam and therefore victimizing Muslims. He himself regrets it to some degree. He got carried away by the movement, which went out of control. When he first started out, you might think, yes, support our troops, but it's been steered into other avenues, because once it went national, everyone wants their say ... It's not just about Luton any more ... It is a monster, really. He's thirty-one now. He started a street movement when he was twenty-six. I know he wouldn't say the things he said back then ... If I had had a crystal ball, I wouldn't have taken any part in it. And I imagine Steve [Tommy Robinson] wouldn't, either. I regret it.

During these years we've talked many times about this ... Once, Steve [Tommy Robinson] had a little drink and told me he was stressed. Again, I told him to quit. When he eventually left, I was glad that he apologized to the Muslim community ...

EDL has changed all of us ... I don't think the EDL's gone away or will go away. The box has been opened ... But if I had the power, I would advise and discourage young people not to go near groups like the EDL. It ain't nowhere to go.

7

THE NEW OUTSIDERS

Press reports and analyses by anti-racist campaigners seemed to suggest that racist ideologies such as those propagated by the EDL have suffered a defeat, as the group has fragmented and its ability to mobilize was left weakened after Robinson's departure in autumn 2013. Hope Not Hate campaigners also claimed in early 2015 that the support for the UK's far right is at its lowest in two decades. In the 2015 general election, the Conservatives, with their mainstream anti-immigration pledges, won a twelve-seat majority as Labour suffered the worst defeat since 1983 and have been almost wiped out by the SNP in Scotland. UKIP, despite aiming to secure a flock of MPs and having won almost four million votes in the general election, didn't manage to gain more than one seat in Westminster. Its leader, Nigel Farage, also failed to win his seat in South Thanet to the Tories. It seems to indicate that race-based politics have not triumphed.

The reality, however, is much more complex. Racism is not the privilege of the far right, but is nurtured, reproduced, kept alive and passed on via ideological state apparatuses, of which the media is a part. It was treated as headline news when the British

Social Attitudes survey found in May 2014 that the proportion of people in the UK who say they're racially prejudiced has risen since 2001.* For those on the receiving end, this came as no surprise. It has been a long, gradual process in which racism grows and manifests itself in a variety of forms, whether expressed through the lens of culture or of religion. The racism that has formed the core ideology of the EDL has in fact been mainstreamed and is permanently echoed in our public sphere.

A BBC survey interestingly pointed out, in the same autumn as Robinson's departure from the EDL, that more than a quarter of eighteen- to twenty-four-year-olds in Britain do not trust Muslims. Of the 1,000 young people who took part in the survey, 28 per cent said 'Britain would be better off with fewer Muslims', while 44 per cent said 'Muslims do not share the same values as the rest of the population'. What the EDL represents isn't a 'counter-jihad subculture', as some people would like to think. The phenomenon it has created isn't an aberration that runs counter to the rationality and morals of modern British society. It is very much part of it.

While the EDL itself becomes more divided between regions, with no strong leadership,† its increasingly more active splinter

---

* See report at www.theguardian.com/uk-news/2014/may/27/-sp-racism-on-rise-in-britain.
† Unite Against Fascism (UAF) commented: 'The EDL are in a stalemate; they are at the level of their demos always being reliant on outside thugs and assorted far-right scum, being bussed in to make up paltry numbers. In this at least, anti-fascists can feel vindicated. Those in the anti-fascist movement who told us "Don't demonstrate when the EDL are in town", and even held alternative events with the aim of trying to undercut effective opposition to EDL, were found wanting. Had we followed such moves, the EDL would be very much with us, and not what they have been reduced to.'

groups and other neo-fascist groups are seeking unity and working together. At the same time, resistance continues. UAF commented on a recent, successful mobilization:

In a fit of pique, [when] they [EDL] announced they were returning to Walthamstow in May 2015, many of us wondered if they had a death wish. Even others on the far right and some in the EDL said this was madness; 'the locals will go for you', was their (for once accurate) view. However, EDL, in their delusions (and knowledge that the police would allow them to enter the borough), ploughed on. On the day, around 100 EDL-ers assembled at Blackhorse Road, surrounded by hundreds of police from around ten forces. All this for 100, out-of-town racists, was an overriding feeling. Hundreds of police also gathered where UAF held a protest; policing was heavy-handed and intimidating ... EDL were glad to get out of the area; their rally was a farce, and ended early. They left, with E17 anti-fascists giving them a large flea in their ears. UAF, locally, in three weeks, assembled around 800 anti-fascists.

What broke the EDL was the mobilizations by black and Asian communities backed up by the power of the trade unions. The EDL was broken in Tower Hamlets and Walthamstow because UAF was successful in pulling this alliance together. We were also able to break the EDL ideologically. When the EDL appeared, it was described as a 'protest movement of the working class'. But it was the working-class movement that broke it.

In early 2015, Pegida UK was formed, as a British extension of the German anti-Muslim movement Pegida that was set up in October 2014. UAF observed:

> The far right and outright fascists in Germany have for some time been looking to forge ahead on the back of Islamophobia. October 2014, for instance, the HoGeSa, Hooligans against Salafists, marched with around 5,000 neo-Nazis and racists in Cologne … In Dresden, from where Pegida formed, a number of weekly demos were held. Pegida was at pains to appear respectable and initially tried to claim they were not neo-Nazis or anything like that. Those unhappy with their lot in Germany and those alienated from official politics made up much of the mobilizations. The Pegida leadership looked to turn such feeling against migrants and refugees. Their largest demo saw over 20,000 march in Cologne …

Pegida suffered a big blow when their founder, Lutz Bachmann, resigned after posting a photo of himself as Hitler, with the words 'He's back' underneath. 'Anti-fascists were very successful in creating the tensions inside Pegida that saw neo-Nazis split away from the more populist, AfD types (akin to UKIP),' commented UAF. 'For now, Pegida is a shadow of what it ominously could have been. But, in Germany, as across Europe, forces exist which aim to capitalize on Islamophobia and anti-immigration.'

Pegida UK is a loose aggregate of ultra-nationalists, Loyalists and white supremacists. As EDL activists reveal, Pegida UK's activists come primarily from splinter groups such as Northwest Infidels and Northeast Infidels. In February 2015, Pegida UK held their first national demonstration in Newcastle. 'UAF, as part of Newcastle Unites, spent several weeks leafleting, holding meetings, having big stalls around Newcastle, working with football fans, Show Racism the Red Card, musicians and more, to try to ensure that the first attempt of these bigots would be well opposed,' said Paul Sillett of UAF. 'On the day itself, a magnificent 3,000 marched with Newcastle Unites/UAF, to where the bigots were. It was Newcastle at its best. In contrast, Pegida UK wilted. They had no more than 250 ... Again, the strategy of broadly mobilizing against such far-right filth worked.'*

---

* UAF observed Pegida UK's latest activities: 'Pegida UK promised that their next demo, scheduled for March [2015], in Edinburgh, would see lessons learnt. They weren't. UAF and others weren't sure what to expect on this one. We guessed that the small Scottish Defence League and some Loyalists would attend but few thought that Pegida UK would muck it up in the manner they did. They said they hoped "several hundred would gather", in the nation's capital. It was clear they were in trouble as just the day before their demo, they were reduced to appealing to "anyone who can make it" to come to Edinburgh. It smacked of desperation. The day itself was a farce, even worse than Newcastle. Just four, or six, if you are generous, made it to their pitch, and for about five minutes. Over 150 anti-fascists demonstrated and celebrated Pegida's effective non-appearance ... Foolishly, the goons said they were going ahead with their London demo, which took place on the Easter Bank Holiday weekend. It seemed that Pegida UK were gluttons for punishment, and were unwise in not taking time to assess their weaknesses. Could it be third time unlucky for the latest fascists to appear ... It was indeed third time unlucky, as events unfolded ...The call went out and on the day, over 300 anti-fascists assembled and barracked the seventy or so goons, who supported Pegida UK ... This was their third fail in three months ... Many of us thought it had been a good three months' worth of work in not being complacent about such efforts to transport the Pegida brand here. Though as some old sweats said, "Not the cleverest thing to do, calling your movement by an overseas name; British fascists don't always like that" ... No one knew if Pegida UK would spark a fire and it was right to take their efforts seriously. We had learnt some lessons from isolating and cutting down the BNP/EDL and tried to put these into practice here, e.g. the attempt to summon and work with wide forces of people open to anti-fascism. It is clear that Pegida UK are licking their wounds and have not called any more demos since their failure in London. No doubt they may seek to venture forth again, but they are their own worst enemies and have little strategic or tactical nous ... The coalitions UAF and others drew on for support still exist and will be essential if Pegida UK attempt a comeback.'

Meanwhile, large sections of the social base of the far right are looking to the more mainstream UKIP to voice their concerns. This was clearly shown in the European parliamentary and local elections of May 2014 as well as the general election of May 2015, in which many of UKIP's votes came from former BNP voters and EDL and Britain First activists and followers. Despite its populist face, UKIP's politics bear similarities to and share substantial common ground with the traditional far right in targeting specific ethnic/national groups in society. According to Raphaël Liogier, a professor of sociology and philosophy and director of the Observatoire des Religions (Observatory of Religious Phenomenon), UKIP's is a populism where 'people become fiction'. It employs the same kind of 'collective emotion' common in the mobilization of the far right. UKIP has seemingly effortlessly secured solid support from the traditional far right. Everyone I've met in the EDL has voted UKIP. Chris, for instance, an activist of EDL's London Division, whom I met on the Lee Rigby Memorial March, told me that he provided administrative help to the English Democrats during the elections and voted for UKIP as his only political alternative.

Throughout my research, it was clear to me that the scope of racism and Islamophobia goes well beyond the far right street scene. Spinwatch, which investigates and campaigns on PR, propaganda and lobbying in politics, is currently investigating the anti-Muslim racism and counter-jihad movement that operates within the British establishment. Through Spinwatch's brilliant research, David Miller, its co-founder and professor of sociology at the University of Bath, argues that the most dangerous Islamophobia is practised by the state and its institutions.

The anti-Muslim racism isn't happening only on the streets. It's also propagated in Britain's political institutions,* such as the House of Lords. EDL supporter Alan Lake, associated with UKIP's former leader Lord Pearson, attempted to help Pearson bring Dutch MP Geert Wilders to the House of Lords to screen his racist, anti-Muslim film *Fitna* in February 2009. Their project finally succeeded, when Baroness Caroline Cox hosted the film screening in 2010 and launched Sharia Watch UK at the House of Lords. Journalist and campaigner Hilary Aked has examined Sharia Watch UK, founded in April 2014 by Anne Marie Waters, and concluded that it is ideologically no different to far-right groups such as the EDL and Britain First. Anne Marie Waters, who joined UKIP in May 2014 and stood as the party's candidate for Basildon and Billericay, works closely with European counter-jihad movements to promote anti-Muslim racism across Europe. Her Sharia Watch UK has gained much credibility from media coverage, e.g. in the *Daily Mail* and the *Sunday Telegraph*.

Since then, Anne Marie Waters appears to have been deselected as a UKIP candidate for reasons unknown, although remaining a party member. Hilary Aked wrote in January 2015:

> Her [Anne Marie Waters'] anti-Islam radicalisation provides supporting evidence for the claim that UKIP is 'a party of Islamophobes' (an allegation made by one Labour MP after former UKIP leader Lord Pearson, who co-hosted the screening of *Fitna* with Cox, said that Muslims needed

---

* See www.opendemocracy.net/opensecurity/david-miller-tom-mills-hilary-aked-narzanin-massoumi/five-pillars-of-islamophobia.

to 'address the violence in the Qur'an'). Other top party personnel including Gerard Batten and Magnus Nielsen have counterjihad links too, and in the days after the Paris attacks, Nigel Farage himself used rhetoric reminiscent of the far-right movement, talking of 'fifth columns', 'Judeo-Christian heritage' and Muslim 'no go areas'. It is clear that UKIP, like Pegida, contains deep wellsprings of anti-Muslim, as well as anti-immigrant hostility.

In the past few years, under Farage, UKIP has made considerable advances in British politics, electorally and ideologically. Its anti-immigration agenda has influenced and been incorporated into the policies of the coalition government as well as into the day-to-day language of a large part of the British media. The enemy is now migrants from Romania and Bulgaria, the new outsiders to the British nationalist dream. In early 2013, and throughout 2014, Romanians and Bulgarians became the focus of a national discourse on the negative impact of immigration. The number game once more dominated, in spite of the evidence. Between 2004 and 2011, 1.32 million migrants arrived in the UK while 644,000 people who were born in the EU left during the same period, according to the *Guardian*. In 2011, Britain took in 566,044 EU nationals, but 350,703 EU nationals emigrated. According to the Office for National Statistics (ONS), the number of Romanian and Bulgarian nationals working in Britain in fact fell in the first three months after work restrictions were lifted in January 2014, and the number has only slightly increased since. Also, there have been 60,000 fewer temporary workers from these two countries since 2014, owing to the closure of the Seasonal Agricultural Workers Scheme. Yet they continue to be singled out as the most important new threat to British employment and way of life.

UKIP has been making an impact in both traditionally Labour and Conservative-voting areas, including some where the party had never previously had a presence. In 2010, UKIP won second place with more than 18 per cent of the vote in three local by-elections in Labour seats in Rotherham, South Shields and Wythenshawe and Sale East, and won by more than 10 per cent in Barnsley Central and Middlesbrough. In 2013, UKIP made substantial gains in local elections across the country, in a year hailed by Nigel Farage as a 'game changer'. Again, UKIP's victory came in traditionally Conservative county councils, while it has also won votes in traditional Labour areas. In May, UKIP won over 140 seats and averaged 25 per cent of the vote in the county councils where it was standing. It came third in the national share of votes. In another clear indication of its growing influence in politics, it secured seventeen council seats in Kent, sixteen in Lincolnshire and fifteen in Norfolk.

UKIP also made huge progress in Hampshire for the first time. In June 2013, a council by-election in Southampton saw UKIP posing a substantial challenge to Labour. In Southampton's Woolston ward, UKIP won 731 votes as compared to Labour's 864 (33 per cent), a decline from 1,607 votes (55 per cent) the previous year. In Newcastle's council by-election in June, the same pattern occurred. In its Walkergate ward, UKIP won 668 votes as compared to Labour's 1,080 votes (44 per cent), a decline from 1,912 votes (68 per cent) the previous year. In these seats, the share of votes among the major three parties has fallen from 95 per cent in 2012 to 65 per cent in 2013, with UKIP being the overwhelming beneficiary.

In Eastleigh, political influence has also turned in UKIP's favour since 2013. In Bishopstoke & Fair Oak, UKIP won 1,824 votes, ahead of the Lib Dems' 1,657; in Eastleigh East, UKIP gained 1,609 votes, compared to the Lib Dems at 1,440; in Eastleigh West, UKIP won 1,604 votes, again ahead of the Lib Dems at 1,533. And in February 2013, Eastleigh saw its former Lib Dem mayor (2003/04), Glynn Davies-Dear, tear up his party membership card, calling the party deceitful to its electorate and then defecting to UKIP. Since then, he has become UKIP's main man in Eastleigh.

The South East, the UK's largest electoral region with a population of over 8,500,000, is now a growing stronghold for UKIP. Nigel Farage has been an MEP for the South East for more than ten years. He was first elected here for UKIP in 1999, and since then the party's share of the vote has gone up to 19 per cent, with two out of the ten MEP seats in the region allocated to his party.

In spring 2014, as UKIP launched its European election campaign with a £1.5 million billboard anti-immigration campaign, it pulled in the support base of far-right parties and groups, i.e. the BNP, the EDL and Britain First, to rally behind its cause. UKIP's Neil Hamilton openly said that his party attracts 'decent BNP voters', referring to those who voted BNP in the 2009 European elections, as they 'feel swamped by immigrants'. Nick Griffin, meanwhile, accused Nigel Farage of stealing his party's rhetoric and called him a racist because 'he didn't discriminate against foreigners equally'. In May, as the party that was given the largest amount of media coverage, UKIP stormed to victory in the European elections, taking 27.5 per cent of the votes and winning twenty-three MEP seats, ahead of Labour's 25.4 per cent and eighteen MEP seats.

During the same ballot, UKIP also did extremely well in the local elections, taking 17 per cent of the national vote, behind Labour (31 per cent) and the Conservatives (29 per cent). Significantly, it turned the tide in traditionally Labour areas. In Rotherham, out of the twenty-one seats on the Labour council, ten were taken by UKIP.

In the South East, Eastleigh is considered UKIP's heartland, the place Farage regards as 'home territory'. His party campaigned for all of the fifteen Eastleigh Borough Council seats being contested in May 2014, in a chamber where one third of the incumbents are Liberal Democrats. Farage himself stood as a parliamentary candidate there in 1994. Although eventually the split of votes led to no seats for UKIP in May 2014, the number of votes was high enough not to be ignored.

Well before the elections, the growing influence of the far right could be felt among Eastleigh's communities. For a hundred years, the town was known as a railway town, being a hub of the railway industry in southern England. In the early twentieth century, Eastleigh was the centre of the locomotive industry, which employed nearly 3,000 people at its peak. The town suffered from the decline of the industry after the Second World War and the era officially came to an end with the closure of the depot in 2006, with further job losses. The death of the railway industry took away the soul of the place, and its 'nothingness' has been repeatedly described by visitors.

'The town itself is so characterless it is almost notable,' said Ian Dunt, editor of politics.co.uk, in February 2013. 'It is entirely without qualities. Most places have at least one spot which make them look passable, but Eastleigh is universally dull. It is not even really ugly. It is nondescript; shattered by the war and then by the decline of the railway industry.'

But I was more surprised when local residents talked the same way about their own town. 'It's dead,' several people said to me. 'All the main industries are gone. It's got nothing here now.' It seems that people are looking to understand and relate to that void.

In spring 2014, when I visited, many in the ethnic minority communities, tiny as they are in Eastleigh, were concerned about the rise of political forces like UKIP. Running away from its influence didn't seem an option, and some were looking to enter into dialogue with it, so as to try to 'contain' it. I attended a local forum meeting where activists from all communities discussed race crimes and racism in the area.

Glynn Davies-Dear, chair of the UKIP Eastleigh branch, was invited to address the audience and explain his new allegiance. He had defected from the Liberal Democrats because he claimed the party members were corrupt and 'a bunch of liars'. He attempted to address the public perception of his new party. 'You may have this idea of UKIP as racially orientated party dedicated to turning things into the early 1950s ...' he said. 'I am myself a second-generation Welsh immigrant and I can tell you that UKIP is by no means racist.'

He then read out a list of local ethnic minority groups that he has associated with. He also took out UKIP membership forms and started to pass round the party constitution which stated, 'Former-BNP and EDL members are not allowed to join UKIP'.

I met with local activists Denis Wong, chair of the Eastleigh Race Equality Forum, Margaret Raff, a Labour campaigner, and Ian Bryan, a visiting fellow at the Faculty of Social and Human Sciences, University of Southampton, to ask them about the context in which UKIP seemed to be gaining a foothold in Eastleigh. 'UKIP came second in the Wythenshawe by-election [in 2013], not far from where I was born and grew up,' said Denis Wong. 'Their presence does make a difference and creates a climate of fear amongst Eastleigh's communities.'

Ian Bryan described the sentiment among many middle-aged working-class men in the area: 'There is an unfocused, generalized frustration, combined with nostalgic nationalism … about a past that Britain once was … and the kind of jobs that their parents had, which were jobs for life, good old skilled, working-class stock … Given those jobs are gone now and given they're squeezed between not having what their parents had and also worrying about their kids … you can see where they might be turning …' But here, as Ian explained, there isn't much of a culture of 'street militancy', represented by football hooliganism, for instance, among the working class that could develop that frustration into a desire to join the ranks of far-right groups like the EDL or the BNP. Margaret believes that UKIP offers a very simple message with which disenfranchised people can easily identify. 'Huge levels of poverty and a widening wealth gap is the background,' she said.

Local activist views fit in with what I saw later. The main basis for UKIP support is the manufacturing working class, although that base is not a secure one and their votes could return to Labour when times change. Matthew Goodwin and Robert Ford argue in their book *Revolt on the Right*: 'One of the biggest myths in British politics is that UKIP is winning support mainly from disgruntled middle-class Tories who care only about leaving the EU.' They rightly argue that 'Nigel Farage and his followers are drawing their strength from the left-behind in modern Britain: old, financially disadvantaged, blue-collar, low-qualified and angry voters marginalised by the country's post-1970s economic transformation and cut out of the political conversation by the new focus on middle-class swing votes'. Indeed, UKIP is not a second home for Eurosceptic Tories. It's in fact becoming 'a first home for the angry left-behind electorate, many of who have been the hardest hit by the economic crisis and austerity'. Results in both the 2014 local election and the 2015 general election made this clear. In the latter case, UKIP came second in a large number of safe Labour seats in the North and in Wales.

Former Labour MP Geoff Hoon commented after the General Election: 'The big change in 2015 was therefore that Ukip, previously seen as a fringe or protest party, was setting out exactly what the socially conservative unskilled working class wanted to hear. No more immigration, leave the EU, cut back on benefits for foreigners. Everyone who has ever knocked on doors for Labour has heard those views from Labour supporters at every election ...'

I visited the Velmore estates, known as traditional Labour territory in Eastleigh. They also have another name locally, the 'drug den', the most run-down part of town. Just by stopping any passers-by on the estates, you'll hear anger and frustration from working-class residents, either in low-paid jobs or long-term unemployment. They are furious at the cuts under both Labour and coalition governments, and see no way out of their miserable situation. Six out of ten residents I spoke to came straight to the conclusion that immigration is the problem and UKIP would be their electoral choice.

However, a higher number of people, despite sympathy for UKIP's politics, said they 'couldn't be bothered to vote'. As I walked past a row of council flats, a man of around forty was sitting on a bench outside, his dog beside him. He looked vacant when I tried to ask him questions, as if he hadn't heard me. Eventually he told me his name was Steve, and he had been unemployed for years. 'I wouldn't vote,' he said, without any expression on his face. 'I used to vote Labour, then switched to Tories, and then back to Labour again. Since the last time I voted Labour, I've given up voting.'

There are many like Steve who feel totally alienated from mainstream politics and have given up attempting to make an electoral choice. In despair, they turn to UKIP. At the same time, despair also means that they don't feel the need to act or to take part in elections and go out to vote. Steve said he doesn't disagree with what UKIP says, but he doesn't want to support them by voting, either. 'It doesn't matter to me,' he said, looking into the distance.

His neighbour upstairs expressed a similar total apathy. He is forty-three and has two children, and has been on the dole since he was made jobless as an engineer six years ago. 'I was laid off from Wessex Engineering, along with fifty others ...' he said, still shivering with anger. 'The company contract was given to cheaper labour abroad, I'm sure.'

Since then, he has suffered from depression and anxiety, and has taken to heavy drinking. His breath smelt of alcohol and I guessed he had been drinking already. It was three o'clock in the afternoon. His eyes were bloodshot and exhausted.

'Are you looking for work at the moment?' I asked.

'Look at me,' he said, pointing to his swollen eyes. 'I'm not fit to work.'

I asked who he would vote for.

'Never again,' he replied simply. 'I think what UKIP says is right. But I won't vote.'

'Why not?'

'Elections don't do nothing for you,' he said.

Farther down the road, I met Joyce Kemb, who told me she'd been a Labour voter all her life. But as we spoke, she was wavering between Labour and UKIP. 'I sympathize with some of what UKIP says, like immigration. I also don't like it when Muslims don't fit in with this country's culture and rules ...' Joyce is a pensioner living on her own. Her two sons are in Lincolnshire and she rarely sees them. Given that she lives alone with limited economic resources, her sense of security and well-being has been challenged over the years.

As our conversation continued, Joyce seemed to soften her views and became uncertain about her previous statements about immigration. 'I know that Britain needs immigration ... My twenty-two-year-old grandson would never take up those jobs that migrants are doing in Lincolnshire; you know, farm work, etc. It's just too tough for him.'

She said: 'This area is mainly Labour and Lib Dem, but some people are changing their mind ... and are likely to go for UKIP, mainly because of immigration and work, although many still vote Labour as a habit.'

Back in town, I met a local man named Gary Harper, in his forties. He is unemployed owing to illness. He seemed certain he wouldn't vote UKIP, although he understood why and how it became the choice for many around here. 'Eastleigh has always been open to diversity and never had a problem with immigration until recently ... In Eastleigh, unemployment has been caused by the closure of major industries, particularly the railway and the Fords. The railway closure led to at least 8,000 losing their jobs. The town has gone downhill since ... UKIP offers a false solution.'

As a result of the decline of industries, unemployment is the town's biggest problem. It is also one of the issues that UKIP has used to attract support, despite the fact that unemployment preceded any significant migration from eastern Europe.

Gary said his two sons are fortunate enough to have work, one of them as a plumber. Many young people, though, have left the town as a result of the lack of options. Some have migrated north, to work in the construction industry, for example. Others have gone abroad. 'I would say to young people that they should leave Eastleigh because there's no work and no future here,' he said, shaking his head.

Gary invited me to come along to one of his weekly meetings with members of the Eastleigh Workers Club, to which he belongs. He does this to catch up with old friends. As this was a Labour club, I expected to meet solid Labour supporters, i.e. working-class men and women from traditional Labour-voting families.

Indeed, they were all born-and-bred Labour supporters. However, at least half of the club's members (between 500 and 800) are now UKIP voters. The first man to approach Gary to say hello was Andrew, a UKIP voter. He didn't hesitate to tell me that he supports Farage and his politics. He said immigration and employment are the key issues that have driven him to support the party.

'But immigration is not even visible in your town,' I said.

Andrew frowned, disagreeing. 'Eastern Europeans are concentrated in Shirley, called Little Poland in Southampton, and some have moved down here.' He feels the pressure of competition from the incomers.

'They're bound to get a council house before me,' he said anxiously.

However, the fact is that very few migrants from eastern Europe live in council housing. Most of them rent privately and share their accommodation with fellow migrants to lower the costs.

Gary said he himself was surprised to see the change of views among the club's members. He never expected this. Their support for UKIP is motivated by a combination of opposition to the EU and immigration.

Just then, another member, Steve, with heavy tattoos on both his arms, arrived. He stood and listened to our conversation, and echoed Andrew's views about immigration. He comes from a Labour family and was brought up to detest Thatcher. 'Thatcher got in when I was nine. My mum was telling me about it when it was on television. She said Thatcher took away everything from the working class. I was too young to understand it all … But later I worked it out for myself …'

But Steve never did work it out. Over the years, he only grew to feel a sense of betrayal by the political elite. He felt a nobody, never listened to. That changed when he watched UKIP on television. 'It used to be always depressing to watch politics … But watching UKIP gave me a sense of hope … At least someone's thinking about us.'

He then looked at me and asked: 'Are you from a privileged background back home?'

'No,' I answered. It was too long a story to tell. Although my parents are middle class, I've practically 'declassed' myself by migrating to Britain, and had to start from zero after graduating. Those first years seeking suitable employment and a secure roof over my head were the toughest I've ever experienced. Back in 1992, my first job in Britain was serving cream tea at a seaside resort. At one point, in 1993, I had to do voluntary work in order to get free accommodation in London. At times I couldn't afford to pay the bills. Building a new life as an outsider to this country wasn't at all easy, but at this point I did not expect Steve to understand.

'If you're working-class, then you'll understand what I'm talking about,' he said.

I listened, not knowing how to respond. I recognize this strong sense of class and class betrayal. The problem is with the analysis that follows. Steve isn't pointing fingers at employers and the bankers, but the few eastern European migrants, a rare enough sight on the streets of Eastleigh, who come to earn a few pounds per hour to feed their families back home.

There is a significant overlap in the support bases for UKIP and those traditionally known as the far right. Followers of the

EDL and the BNP, for instance, tend strongly to vote UKIP, often perceived as the only realistic option available to them. The BNP collapse in the May elections of 2014 was proof enough. Andrew told me he knows that EDL activists in Hampshire vote UKIP. Steve nodded, and added that, although their support base overlaps, UKIP isn't the same as the BNP. 'UKIP are professional politicians whereas the BNP has a lot of thugs and people like that,' he said.

Another club member, Chris, agreed. He's a self-employed window cleaner. He used to be a Labour man, but is now behind UKIP, particularly on immigration. 'I'm so fed up with the lot of them, I just thought, what could be worse? Why not give them [UKIP] a chance?'

I asked him how immigration affects him. 'Have you been out of work?' I asked.

'No, I've always had work since sixteen. But the Polish come here and start doing cleaning; I don't want competition,' he said.

'But as you're experienced, you haven't lost work,' I said.

'Yeah ... but there are so many of them here. When I walked down East Street in Southampton, I was the only English there. They [immigrants] done me no harm. My kids got jobs, touch wood, one of them is a chippie, the other one is an engineer. But other people ain't ...'

This feeling of fear and threat from 'outsiders' originates from deeply insecure economic circumstances where job security becomes history and casualization in the labour market becomes the norm. Chris said some of his friends who worked in the Ford factory had been laid off. Since then, they've been doing casual jobs around town. 'All that the companies are doing now is to get part-timers in, two hours here and four hours there; there're no full-time jobs any more. You've got people with four jobs ...'

Some of the other members of the Eastleigh Workers Club were laid off from Ford, too. Martin is one of them. He introduced himself with confidence as a UKIP voter. He sat down for a beer, and told me that he was made redundant by Ford in August 2013. He had worked there as a forklift driver for ten years. As he was on contract, he received only £10,000 as severance. He was one of the longest-serving contract staff, and some staff didn't even get that money. Prior to Ford, Martin worked on the railways for fifteen years, but he lost that job as the railway industry closed down.

'I've always worked in my life ... Now I've walked around and there's no jobs,' Martin said, angrily. 'Only working on zero hours – that means I'm struggling to pay my bills. I don't sign on, and my savings have dwindled ...' I looked at this frail-looking man and wondered what life has done to him. I had also had my financial struggles. I also know what it feels like to not know what the next week will bring.

Since 2008, 80 per cent of all jobs being advertised in the UK are zero-hours contracts. According to the Office for National Statistics, at the end of April 2014 there were 1.4 million workers on these contracts in Britain. Unite the Union estimates the figure to be closer to 5.5 million. Under the coalition government's 'welfare reforms', jobseekers who refuse zero-hours contracts face a temporary benefits ban. This is a situation destined to trap even more workers in low-paid, casual employment.

For Martin, low-paid and casual employment seems the only option.

I see my job [at Ford] goes to Turkey, paid for by the EU. Ford relocated with the money from Brussels and the British government. They've been knocking it down in the last five years ... My dad used to work for them in the 1970s ... They employed nearly 3,000 men. Now it was down to 500 men, and just before the credit crunch, they made one shift redundant and just ran on one shift ... And slowly that went, too. Around 2,000 people lost jobs alongside me. I know people who are still struggling for work, like me. And those who have got work are on a very low rate of pay. It's anything, construction work or anything they could get.

Since last August, Martin's been given only six weeks' work.

I go to the jobcentre each day ... The government made it so awkward. There's no help there. They might send you off for an hour a week on a computer somewhere ... I'm sixty and it takes a bit longer for me. So I stopped signing on and am living on my savings ... My children are all grown-ups now and I don't have to support anyone, but I have to support the rich running the gas, electricity and water companies for their big fat cheques ... If I don't pay my bills, they switch me off, and I'll end up with a court order. [I'm on] £6 an hour. I'm bloody sixty. I used to be on £12 an hour ... The rate has come down so low. People are struggling, on zero hours, and some of them are married and have families ... and they can't get a mortgage. This government loves it.

Martin's deep anger turned to bitterness and despair. It was then he began to feel threatened by those visibly different. 'Just before Christmas, I was working for an agency outside of Eastleigh … a small factory unit … When I went into the common room to have my sandwich, not a word of English was being spoken in there … They were all Polish. And I felt really uncomfortable … Not intimidated, but just didn't want to sit there. So I walked out and sat outside to have my sandwiches … And I hear that there's another million coming over … from Spain and Portugal because their countries are in dire straits … They're coming over to look for work.'

Of course, 'another million coming over' was a story manufactured by the popular media. It tapped into Martin's bitterness and offered him an effortless analysis of a difficult situation.

'There's no work. The door's got to shut and I'm voting UKIP,' he said firmly.

Then he shook his head, again and again. 'I've always been a Labour voter; I'm a working-class man. But since Tony Blair's New Labour, I became fed up with them … It's not a working-class party any more. The Tories are for the rich, and the Liberals would sleep with anyone; we've got no one. UKIP's offering a solution at the moment. I'm not saying they could run the country. But what I do know is they're saying what needs to be said.'

'There's nothing here now,' Martin carried on. 'A bit of service industry, construction and that, and nothing else. Twenty years ago this town was vibrant. A lot of work here. You had the railway works that employed thousands of men … The railway was owned by British people and they sold it off … All good jobs were gone.'

However, Martin has chosen to lay the blame for the decline of industries on the tiniest wave of migration into Eastleigh in recent years.

'It used to be a nice town. You walk around Eastleigh today, you see that immigrants are slowly coming here. It's full of outsiders ... It just feels like I'm an alien in my own land. Under a British government, you can't even say you're English ... When I applied for a job, I put down "English" and got pulled up for that. They said I can't say that.'

'When did you begin to feel like this? Feeling "English"?' I asked.

'It's been a slow process, I suppose ... At the beginning of the recession, a lot of people were losing their houses, good people. I saw UKIP come and stand up and say what we needed to say ... that was four years ago when they had an office down the road ... The press ... it's like a witch-hunt ... Every day you read in the press about UKIP, but you don't hear about the other three parties when they wiped their noses in a trough, robbing the taxpayers ...'

I followed Gary and talked to more local workers later that afternoon. Only one man among the many I spoke to that day said he disagreed with UKIP politics. His name was Dan. He works as a builder in town, born into a Labour-voting family; even he has given up voting and stopped believing in electoral politics years ago. Disillusionment, however, has not led him rightwards. 'I don't feel threatened by eastern European workers at all,' he said calmly. 'UKIP's talk about immigration is misleading. No one's talking about emigration from Britain. If British people can move wherever they want, why can't people from other countries come here?'

Nigel Farage was coming to town, they said. He was going to hold a public meeting in Eastleigh with another UKIP candidate, Diane James, two days before the European parliamentary and local elections of May 2014. That evening, there were around 200 UKIP activists and supporters gathering at the town's leisure centre. Morale was high, as if to defy Farage's recent bad press.

Many have travelled from outside of Eastleigh to support the party. Scott Cross, for instance, was an activist from North Bordon, East Hampshire. He was a librarian all his life, and now, since retirement, has devoted all his time to campaigning for UKIP. He voted for the Conservatives and Labour in the past, but now supports UKIP because of their position on the EU and immigration. Like most others in the party, he says UKIP is not against immigration, but just wants it controlled.

As we sat waiting for Farage, a man next to me began to talk. He was probably wondering why a foreign-looking person like me would be sitting here. His name was Paul Cadier, UKIP branch secretary in Romsey, a small Hampshire market town seven miles north-west of Southampton. He told me that Romsey has just under a hundred activists and most branches in the region are made up of similar numbers. UKIP has a membership of 38,000 in total, he told me proudly. 'We have 1,000 new members every ten days,' he said.

Paul Cadier came to Eastleigh to help out with the local election campaign. Eastleigh is home to a couple of hundred of activists, he said, and the number is likely to grow. Cadier himself joined UKIP in 2006, and has been active for two years. What he has found most noticeable is the growing number of working-class supporters who used to vote Labour. 'People who support us in working-class areas are those who say their children can't get work ... and two parents who are working full-time but they're not earning enough to keep their heads above water. They're not interested in whether we're racist and what the press says about us.'

Cadier campaigned for UKIP in Southampton, where immigration is the major issue among the white British electorate. 'It is the first thing people want to talk to us about at their doorstep,' he said.

It never used to be a big issue in UKIP because at the time there weren't that many eastern Europeans coming in. A Polish or Bulgarian person can earn four times as much just by moving to this country ... and you can't blame them because they are poor countries. If I were unlucky enough to be born in East Germany or Poland, I would have gone on the first bus to go to West Germany or Britain. This is a sensible thing to do. The problem is, can the host country accommodate such large numbers of people? I'm campaigning in the Flower Road section of Southampton, a particularly run-down area, and there are no Conservatives here but Labour and Lib Dems ... Quite a lot of Labour voters have turned to UKIP, as they feel they've been let down.

There are large numbers of eastern Europeans here. If you're Polish, you can almost get by without learning English. This is in contrast with the Commonwealth migrants, for instance from places like Uganda in the 1970s ... The Ugandan Asians set up corner-shop businesses

that continued to open after five p.m. ... They provided
a service which had never been provided before. They
created employment and didn't put any British people on
the dole ... Unfortunately the system we have now in the
UK discriminates against Commonwealth citizens in favour
of Europeans ... We're not against migration but welcome
people to come in when there are actually shortages and
when there isn't enough local workers to do the job ...

In other words, the managed migration system UKIP argues
for is a rigid Australian-style points-based system in which the
number would be determined by assessed needs of British
industries. Attributes like language proficiency and cultural
affinity become part of the process of determining who is 'good
for Britain' and who is unwanted. The idea of managed migration
proposed by UKIP is in fact not very different from what we've
had under New Labour – and what Blairites are proposing now*
– and the Conservatives, but merely amplified.

Thirty years ago, Cadier became a decorator. He became
self-employed during the Thatcher years when he heard
Norman Tebbit saying, 'We should all go out there, get on our
bike, and if we can't find a job, then become self-employed.'
He acted on that piece of advice, and set up a business together
with a friend. 'This Thatcherite stuff actually worked for me
... I ended up earning a decent living, buying my own house
... What the politicians said actually worked for me. So I got
interested in politics.'

---

* See report at www.independent.co.uk/news/uk/politics/liz-kendall-says-she-
wants-an-australianstyle-pointsbased-immigration-system-10328214.html.

But the Thatcherite dream turned out, in later years, to cause a nightmare for Cadier. The unregulated industries such as construction are where local workers suffer the most, as a result of the prevalence of casualized, cheap labour under the disguise of self-employment, which really only benefits employers. Construction bosses looked around and saw an exploitable workforce in the migrants who are new to Britain's employment laws and who are not protected. They become a target for abuse and exploitation, and are subjected to lax health and safety enforcement and low wages, in the name of the 'self-made, self-employed'. In these circumstances, both migrant and local workers are victimized.

Being at the front line, some local workers can easily put the blame at the feet of foreign colleagues in the same trade. Cadier said: 'I had competition from self-employed people from the mainland of Europe who were paying themselves less than the minimum wage ... so they could undercut my prices by two-thirds. I got my customers coming to me and showing me the quotes, saying if I could come close to the quote [offered by cheaper, self-employed migrants], they'd give me the work ... I said to him, I can't afford to work on those terms. I got to earn enough to pay my mortgage.'

Cadier escaped the hell of self-employment in the British construction trade by migrating to Italy for decorating work. Ironically, he was soon faced with local hostility which resembled the resentment against eastern European workers in similar trades in Britain, the only difference being that Cadier was actually paid a lot more than the local Italian workers. 'You'd better pack your bag and leave now,' an angry Italian decorator once said to him in Italian. Cadier's employer had to buy him an expensive bottle of wine to keep him at work.

Eventually, as he became a relatively successful self-employed decorator, he decided to join UKIP, believing it was the party to protect small businesses, in contrast to the Tory support for big corporations. Cadier said: 'We've got capitalism for the poor, and for the rich we have golden parachutes, bonuses, and if their enterprises fail, the poor taxpayers like people on Flower Estate will have to pay. If you think that is right-wing, then I'm a Chinaman.'

It became clear to me in my time researching this book that, although UKIP is primarily a party for the entrepreneurs and not for the working class, and in fact puts forward policies that would impact negatively on working-class people, it has been immensely successful in its use of populist, emotive language that evokes working-class concerns. In the 2015 general election, while the Conservatives took over Eastleigh, UKIP came third, above Labour (UKIP won 8,783 votes, 15.8 per cent, above Labour's 7,181 or 12.9 per cent). Amplifying a racism that has already become acceptable in mainstream politics (mainly in the form of anti-immigration rhetoric), UKIP has managed to win the hearts and minds of many working-class people who feel like outsiders in Britain today.

The growing influence of racist ideologies has been felt in a variety of migrant and ethnic minority communities in Southampton, from where many in Eastleigh claim the effects of migration have originated. Southampton is a city that boasts a long history of immigration over a period of 500 years, from the Huguenots in the seventeenth century to the West Indians and Asians of the twentieth century and the new migrants from eastern Europe this century. The diversity of its population has grown over the years. Today, about a fifth of the city's 237,000 population was born outside the UK.

A short walk around town will instantly tell you that cultural diversity is the norm today. Shirley Road, nicknamed Little Poland and Beirut, for instance, is lined with businesses catering for the new migrant communities. The churches in this city are also a good reflection of how ethnically diverse Southampton has become. You see Filipino priests offering church services to Polish and Romanian migrants. The cosmopolitan character of the place and the abundant work opportunities have pulled in migrants from afar. Filipinos, for instance, come here to work as domestic helpers and care workers in hospitals and care homes, as well as sailors.

Father Claro V. Conde, a well-respected community activist originally from the Philippines, appreciates the diversity that brought him here. His church services have provided support, including offering shelter when needed, to many migrants to this city, not only to many in the 5,000-strong Filipino community but also to European newcomers. A third of his parish consists of Polish migrants. His church has therefore offered programmes and exchanges to welcome Polish migrants to help them settle better here. To the migrants who have suffered labour exploitation, he has not only offered them emotional support but has also referred them to trade unions.

In the past decade, however, the recession and economic downturn have contributed to a growing resentment against new migrant communities, and even ethnic minority communities that have long been part of this city's history. The non-white British population has increasingly been described with words like 'flood', despite the fact that the 2011 census still showed 'white British' to be the overwhelming majority, at 78 per cent of the city's population.

In recent years, racism has manifested itself in growing numbers of racist attacks and incidents of racial abuse. When I visited, I had my first taste of local racism from several conversations with taxi drivers who complained about the 'influx of foreigners'. The 'British jobs for British workers' rhetoric of the establishment has had an impact. For migrant workers who take up a small number of local jobs, such as the Filipinos, workplace racism, in the form of long-term racial harassment, has become a common occurrence. Worse still, there are the direct, physical racial attacks: both Polish and Chinese communities have reported increases. The London-based community activist Jabez Lam, along with Eastleigh-based Denis Wong, has worked on numerous cases of racial attacks and harassment in Southampton throughout the 2000s, the victims being mostly Chinese catering businesses and Chinese students.

And then I heard about people getting badly hurt. In February 2010, forty-one-year-old restaurant owner Mohammed Mazumder was brutally attacked, unprovoked, in Southampton, by a gang of seven white men who threatened to kill him and his family. In June 2011, a thirty-year-old Latvian man was attacked by three local white men in the city's Palmerston Park, the much-quoted site of numerous racist attacks. He was hospitalized by a deep cut to his face and bruises all over his body after being kicked and punched to the floor – again, completely unprovoked. The list of attacks goes on.

How have communities responded to the rising levels of racial hatred? What is being done about it? Activist Denis Wong and his colleagues have been doing what they can to highlight the issue and provide self-defence mechanisms via the Race Equality Forum. But he also said that, despite the impact of far-right politics, the local Chinese communities weren't responding. He feels frustrated with their attitude of indifference.

Denis identifies himself with Britain – his father originally came from Hong Kong and fought during the war for Britain – and has recently stopped defining himself as 'Chinese' because the only Chinese community organization in Southampton rejected his active approach to addressing racist attacks on Chinese students and residents, instead choosing to do nothing about it. Denis, as a result, became an 'outsider' to the community he wanted to serve. 'The Chinese community organization is there to get people to jump around in lion suits every Chinese new year ... There's not a community as such, but a huddle ... When there were many cases of race attacks, Jabez Lam who set up Minquan used to come down here a few years ago, to visit Chinese people who were attacked or had their shops attacked ... The police didn't respond properly. That was why and how Eastleigh Race Equality Forum was set up, and at the Forum we hear of and discuss race attacks in the area.'

Other migrant communities have dealt with challenges and responded to the impact of anti-immigration politics in different ways. The Polish migrant communities, for instance, have managed to build up strong community networks. Many have been living here since 2004, and they continue to offer themselves as support networks for newcomers. SOS Polonia is one such community organization. Based in the heart of Southampton, where tens of thousands of Polish migrants live and work, SOS Polonia has been the focal point of community support. The organizers say of their role: 'Migration is a leap into deep and unknown waters ... We need a safe place where we can share our knowledge and experience, drawing comfort from learning together how to live and work here peacefully and successfully.'

Barbara Storey, chair of SOS Polonia, has a motto for migrants: 'Out of traps, back on track', which says much about the struggle of Polish migrants in the past decade. 'The Poles were not well prepared at all in May 2004 when the EU was enlarged,' she said in summer 2014. 'It took us two years to manage to establish a community network ... to help people with the skills and knowledge, to stand on their own and to integrate and contribute ... to achieve financial security and to find sense of belonging in this country.'

Life can be isolating abroad and migrants often have to find their own ways to survive adversity. Barbara knows this well from the disadvantaged Polish migrants she's offered help to, particularly those who lost jobs and therefore their accommodation, which came as part of their work package, making them homeless. Barbara held back her tears as she remembered the twenty-five-year-old Polish man who took his own life at the end of an unbearable time spent homeless on Britain's streets.

David used to come to us a lot. I knew him for about a year. When he committed suicide, they rescued him and he was in a coma. His dad came to us and I went with him to the hospital to see his son. That day, the doctor came to the room and switched the life-support machine off. He said David would still be alive for fifteen to twenty minutes. David's father ran away. We couldn't find him. I was left alone in the room with David. The doctor asked me if I wanted to stay in the room. I said yes. Maybe he could still hear something, I thought, so I stayed. 'Don't worry,' I said to David, 'you're going somewhere nice and all your trouble will be over.' I prayed in Polish, and sang a song, a lullaby in Polish, for him. Later, his dad wanted to see where he committed suicide. So we went to this park with him. Horrible place, a place where some homeless people stayed. David hung himself there.

Barbara continued to offer support to homeless Polish men in Southampton. Sometimes she visited them in the car park where they slept. She led twenty of them to the Majesty Church, which provides care for the homeless, and as a result they managed to get off the streets. One day, they came to her office and offered her £5 from each of them, as a thank-you gesture. 'I was moved to tears, and yet they were so apologetic about the amount of money they tried to give me,' she said.

Barbara said that Polish Roma are the most victimized among Polish migrants, which keeps them in an extreme poverty trap. Many of them have had to rely on casual employment and the charity of community groups like SOS Polonia to survive. Gosia is one of the few who got out of that trap. She used to live on the streets with her family when she was a child. Now she's married with two children and working as a part-time dance teacher at SOS Polonia, for £15 per hour.

Although she's no longer homeless, Gosia has never forgotten the Polish Roma families she used to know that are still living on the streets. She and her husband often make sandwiches and hand them out to those families. Every time Barbara holds an event at SOS Polonia, she always remembers to take the food leftovers and bring them to Gosia for her to distribute among the homeless Roma families.

Over the years, SOS Polonia has given emotional and economic support to Polish migrants who have been subjected to abuse and exploitation at work in Hampshire's farms and factories. I have many times seen Barbara and her colleagues listening and talking to Polish men and women who come through the door to ask for advice and help, to challenge their abusive employers.

Most Polish migrants either work antisocial hours and have little time to learn English, or cannot afford English lessons. SOS Polonia has filled the gap by offering low-cost language learning. Barbara said: 'The British encourage all migrants to speak English and we took it seriously. We accept the challenge and try to do it ourselves ... It was very moving to see people working hard all night and still have the energy to come to our "English for survival" lessons in the morning ... At that stage, we had help from our Romanian friends who acted as our trustees advising us. We had Laura teaching English here, a Romanian migrant teaching English to Polish migrants. And we had help from the Filipino community, who welcome us to their church here.'

It is by working with other migrant communities that organizations like SOS Polonia are able to support Polish migrants in adjusting to working life in Britain. Barbara Storey said it's solidarity which has set them on the right footing, and it's now time to offer that solidarity to new migrant groups. She has a vision of extending the support to new migrants from Bulgaria and Romania, especially as they are faced with growing hostility from British society and media following the work restrictions on the two countries being lifted in January 2014. She now works closely with Romanian and Bulgarian community activists in order to achieve that vision. 'We want to explore opportunities of sharing and building that solidarity ... We have always to learn from mistakes ... and a wise man learns from others' mistakes. We welcome Romanian and Bulgarian people to learn from our mistakes, how to do better than us in 2004.'

As a relatively nascent migrant community, the Romanians in Britain are still searching for ways to voice their concerns and their opposition to British racism. Roxana Carare, of the Honorary Consulate of Romania, UK, said the fear of an 'influx' is completely irrational. 'Traditionally the Romanians are of Latin background and they relate better to Latin-speaking countries ... and there are over one million in Spain and Italy already, so that's where they normally gravitate. And also Germany, because it is geographically closer ... Most Romanian migrants are of working age, and they are much less likely to claim benefits than the UK nationals (6.6 per cent compared to 16.6 per cent in 2011).'

Confronted with the increasing criminalization of Romanian migrants since the beginning of 2013, Daniel Profir, cultural adviser to the Honorary Consulate of Romania, said that austerity measures have created a culture of blame whereby Romanian migration becomes associated with crime. 'To associate criminality with certain nationalities fuels racially motivated incidents

... Allegations were made by certain politicians that 27,725 Romanians were arrested in the last five years. In 2012, more than 5.6 million crimes were committed in the UK by British nationals. If multiplied by five years, one can reach the conclusion that twenty-eight million Britons have committed crimes. That's one in two Britons. Of course that is nonsense. And it's nonsense to say that one in three Romanians are being arrested.'

Daniel Profir calls himself 'a double migrant', having become a French national before landing in the UK to teach French to English children in a pilot programme for the British Council. From his own experience, he recognizes that migration is what drives social progress. He said: 'The great majority of Romanians living in the UK are very well integrated into local communities. Their presence is mainly the result of a British labour market demand. Forty per cent of Romanian migrants have university degrees; they work hard and pay taxes and are valued by their employers ... They put in the British public purse more than they take out.'

Profir knows of a Romanian Roma man working as a pizza delivery worker in Portsmouth. 'He's a family man, a churchgoer. He started out as a driver in Domino Pizza and he was the only foreigner among the twenty drivers there. He worked hard and was the only one helping out with cleaning and tidying up after work ... Two years later, he opened his own franchise in Portsmouth. He's totally committed to his work. That's the kind of contribution Romanian Roma are making here.'

Bulgarian migrants have also completely relied on their own networks to find ways to adapt to a new working life in Britain and develop coping strategies when they find themselves in difficult circumstances. I talked with Eugeniy Kaydamov, editor-in-chief of *BG Ben*, a biweekly Bulgarian community newspaper in Britain. The forty-four-year-old Eugeniy worked as a journalist in Plovdiv after graduation and has been writing for *BG Ben* since coming to the UK. Not a 'typical' 'Bulgarian migrant', he's nevertheless well connected in the Bulgarian community owing to his profession. He said that, prior to January 2014, most Bulgarian migrants worked in low-skilled, low-paid work; 60 per cent of Bulgarian women were agency workers with 'self-employed' status, in domestic cleaning work. They had few rights and little protection against exploitative conditions. 'It couldn't be different because Bulgarians and Romanians were subjected to different rules in employment,' said Eugeniy.

> They didn't have much choice. They were forced by law to become self-employed. If you came from Bulgaria and Romania, you could only legally be here if you registered yourself as self-employed.
>
> Many didn't have the money to start a business or apply for loans. So agencies offered these people contracts ... and agencies were abusing and using the situation to exploit Bulgarians and Romanians and offer them 'slave' contracts ... It means you have only duties but no rights. Agencies can get rid of you any time. Bulgarian agency workers never had the same rights as the British agency workers. You can't make a complaint [against bad employers or agencies] because of your own status ... Many Bulgarians were working in medieval conditions ...

The blue card was given as a proof of your right to work as an employee and it was required for someone working on a contract. This blue card was very hard to get: it was an efficient discriminatory mechanism to demotivate people ... to make people make up their minds about leaving Britain. If you're out of money and you're kept waiting by the administrative procedures here ... for NI card, etc. ... Cost of living is very high and in this way their enthusiasm goes down and eventually they pack up and leave Britain.

We're a relatively young migrant community. We don't have the resources to protect ourselves ... Yet the media here kept on their headlines about Bulgarian and Romanian migrants. We've been singled out in the media campaign that started from early 2013. The problem is, you can sue someone for calling you a racist word, like the n-word, but you can't take the discriminatory bureaucracy, the law-makers, to court. You can't struggle with the state.

In May 2014, the coalition government announced the UK Immigration Act, as the Immigration Bill became law. Under the Act, family migration rights were curtailed, private landlords were given the power to act as immigration officers to check tenants' status, and all migrants were now obliged to pay for healthcare in the UK. Migrant communities feel powerless in the face of this draconian law. It is the state they're up against, not just Nigel Farage and the popular media.

For migrants who have contributed for some time to Britain's healthcare system, the Immigration Act is a direct insult. Among Southampton's few hundred Bulgarian migrants, many have served in Britain's care homes and other healthcare institutions. They are well qualified and hard working, and contribute enormously to their local community. Forty-six-year-old physiotherapist Milena Petrova is one of them. She came on a work permit in 2003 to work as a senior care assistant in a care home, My Care Home, in Southampton. At the time, she was the sole breadwinner of the family. 'Then, it was the only way for Bulgarians to come to Britain legally,' Milena told me as we sat in a café in central Southampton.

> There were a few hundred Bulgarian women who came to work for the same care home … A lot of English employers came to Bulgaria to get workers for the care homes, because Bulgarian people are very qualified, good workers and the payment was minimum [no more than the national minimum wage].
>
> We worked long hours, around twelve hours a day … A sixty-hour week was the norm. And sometimes I worked up to eighty hours a week. Overtime and night shifts were the same rate as normal shifts. There are many care homes like this.

Milena sighed as she recalled her toughest time working in Britain, between 2003 and 2008. On top of this, Bulgarian care assistants also had to put up with older customers at the care homes who might make racist comments to them.

'The verbal abuse got too much sometimes, especially when you have to work such long hours,' she said. 'The problem was, you couldn't change your occupation and had to stay in care work until the five years were up, as it was the requirement of the work permit, no matter how bad the conditions were. I wanted to change job and became a physiotherapist like I was in Bulgaria, but I couldn't.'

Being away from her family for years and earning on her own to support them was the hardest thing she'd ever done in her life. Back then, Milena couldn't even telephone as it was too expensive. Sending emails was the usual way she communicated with her family. She worked at the care home for five long years. The hardship was worth it in the end. In 2008, Milena was able to leave the care home and became a physiotherapist for a private company. 'Things improved after 2007 [when Bulgaria joined the EU],' she said. 'But the work restrictions imposed on Bulgarian nationals meant that most Bulgarian men could only work as builders and Bulgarian women as cleaners. It became extremely difficult to get a work permit for care homes. When the government makes it difficult for migrants to get work in these places, care homes continue to find it hard to recruit local workforce.'

Milena believes this is due to the flexible working hours required in care homes. 'There's no point talking about "British jobs for British workers". There are jobs out there, like in the care homes, if British people want to do it. But many of them don't.'

Faced with so much hostility from society, I wondered what attracted Milena to remain in Britain. She smiled and said with ease: 'What I like about the UK work environment is that as long as you work hard and are good at your job, you will have the chance of promotion, of going up ...' Then she added that Bulgarians still prefer to go to Germany and southern Europe, even after work restrictions on Romanians and Bulgarians were lifted in January 2014, despite UKIP's warnings of an 'influx'. 'When Farage went to Bulgaria to try to show the possibility of many Bulgarians planning to come to the UK, he didn't see what he wanted to see,' she said. 'No one he met actually wanted to come here. And despite what UKIP says about us, I don't know any Bulgarian person on benefits in Britain. And we've had no problems with our neighbours and local people, some of whom have visited Bulgaria and even bought properties there.'

I asked Milena what changes she'd like to see in the British media in their representation of Bulgarian and Romanian migration. She did not hesitate in her reply: 'The truth.'

In spring 2014, Dr Razvan U. Constantinescu, chair of the European Movement in Bristol, watched the growing hostility towards and scapegoating of Bulgarians and Romanians with amazement. He came to Britain as a political refugee in the midst of the Romanian government's crackdown on opposition forces.

> The Romanian communities in the UK at the time were made up of those who came from previous waves of political refugees ... They sought asylum here during the Second World War when Romania became a dictatorship ... It began with Romanian intellectuals, students, diplomats, business-people, especially those with Jewish origin ... between 1939 and 1940. At the time of my arrival I felt very lonely ... and had to learn English fast and adopt the British way of life fast ... There was no community support network to

fall back on at all, not like now; at least you have several churches, Romanian restaurants, hairdressers, delicatessens … Back then, these were non-existent. There was little cultural representation … We didn't even have newspapers. And people were afraid to even go to the church because they thought there might be spies there.

This situation motivated Dr Constantinescu to found the Romanian Culture Centre in London and a church in Bristol, both of which are still active today.

In those days, we were so rare. I was studying in the University of Brighton where there were no Romanians. And there were no Romanians in my village where I lived for four years … I interacted mostly with local British communities. Many people knew very little about Romania at the time and I was a little curiosity. There was even compassion, in those days, for Romanian refugees … The change of local attitudes definitely has a lot to do with the portrayal of Romanian migrants in the press who at the time didn't see us as a threat yet. The Brits were more interested in their relationship with people from India and the Caribbean at the time … We weren't seen as posing any danger yet. Later, the Brits were more irritated by the 'Polish plumber', and not so much the 'Romanian builder', who might take their jobs. The attitudes towards Romanians changed and hardened with the accession of certain countries into the EU, which started with the first wave of the first ten countries from the Eastern bloc … the main one being

Poland. Once borders opened to these countries, I started to detect the hardening of local attitudes towards European migrants. By now, we're no longer a curiosity or object of charity. We've become a nuisance in the British eyes. The hardening of attitudes and negative press got from bad to worse in the last three to four years ...

The initial labour market restrictions on Bulgarians and Romanians was two years ... and the subsequent government increased those restrictions to another two years ... until eventually the EU said that it's no longer permissible and that Bulgarians and Romanians must be treated like all other EU citizens ... So the press started to say that there will be planeloads of people coming from January 2014, with the UKIP jumping on it ... By January, everybody expected the massive influx of Romanians to unsettle the thousands of years of the British way of life!

As an educated, resourceful and well-established British Romanian, Dr Constantinescu said British racism hasn't affected him as much as it has affected working-class Romanians.

It pains me to hear that my fellow Romanians are being discriminated against and to see outrageous stories in the papers ... It pains me to see the erosion of British values. My daughter's born here. She's British Romanian. Her mother is English. She still has a Romanian name. And of course I'm concerned about her and how she will be treated in life ... She has a flag of Romania on the wall and she's very keen to go to Romania and she loves going there on holidays and loves interacting with children in the village. She speaks and understands Romanian very well. But like other children, she'd like to be anonymous; she'd like to be like everyone else. She wouldn't want to be identified as different. She likes to be told that she has a name of a princess ... but when it comes down to it, in the schoolyard, I'm sure she prefers to be Mary Smith. Like other children, she'd like to be seen as ordinary. She's predominantly an English person with a Romanian heritage and that's what I encourage her to be ...

When some Brits talk about migrants taking British jobs, they are in fact arguing against the principles and values upon which this country is based ... Their argument undermines equality and fairness and it erodes the very British way of life that they wish to protect. It is also a double standard: the same people who are advocating against Romanian labour accessing their market are actually promoting British goods accessing the Romanian markets. Romanians can say to you, we don't want your engines, your tractors, your cars or your financial services. Who will gain out of this? Nobody.

To change perceptions, Dr Constantinescu is working to promote exchanges, to 'engage with the local British communities, recognize their fears and work with them to increase their knowledge about the incoming communities'.

Currently, Dr Constantinescu is concerned about social segregation and the consequent possibility of the ghettoization of Romanian communities in Britain as a result of racism and discrimination, particularly so as regards Romanian Roma communities, who have been the major focus of media scaremongering and racism in Britain. There are ten million Romani people in Europe, the majority of whom live in poverty without adequate access to education, housing or healthcare. Many Roma people have left Romania as a result of long-term institutional and social discrimination against them. Britain appeals to them because it is seen as a relatively liberal country with rules of law where discrimination can be challenged. Blogger Filip Borev, who defines himself as a second-generation Bulgarian Roma immigrant, tells his grandmother's story: 'She came to England in the late 1970s. To her England was a golden land full of opportunity, worlds away from the poverty and destitution of her Varna slum. England was a place of equality where her children would be educated, not segregated, and where they would have access to healthcare which meant they might live past middle age …'

Sadly, however, on arrival in Britain, Roma migrants find themselves further discriminated against and labelled as a burden on society. Britain's popular media plays a large part in creating and reproducing inaccurate and biased information about Roma migrants. First, the majority of Britain's media fail to make distinctions between the huge variety of Romani communities; among the 90,000-strong Romani population in the UK are English Romani (Romanichals), Welsh Romani (Kale) and European Romani (Roma). The media often choose to lump them altogether, under the name 'Gypsies'. The media are obsessed with numbers, or more accurately distorted impressions of the numbers. In fact, the overall number of Roma migrants entering the UK is comparatively small. For instance, most Roma arriving in Britain came from Romania, representing less than 5 per cent of all refugees.

Roma people are the most disadvantaged and discriminated-against ethnic group in Britain. 'Romanian Roma migrants don't really have anywhere to turn to when they need help to deal with incidents of racism,' Dr Constantinescu told me. 'The only institution outside the family for them to seek support [from] is the church ... They have few social networks or the social capital to be able to build those networks. They are very isolated even within the Romanian community ... The Roma are in many ways victims of multilayered isolation and segregation ... The Romanian Roma are discriminated [against] by some Romanians themselves.'

This is the background against which Dr Constantinescu founded the Romanian drop-in centre in partnership with the Polish communities in Southampton. 'The Polish have had experience ... an absolutely wonderful development,' he said, referring to the work centred around SOS Polonia. 'Nothing of that scale is happening anywhere else.' Following the Polish example, he co-founded a similar drop-in centre in Bristol, and has been running it for the last four years. The centre offers support particularly to Roma people, providing legal advice and education.

This support is extremely important to a much-victimized community. In Southampton, for instance, you frequently hear of racist abuse and attacks on Roma people. Romanian Roma make up one third of *Big Issue* vendors in Southampton. They stand outside the city's shopping centre, disrupting nobody, but sometimes, it seems, simply speaking in an unfamiliar accent is enough to invite abuse. Gareth Hughes, senior outreach officer for the *Big Issue* in Southampton, said that Romanian Roma sellers work extremely hard. 'They have very strong work ethics ... and contrary to popular myth, they are the group that needs the least support. They are self-sufficient and hard working.'

Despite this, racism is a common occurrence. Hughes said:

> The Romanian Roma vendors often receive racism or complaints from the public. Those complaints are largely based on prejudice about Roma people ... There have been racist attacks on Romanian Roma vendors. But they don't tend to report this to the police because the response from the police hasn't always been positive ... The press are stirring up hatred. You'll read a piece of news in the papers against the Roma, and then soon after that you'll hear of a racist attack. I myself saw this happening. Following a particular *Daily Mail* report, there were incidents of verbal abuse inflicted on our Romanian Roma vendors.

The *Daily Express* is one of the newspapers to have consistently taken an anti-migrant position, particularly against Romanian and Bulgarian migrants, among which the Roma were a particular focus for the tabloid. In 2013, the *Daily Express* launched a campaign against a surge in migration from Romania and Bulgaria. It claimed that 98 per cent of its readers who took part in the newspaper's phone poll agreed unanimously that 'Britain should close its borders to all new migrants'. This campaign received backing from Conservative MP Peter Bone, whose Private Member's Bill also called for restrictions on Bulgarian and Romanian migration. In November that year, the *Express* ran an anti-Roma story with the headline 'A multicultural hell hole that we never voted for'.

The news article focused on Roma communities in Page Hall, Sheffield, where the reporter quoted an unproven case of two Roma migrants attempting to sell babies, and said, 'Page Hall's descent into social breakdown is just a foretaste of what will happen across Britain as the final restrictions on migrants from eastern Europe are removed ... 29 million Bulgarians and Romanians will gain the right to settle here, bringing a large number of Roma to our shores. This wave of mass immigration from two of Europe's most impoverished countries will be a disaster for Britain, hastening the collapse in national identity ...'

The media scapegoating of Roma migrants was backed by politicians of all parties, including David Blunkett, who said, 'we've got to change the behaviour and culture of the Roma community'. Nick Clegg added: 'We have every right to say if you're in Britain and are coming to live here, you have got to be sensitive to the way life is lived in this country. If you do things that people find intimidating, such as large groups hanging around on street corners, you have got to listen to what other people in the community say.' Meanwhile, Jack Straw, former Labour Home Secretary and Labour MP for Blackburn, said that he regretted opening doors to eastern Europeans and that 'having no work restrictions on eastern European migrants in 2004 was a spectacular mistake'.

Media racism was at its peak when stories of Roma parents 'stealing babies' hit the tabloid headlines. In late October 2013, two Roma children in Athlone and Dublin were snatched from their families because they looked blond and were believed to be stolen, following the sensationalist news story about the four-year-old 'angel Maria' being stolen by Bulgarian Roma couple

Sasha Ruseva and Atanas Rusev (who were later proved by DNA tests to be the biological parents of the blonde Maria). As blogger Filip Borev commented, the notion of 'The baby-snatching Gypsy is an old racist stereotype'. Yet it has been recycled time and time again in the popular media of twenty-first-century Britain.

Bulgarian Roma migrate primarily to escape from segregation and the harsh reality of racism in every aspect of their life. They constitute 10 per cent of Bulgaria's population, the largest proportion in Europe. They are also one of the most victim-ized and marginalized Roma groups. During the Stalinist era (1946–90), assimilation policies put an end to nomadism, self-employment and the Romani language. Roma people were forced to settle in poorly equipped neighbourhoods. Their housing conditions didn't improve after the fall of the Stalinist dictatorship. As a result, as Filip Borev observed, much of the housing found in Roma neighbourhoods today has been built illegally, which has led to a deterioration in living conditions in these neighbourhoods, where many Roma families were left without water, electricity and adequate sewage systems.

I witnessed the level of systematic segregation Bulgarian Roma endure when I visited the country. There in Sofia and Plovdiv, I saw the denial of basic rights to freedom from deprivation and hunger, as well as the denial of opportunities for education and general well-being. Education is often the way out of the ghetto, but access is being denied to most Roma children. In Bulgaria, there are 106 segregated Roma schools; 70 per cent of Roma children are currently educated in poor 'ghetto schools'. Accompanied by Human Rights Watch activists, I visited the

75th School, known to be the best among all four Roma schools in the capital. However, as in all ghetto schools, overcrowding is endemic. There were few facilities for learning, and no teaching materials in Romani. The headmaster explained: 'In some schools we don't even have textbooks … The Turkish minority can get their textbooks and materials from Turkey. But we can't go all the way back to India!'

State schools tend not to enrol Roma children. Few children from these ghetto schools will be accepted into colleges. In the Stolipinovo ghetto of Plovdiv, only some ninety people have a secondary education, out of a Roma population of 55,000.

In the Facultie neighbourhood to the west of Sofia, 30,000 residents struggle as they live in subhuman conditions. This is clear evidence that the government endorses Roma segregation. This neighbourhood is totally separated from the outside world, and some taxi drivers even refused to take me there. It is not incorporated into city planning and is seen as an illegal quarter of Sofia. For years, it has been left on its own to rot, down to the level of basic garbage disposal, which is not covered by local authorities. My first experience of the district was people in ragged clothes riding carts, the main transport in the ghetto. Buses to town are infrequent – one every hour – and are too expensive for Facultie's residents. Besides, they are only too aware of the danger of racial violence from skinheads. It's best to stay where they are. Roma people even fear speaking their own language on public transport. And if they do get into town, there is a colour bar that prevents them from functioning normally: coffee bars and public places often do not allow Roma people in, for fear of 'affecting business'.

The Stolipinovo neighbourhood of Plovdiv also shocked me. It is home to 45,000 Roma people, 90 per cent of whom are Muslim Roma (Horahane Roma) and 10 per cent Eastern-Orthodox-Christian Bulgarian Roma (Daskane Roma). The neighbourhood is a completely segregated ghetto, cut off from the rest of Bulgarian society, with an unemployment rate as high as 90 per cent. Water is limited here, and electricity is supplied only two hours daily. Residents told me that a private company has started selling electricity in Sheker Mahala, the second-largest Roma neighbourhood in Plovdiv, because the state company refused to supply electricity to the community.

Stolipinovo's Roma residents live in darkness most of the day. The worst dwelling I saw was only one square metre in size, in which seven people made their home. It was pitch black. Someone used a torch so I could see inside. There I saw a baby, lying on a mattress. A young man was sitting against the wall, which was piled high with water bottles. The baby's mother showed me the sort of food they live on: some bread collected from the rubbish dump. 'We'll have these for dinner tonight,' she said. More than a hundred families live in these conditions in this neighbourhood.

It would only be human to want to escape this inhumane existence. But Bulgarian Roma people in these ghettoes find it extremely difficult to migrate abroad. They do not have the resources or networks to make migration a viable option.

While the European parliamentary and local election campaigns of May 2014 were heating up and Nigel

Farage's face greeted me every day from the front pages of Britain's newspapers, I heard surprising news from Darren in Luton: he was considering voting Labour, after years of disillusionment and alienation from mainstream politics.

'My dad used to think it was his duty to vote Labour ... and in my heart of hearts I wanted to vote Labour, too, but it was just what they did really frustrated me. I'm never to vote for the Tories, it's not in my blood ... and farther right is no option for me,' he said. 'Having few options, I wouldn't give up my vote, though. My grandad used to tell us it's our duty to vote. What I want to see is our people, working-class people, there in politics ... Labour really needs to reconnect with working-class people.'

I knew Darren had been doing a lot of thinking about his future and what he'd like to do politically. I had sensed that he was eager to find his place in the world again. He told me that our conversations over the months have been like therapy for him, going through his past and all the issues that have concerned him. It was reassuring to hear him say that he's completely opened up, which allowed him to reflect on the past.

You came to my home and I was always able to talk freely without being judged ... You didn't just come to get a story and leave. It has made me trust – I've never trusted to this degree because I didn't want my feelings to be hurt. But this time, for the first time in my life, I gave everything out. You heard what's deep in my heart, the truth.

Our talks made me analyse myself, on a much deeper level than I'd ever done. After every 'consultation' we had, I'd gone away and thought about what I'd said ...

Sometimes after our meeting, I felt bad, because our talk made me confront what's deep in me. I asked myself, who was I? Who am I?

A few days later, Darren sent me a text, telling me his decision: 'I've been thinking a lot about the options available to me. I'm not a fan of Luton Labour, but I'm definitely going to vote Labour, in the hope that the party reconnects with the likes of me.'

'Are you sure?' I asked.

'I should put up and shut up, or get involved and have a go at reconnecting myself, instead of shouting from the sidelines,' he wrote.

'What do you want to do, exactly?' I asked.

'I'd love to engage with Luton people on a civil level. It's always been about Luton for me ... and I ended up feeling on the outside of my own town ... It was painful. It's a barren place to be. I think getting involved is the only thing that will cure me.'

I understood immediately what Darren meant. He needs to feel connected again with the outside world, and to feel that he can make a difference in the right direction. Only then he will be able to clear away the past of which he is ashamed and really move forward.

Darren understands that it won't be easy. His involvement in the far right, just like his football days as part of the Migs, will stay with him, mainly because it will remain in the minds of others. 'Local politics may not want me,' he said sorrowfully.

Meanwhile, Tommy Robinson was released from Winchester prison. He called me from a new mobile number. Now a free man, he was eager to get back to spending time with his family and his ill mother, who has suffered a lot from the knowledge of his involvement in the EDL. Robinson told me that he has no real plans at this stage. 'I've always had a focus in my life. Now the EDL's all behind me and my jail sentence is over, I don't actually know what I want to do, apart from trying to return to normality for a while, the normality that I didn't have for five years.'

When we met again in Luton, Robinson looked exhausted and talked in a hushed voice as if he had run out of energy to even speak. He has been catching up with sleep, he told me. His prison term felt long, but he's glad he served his time. Like his previous jail term, it gave him time and space to reflect.

Robinson told me he's working on a BBC documentary, in which the producers would like to see him work with think tank Demos and establish a dialogue on 'community cohesion'. 'This is what they want to see and how they want to end the documentary,' he said. This interestingly suggests that the mainstream media are forging links on his behalf, helping him to reshape his public image.

Robinson explained to me that he changed his mobile number to avoid his old friends in the EDL. He's been banned from having any contact with them for a year. 'If I send anyone in the EDL a text, I'll be back in jail,' he said.

Reflecting on his time inside the group, Robinson said he recognized his mistake. 'I'm guilty of generalizing ...' he said, referring to the speeches in which he equated Muslim communities with 'extremism'.

A couple of weeks later, he revealed to me that a man called Dave was the one who proved instrumental in getting him to leave the EDL and change his path, not Quilliam.

In Luton in 2011, after a demo he organized against a meeting in the town which was to discuss 'extremism', Robinson was introduced to Dave by a councillor whom he called a 'proper Lutonian'. He has been meeting with Dave every two weeks or so since then and speaking on the phone most days for the past few years.

'I'd been surrounded by "yes" people for five years. I'd never had a balanced view from anyone. And Dave gave me that. He gave me advice but never told me I shouldn't be doing what I did. He's like one of us, a working-class man, and he understands us. While all of the commentators, "experts" and academics were pointing the finger and calling me names, he came to Luton, met with me and listened to me and other lads. He's supported me through everything ... I see him as a mentor.'

But Dave has not been willing to talk to the press since Robinson left the movement. I met with Dave during my research. He has been active in this field of work for twenty-five years, with seventeen years of experience in heavy industry prior to his change of direction. He delivers training for professionals and works in schools and with youth organizations, as well as on a one-to-one basis with individuals nationally. His approach is to counter racist myths with factual and practical evidence. It tackles racism on a more fundamental level by denouncing and deconstructing 'race' itself as a false social construct. Through one-to-one mentoring, his aim is to de-programme the individuals.

Dave recalled that he took one of the 'extreme far-right individuals' on a visit to the International Slavery Museum in Liverpool. That was an education for him. 'He's now reading literature on where racism came from and he acknowledges that race is a false social construct and hence racism based on skin colour is ludicrous,' Dave told me. 'There is also a member of a neo-Nazi group ... I took him to meet a Holocaust survivor and he was very humbled by the experience and is now having serious doubts about what he was involved in.'

However, Dave said he has never treated Robinson as his 'project' or even set himself the goal of getting him to leave the EDL, but simply spent time talking to him and addressing his issues. In the course of a few years, as a result of their constant communication, Robinson became more aware of the impact of his group's activities on the Muslim and wider communities and eventually 'softened' his stance, before leaving the EDL all together.

I talked to Arun Kundnani, author of *The Muslims Are Coming*, about the possibility and effectiveness of changing individuals who have followed the far right. He believes that it can be done and he himself has interviewed youth workers who have undertaken such work.

> However, I think most mainstream work in this area [Exit programmes in Europe] tends to operate with an idea that the problem is a kind of psychological vulnerability that leads to a 'fanatical' mindset in which a young person adopts far-right ideology. The aim then is to address the emotional problem in order to bring the young person back to a 'normal liberal', with a depoliticized mentality ... I think a better approach is to try to convert the young person by more deeply politicizing them – i.e. not seeing their politics

as a sign of 'fanaticism' but as an incomplete attempt to make sense of an unequal world. On this approach, deepening their political education takes them away from a narrow 'them and us' ethnic-identity-based politics to a more sophisticated and empowering understanding of the real injustices they experience. Providing opportunities to engage in hard political discussions with people from other ethnic and religious backgrounds can be a part of this ... If the contact [between them] is about real political matters, I think that can play a role, as people realize they have similar concerns about housing, education, jobs, etc.

Despite Dave's influence, I have always wondered whether Robinson has really broken away from the ideology of the EDL. Europe's Exit programmes have not always been as successful in transforming those on the far right as they claim. In some cases, far-right activists even manipulate the programmes and use them for their own benefit. It seems that Robinson's change of heart is due primarily to the issue of tactics. He no longer believes the right way to address the issues at stake is through a street movement. 'The way we did it was good to get the message out ... but there's much more constructive ways to address issues. And society's attempt to isolate us isn't the way to resolve them. The reason why the EDL exploded the way it did was because people were isolated. This is why I hope that society will support the idea of building dialogues.'

Robinson once again emphasized dialogue, that they needed to talk and work with British Muslims. 'There's nothing much about what Quilliam says that people in the mainstream EDL wouldn't agree with. It would be productive to bring some of those people in the EDL to Quilliam, so that they can start to challenge their *tactics* ... But the problem is that the majority in the EDL wouldn't want to dialogue with Muslims. I can see a chance that EDL's current leader Steve Eddowes might agree to work with organizations like Quilliam. But he may face a backlash within the EDL.'

It sounded as if Robinson was keen to change people's minds in the EDL. I wondered whether he would actually consider working with the group in the future. His answer was a firm 'No'. 'If I was able to change things from within the EDL, I would have stayed. But there are just so many different people, taking different things from the organization.'

The old dynamics remain. Robinson said that Eddowes is currently experiencing the same kinds of problem that he himself faced for years.

Steve Eddowes is the best bloke I've met in the EDL for five years. He wrote to me when I was in prison, telling me about the hard time he's had leading the group ... He said he can't cope with all the infights. He talked about the different directions people wanted to take and how difficult it is to drive away the idiots [neo-fascists] ... The EDL hasn't got rid of them. But to be honest, I'd expected that EDL would have been taken over completely by them since I left, but they haven't. The idiots are still there, though ... Hearing his problems, I know I don't miss it [EDL] at all; it's like babysitting 10,000 people.

The neo-fascists within the EDL are looking to groups like Britain First as an example of 'success'. 'Britain First and their paramilitary tactics have the potential to cause great damage,' said Robinson. 'A lot of the EDL men would be attracted to their tactics. Some of them will be watching videos of Britain First invading mosques and thinking, that's the way we should be doing things. Britain First has been looking at the EDL membership for years and they wanted to recruit from the EDL.'

As we talked, Robinson revealed to me that his time in prison seems to have deepened some of his previous beliefs. 'All the views I had of Islam and all that I was talking about in the past few years were all in my face, in prison,' he said. 'In Woodhill prison, there was a lot of radicalization going on ... France has segregated the jails. That's what they need to do in this country.'

Muslims are over-represented in Britain's prisons, making up 40 per cent of the prison population. A higher level of religious activities inside prisons shouldn't be a surprise. However, it would be a huge assumption to claim that recruitment of prisoners into the ranks of more radical groups is the norm. In fact, politicization of prisoners takes place primarily in prisons where Muslims convicted of serious crimes are concentrated. This is evidenced by Robinson's own experience that politicization among Muslims did not happen in Winchester prison, where he stayed after the transfer from Woodhill. In fact, during his time at Winchester prison, Robinson said he met 'moderate Muslims' with whom he talked regularly. One of them was in the cell next to him, and they spoke every day.

Robinson drew the same conclusion about schools and said that Britain's schools are 'infested with radicalization'. He said his convictions about 'Islamification', which informed his activities in the EDL, were confirmed time and time again by what he read in the daily newspapers. A lot of Robinson's time in prison was spent reading newspapers. When cut off from society, ironically, his views about Islam were reinforced by a daily diet of mainstream political discourse.

'When I read the papers, I said to myself, "That's what I've been saying for years!" The government's talking about Islamification in British schools. It was me who told Theresa May about this issue in Luton's schools, particularly Olive Tree Primary School [an independent Muslim school. In June 2011, Robinson 'ambushed' Theresa May in a constituency meeting in Maidenhead and asked her what she planned do about Luton's schools and 'Islamification']. I asked her, how could these lunatics be allowed to run my town?'

Robinson's radio interview with Abdul Qadir Baksh, the headmaster of Olive Tree, apparently prompted the beginning of an Ofsted investigation into 'Islamification' in this particular school. Ofsted inspectors subsequently criticized the school for promoting Salafi, a conservative form of Islam most associated with Saudi Arabia, and rated the school as inadequate. According to the school, the inspectors came in questioning nine-year-old pupils about their attitudes to gay marriage and terrorism. The Ofsted report of June 2014 claims that the school library contains books that are 'abhorrent to British society' and that the school 'fails to prepare pupils for life in modern Britain'. According to the school, the inspectors found in the staff library a book that contained a paragraph from the Prophet Muhammad that mentioned 'stoning and lashing' as the punishment for adultery in an Islamic society. 'The book was providing information about a point of law in an Islamic state, not promoting its application,' the school said. 'We do not teach or promote this view in our school … The Bible states stoning to death for eighteen different crimes and burning to death for a number of crimes. Would Ofsted object to the presence of a Bible on the basis that the Bible contains literature that promotes extreme views about punishments such as stoning, physical beating, burning alive and execution within biblical law [which] do not comply with British law?'

Farasat Latif, chairman of governors of the school, said in June 2014 to the BBC: 'Ofsted came into the school looking for problems of extremism and intolerance and didn't find any.' He said the inspection was part of the state's Islamophobic stance under Education Secretary Michael Gove.

This was part of a nationwide witch-hunt known as 'Trojan Horse', which began with a letter, widely considered a hoax, sent to Birmingham City Council in November 2013, purporting to be a plan of attack sent from a Birmingham circle of 'Islamist plotters' to their counterparts in Bradford, advising them how to carry out a similar takeover of Bradford schools. The letter was then forwarded to the Home Office, then the Department for Education, and then leaked to the media. This letter subsequently led to four inquiries, three of them ordered by Michael Gove, and a crisis at the top of the Conservative Party.

The claims about 'extremism', however, have been more than vague. As little evidence of 'extremism' can be found, the definition of 'extremism' from the Department for Education has shifted from applying to terrorists to applying to religious conservatives, and the focus of the investigation has shifted from actual 'extremism' to 'awareness of risks [related to extremism]'. Twenty-one schools in Birmingham have been put under state scrutiny as a result. The subsequent Ofsted report in June 2014 shows that three of the targeted schools put into special measures amid allegations of 'failing to safeguard children from threats of extremism' were in fact previously praised by Ofsted. Park View Academy, for instance, had actually hit the headlines in 2013 for achieving an 'outstanding' ranking from Ofsted. However, the 2014 Ofsted report rated the school 'inadequate'. It says the school has failed to 'raise awareness' among students of the 'risks of extremism'.

David Hughes, Park View's vice-chair, said on 9 June 2014: 'The Ofsted inspectors came looking for extremism, looking for segregation, looking for proof that our children have religion forced upon them as part of an Islamic plot. The Ofsted reports find absolutely no evidence of this ... The problem was not extremism, but the knee-jerk actions of some politicians who had put Muslim children from these communities at substantial risk of not being accepted as equal, legitimate and valued members of British society.'

Lee Donaghy, assistant principal of Park View, was reported in the *Guardian* (in June 2014) to be opposing the inspection and its report. He said that the respectful attitude of the pupils and the well-above-national-average exam results (75 per cent achieve five GCSEs graded A*–C) gave him the confidence to say that the school was a place that shared his belief that 'education was the key for disadvantaged, marginalized young people'. However, under the government's Trojan Horse inquiries, 'accommodating their faith in our non-denominational school –

allowing pupils to pray at lunchtime if they wish to and wear the hijab if they choose to, or shortening the school day during the Ramadan fast – is not an attempt to meet their spiritual needs as one tool to raise their achievement. Rather, it is extremism.'

Donaghy also challenged the way inspectors disrespectfully asked questions of pupils and staff at the school. For instance, female pupils were asked whether they were 'forced to wear the hijab', and a staff member was asked 'Are you homophobic?'

Salma Yaqoob, former leader of Respect, head of the Birmingham Stop the War Coalition and spokesperson for Birmingham Central Mosque, said the unjustified level of scrutiny carried 'more than a whiff of McCarthyism'.

The McCarthyite-style inquiries proved a waste of resources. The Commons Education Select Committee looked into the official Trojan Horse inquiries and the committee chairman, Graham Stuart, launched a report in mid-March 2015 announcing that 'one incident apart, no evidence of extremism or radicalization was found by any of the inquiries in any of the schools involved'. The committee report also said: 'Neither was there any evidence of a sustained plot, nor of significant problems in other parts of the country.' The Trojan Horse claims proved to be groundless.

The McCarthyite-style witch-hunt continues with the government's latest Counter-Terrorism and Security Act, aimed at Muslims, with nursery workers, schoolteachers and universities expected to look out for signs of increased 'Islamic practice' as signs of 'radicalization'. It went so far that in an east London primary school, Buxton School, questionnaires containing 'counter-extremism tests' which targeted the religious background of students were handed out in classrooms in which they were asked to choose an identity among labels such as 'student', 'British' and three faith identities (Christian, Hindu and Muslim). Other questions included whether students agreed that 'God has a purpose for me' and 'I believe my religion is the only correct one'. The discriminatory practice of singling out Muslims for the purpose of 'preventing extremism' is now the norm in Britain's institutions.

Hearing that Robinson's views have not fundamentally changed from his EDL days, I wondered whether he would have led the EDL if given the chance to start anew? He didn't hesitate: 'Yes, I would. I probably would have done it differently, though.'

Then he took up a pen and piece of paper and drew me a chart, with a line going upwards. 'Look, before the EDL, the number of arrests of Muslim men who groomed young girls was small. After the EDL, the number has gone up and up.'

The same old Tommy Robinson, surely.

Meanwhile, he told me he wouldn't let his children near groups like the EDL and he wouldn't advise young people to get involved in its activities.

Robinson said he knew he has lost a lot personally in the past few years. He talked about his ill mother, and it was probably the only time I saw real regret in his eyes. 'My mum's only little. She's a fighter,' he said. 'The operation was very serious … She's in a lot of pain. When I was in jail, I couldn't see her. It was really difficult.'

During his prison sentence, his wife wrote to him, telling him how scared she was for their children. She always hated his involvement in the EDL. 'Even when I was on *Newsnight*, she didn't want to watch it,' he said. 'But she could never stop me doing what I wanted to do. I even said to her once, "Don't make me choose." I didn't listen to my family.'

To this day, his three-, five- and six-year-old children have no idea about their father's activities of the last five years. They don't know their father led a far-right group. They have never heard of the EDL. 'They asked a lot of questions, but I've never told them anything,' Robinson said, then searched through his mobile phone and showed me the scan of a card. His children made it for him just after his release from prison. It said: 'We're so happy that you can come home from work for father's day!'

'Sooner or later they are going to find out, and I will have to explain everything to them,' he said quietly. 'Now I'm going to spend a lot of time with them … I've been banned from football for four years. Now the ban's lifted, I'll be taking my kids to see matches. I love football and I love Luton. I'm really looking forward to taking my kids there …'

When I met with Darren again in the summer, he gave me more news. 'I've joined Labour. Now I'm waiting for membership material to come through.'

I was amazed that he had actually joined a mainstream party. It must have been difficult, I imagined. Labour Party membership means a fundamental break with his EDL past and the 'the Carrolls in Luton' that have linked him with the origins of a national far-right street movement. I asked him how he felt about it. I wanted to know whether it had been an emotional decision.

'I feel good about it,' he said confidently. 'And all being well with the membership, I look forward to getting involved.'

He told me he'd been watching the elections with intense interest. 'What is worrying is the growth of the far right, like the National Front, across Europe,' he said. 'In this country, a strong argument needs to be put forward and win over the fringe and disaffected voters. As a Labour member now, I'm up for that challenge.'

Darren's concern about the growing racism across Europe was shown to be justified in October 2014 when Pegida was founded in Germany as a threatening force on the anti-Muslim far right. It has since mobilized tens of thousands to march on the streets. In early 2015, following the *Charlie Hebdo* attack in Paris, the 'clash of civilization' argument dominated in the mainstream media in an aggressive manner rarely seen before. 'Je Suis Charlie', a campaign followed by liberals and conservatives alike, found resonance in the far-right rhetoric about free speech, culminating in Nigel Farage's claim about British Muslims being 'the fifth column living within our country, who hate us and want to kill us'. (Farage said this during his March 2015 interview with the former equality and human rights commissioner Trevor Phillips for Channel 4.) The religion/radicalization narrative prevalent in Britain's political discourse has further consolidated the far-right propaganda about Islam and 'Islamification'. For instance, the BBC *Panorama* programme 'The Battle for British Islam' is much cited among far-right activists.

At this time, Tommy Robinson became increasingly more confident in predicting the growth of the EDL and the anti-Islamification movement across Europe. 'When we were talking about these issues five years ago, we were shunned and called racists. Now, in the last twelve to eighteen months, they, the politicians and media, are all talking about the same issues. My speech at the Oxford Union* was very well received. These ideas become more mainstream. People are listening to us now. We've been proved right.' Many EDL activists on the Dudley march on 7 February 2015 expressed the same kind of growing confidence.

Meanwhile, Robinson's idea of 'dialogue' has evolved with organizations like Quilliam. Quilliam's Maajid Nawaz introduced Robinson to Afzal Amin, Tory parliamentary candidate for Dudley North, in 2014, as part of the exercise in promoting 'dialogue'. In late January 2015, Robinson told me that he saw Amin as one of the few British Muslims who 'understand the issues' and introduced him to EDL chairman Steve Eddowes. 'When others came out to oppose EDL marching in Dudley, Amin said, "You can't tell an Englishman where he can and can't march in a democracy" ... Amin said we should try and reform what's happening within the EDL.'

Initially, Amin's intention in organizing meetings with him, as Robinson understood it, was for the EDL to cancel their planned demo in Dudley in February 2015. The twist to this 'dialogue', however, was that Amin allegedly made an offer to Robinson during their second meeting to which he brought with him a so-called 'money man' (who, according to Robinson, owns more than fifty businesses in the country). It became clear that Amin desperately wanted to win votes in his constituency and was prepared to 'do a deal' with the EDL via Robinson: he pledged to make EDL mainstream if its leaders would stage

---

* I asked the Oxford Union to comment on the reasons behind their decision to invite Tommy Robinson to speak about the EDL and its origins, at their event in December 2014. The Union did not reply.

a demonstration in Dudley against the building of a mosque, and then let Amin claim the credit for cancelling the demo. Robinson revealed that Amin also needed his help to access EDL's resources, i.e., in Robinson's words, 'to get him in'. It seemed that Amin never expected that Robinson would expose him. According to Robinson, BBC documentary producers furnished him with £6,000 worth of cameras to undertake secret filming of Amin. The *Daily Mail* got hold of the footage and soon ran the scandal story. As the story hit the headlines, Amin resigned as a Tory candidate within two days. As people start to look for the link man between Robinson and Amin, this scandal certainly leaves a huge question mark over Quilliam's approach to 'dialogue' – if not over Quilliam itself.

In summer 2015, Robinson carried on with his idea of the 'dialogue', planning a public debate with local Muslims in Sheffield; owing presumably to the sensitive nature of the debate's subject, i.e. grooming of girls, the police have not permitted the event. What is clear is that, despite the change in tactics, Robinson's race-based politics haven't really mellowed.

As for Andrew in the Southend Division, he's now devoting half of his time to training as a care worker. He talked about his course with pride. 'I'm going to college today,' he often told me on the phone. However, when I asked about his EDL activities, he would always return to feeling bitter and angry.

Meanwhile, 'Viking' in Reading continued with his local stunts – he recently sent a recruit to 'infiltrate' a local mosque, recording lectures given by imams. The depressing thing was the positive tone of voice with which he spoke about it – it was as if he believed he was engaged in society's monitoring of Muslims' religious life for what he believed to be the 'common good'. In the same way, he talked about the marches he went on, such as the one in Walthamstow.

At this time, Darren felt that his first step in trying to change things should be to get involved in the labour movement. He does not want to remain an isolated 'outsider' any longer. We then talked about the idea of taking part in seminars and workshops organized by the unions. He discussed this with several Unite organizers. He believes that workers need forums in which they can learn and discuss politics, that this is the way prejudices can be challenged. He has an education programme in mind, which he has named Stand Against Far-right Extremism (SAFE). He also joined the construction workers' union UCATT.

Meanwhile, Britain's 'immigration debate' carried on, all the way through the election campaigns in spring 2015, in which mainstream media and political parties took part in recycling the discourse of race. UKIP attempted to outdo the regressive immigration policies of 2014 introduced under the coalition government. UKIP's website says: 'Immigrants must financially support themselves and their dependants for five years. This means private health insurance, education and housing ...' What do they mean by 'immigrants'? Farage confirmed to the press in March 2015 that 'the children of the new immigrants [he meant 'migrants'] coming to Britain should not immediately be allowed to attend state schools'. In other words, new migrants who will be working their hearts out will not be able to feed their families because all their earnings will go to paying for healthcare, housing and even their children's education for five years. This will no doubt ensure the separation of many migrant families (with children staying behind in migrants' home countries, separate from their working parents) as costs become unaffordable for them.

During Farage's interview with Trevor Phillips, he also said that race and other anti-discrimination legislation is no longer needed in the UK. He insists that the aim is to keep 'British jobs for British workers'. Clearly, he was referring to *white* British workers – putting an end to anti-discrimination legislation will impact negatively not only on EU workers but also on non-white British workers. This is the farthest Farage has gone to reveal the racial nature of his ideas.

To challenge UKIP's anti-immigration politics prior to the general election, Darren tried to introduce the idea of the 'I'm an immigrant' campaign (organized by the Joint Council for the Welfare of Immigrants) to local Labour councillors. There was little positive response. As Darren put it, 'Their reaction was basically, "that's a nice idea, but we're not going to do anything about it".' Obviously, Darren's suggestion didn't sit well with Labour's 'immigration mug' campaign and its anti-immigration pledges. Although he helped with canvassing for Labour, Darren came away from the election disappointed with the party he had only recently joined.

Since the Conservatives won the general election, an even tougher immigration bill has been introduced, in which 'illegal working' becomes a criminal offence and the police are given powers to seize the wages of undocumented workers. While taking away rights for migrant workers, the Tories' trade union bill aims to restrict British workers' rights to strike. Following Labour's electoral defeat, Darren believes that Labour desperately needs to reconnect with the working class and regain that identity.

I know that Darren will not just sit and wait for things to happen. He's now exploring alternatives to the left of Labour. In June 2015, he went on his first anti-austerity demonstration in London. In the near future, Darren wants to be able to tell his story to fellow working-class Britons, instil in them the importance of collectively resisting racism. He will continue to try to find his way.

AFTERWORD

S ince working on the project, I've been asked this question: 'What got you into this?' I suppose this is traditionally a territory for white journalists – not least because accessing the world of the far right can pose particular difficulties if you are of ethnic minority background.

So, a bit about myself and my own 'politicization'. I came to Britain in 1991, more than twenty years ago, as a postgraduate student of critical and cultural theory. I was young and adventurous, and I wanted to see the world beyond the small Pacific island where I grew up. So I travelled halfway across the globe, from Taiwan to the UK, from one island to another.

It didn't take long for me to see the two sides to my new home. At first, I was struck by a local resistance to the changing cultural landscape of modern Britain, which manifested itself in considerably negative attitudes towards us 'outsiders', not only in the way overseas students were housed separately from the home students and rarely had the chance to interact with the local population, but also in the frequency with which overseas students and workers experienced racist abuse from local youths.

Yet I also began to appreciate the strength of collective opposition to racism in Britain's ethnically diverse towns and cities, where people of all sorts of backgrounds were working and living alongside one another. Students stood outside the Union, distributing newspapers condemning racist attacks and the government's immigration policies. I'd never seen anything like it back in Taiwan. I saw people organizing Anti-Nazi League demonstrations and marching for what they believed in. This vibrant civic life and the genuine mix of cultures inspired me, along with the wide range of opportunities and potential they offered for an alternative space to be myself that I couldn't find back home. It was this spirit of individual freedom and pursuit of fulfilment which made me stay.

But after I had chosen to settle in Britain, people automatically began to define me as 'Chinese'. This is a complicated term, an ethno-cultural marker that ironically has no direct equivalent in Mandarin or any of the Chinese languages. For to be 'Chinese' does not have to mean being a citizen of China. In the Chinese-speaking world, people often use the word *huaren* to refer to a Chineseness not defined by national borders. 'Overseas Chinese' (*haiwai huaren*) is commonly used as a term that includes every Chinese-speaking person wherever their country of origin. To be known as 'Chinese' in the UK, or automatically as one of the 'Chinese community', felt like being put into a racialized ghetto. It is a form of racism in its gentlest definition, an identity in many ways required of me that kept me on the outside.

I became an outsider among British Chinese, who were primarily settlers from Hong Kong. Although I have had to tick the 'Chinese' box on every ethnic monitoring form I've ever filled in since arriving in the UK, and despite being called 'Chinese' everywhere I go, I have had to adapt just as much when working or interacting with British Chinese as with anyone else.

During my first decade in Britain, I tried to learn Cantonese in order to fit in, and so that I might write for a leading Cantonese newspaper. But at the job interview I was told that their concern wasn't actually whether or not I could speak Cantonese, but whether I could accept their China-directed editorial policy. In recent years, as migration from mainland China increased, I was finally able to use my native tongue to my advantage by working for the Mandarin-speaking press, although I was frequently boxed into writing about 'UK issues' concerning British Chinese communities instead of international affairs. I have had a Chineseness imposed upon me, while at the same time been treated as an outsider among the very community to which I am supposed to belong.

Meanwhile, as I travelled frequently to China and spent a substantial amount of time there for my work, my own experiences, ironically, have not drawn me closer to 'being Chinese', but have made me more and more reluctant to identify as such. I will never forget an experience I had while doing the research for my book *Scattered Sand*. I was standing outside a half-open dormitory gate in Baitu village, Guangdong Province, south China, trying to get the attention of a young Uighur man. He was scuttling past, his head down.

'Excuse me!' I called through the bars.

I wanted to talk to him about the horrific racially motivated murder of two of his colleagues, both Uighur factory workers, who had been brutally beaten to death outside their dormitory not far from this village. To my surprise, a Han Chinese security guard approached, waving me away and shouting at the Uighur man, as if giving orders to a dog, 'Go and shut the door!' The man obeyed and walked quietly towards the gate. He looked at me, frightened. He pulled the gate closed, and said nothing. But his eyes spoke of fear. I will never forget those eyes.

Those eyes told a story of centuries of repression of the Uighur people in China. They have become a politico-economic minority in their own land, known as Xinjiang today, in the north-west of China. The Uighur man at the gate in Baitu, along with his colleagues, had been moved to the village from the factory five miles away after the murders. No one was able to reach them to hear their side of the story.

The reality of racism that I have witnessed over the decades in China – including those four months of living in Xinjiang – made me question what for many Chinese-speaking migrants and settlers in Britain is an important part of their identity. For me, being 'Chinese' seems to symbolize some level of participation in maintaining China's secrets of national oppression. During my twenty years living in Britain, experiences of racism, such as those affecting Uighur workers, have returned to me as flashbacks, making me very uncomfortable about calling myself Chinese, whether to friends and acquaintances, or when ticking a box on a form. The facts seem plain: I am a native speaker of Chinese, my mother comes from China, and I have been educated in Mandarin up to university level in Taiwan. And yet I cannot feel connected to my supposed Chinese origins.

Over the years, I've tried to build a life for myself in London, with its long history of multiculturalism and where identities can constantly change and be reshaped. Many British people who don't live here say that 'London isn't England' and many Europeans I've met in the city have told me they're surprised to find it so 'un-British'. But it is here that I find it easiest to be myself. Self-exile in a global city such as London gives me more freedom than anywhere else to choose to define myself on my own terms.

I have become accustomed to living in this city of world cultures and I have made my home in the East End. London's multicultural reality is the air I breathe, as I continue to say proudly, and I am reminded of how fortunate I am whenever I visit a relatively mono-cultural place abroad. Visitors always ask me 'What is Britishness?' when they come to my part of town, to which I merely shrug my shoulders and smile. What is Britishness? I don't feel the need to answer such an essentialist question.

Without being fully aware, we are immersed in a huge variety of cultural influences and interactions on a daily basis. Living, working and communicating as a global citizen has become the norm for many. Nine per cent of children in Britain are of mixed cultural heritage. More than 300 languages are spoken in London. My friends and acquaintances come from everywhere and work in every kind of job: carers and managers from Bangladesh, writers and chefs from China, builders and nurses from Bulgaria, translators and academics from Poland, engineers and service workers from Spain ... the list goes on. It is inconceivable that we could exist without influences from outside of our so-called cultures of origin.

In the midst of this transformation, 'race' is no longer seen as a scientific and immutable concept. Few could use the word in his/her language without being contested. One of the few places we find the word formally used is on our census questionnaires. And the census results have themselves pointed to an ever-growing mixing of cultural and ethnic groups: as reported widely, the data from the 2012 census has told us that Britain's mixed-race population probably now exceeds one million and, being the largest 'ethnic group' among the under-sixteens, is among the fastest growing in this country.

Yet it would be naive to assume that everyone is aware of, or comfortable with, this globalized culture and the multicultural way of life. That everyone is free and mobile, living this fulfilled and globalized life, is a fairy tale at best. The reality is that some are more free and mobile than others. The old borders and controls are still there, *between* and *within* nations, all the time strengthened and tightened, to keep out those deemed unworthy of the freedom of mobility.

Over the years in Britain, I have seen people having their freedoms of mobility, association and family life taken away by the state. Some have even lost the freedom to live. The murder of Stephen Lawrence in 1993, just two years after my arrival in Britain, opened my eyes to the frightening level of racial hatred that existed in what was on the surface a civilized society such as Britain. The cover-up following his murder taught me about the horrendous hypocrisy and complacency that exist in some parts of British society, which allow room for racial hatred.

And the circumstances behind Stephen Lawrence's murder two decades ago have not gone away. It could be repeated. In fact, it is being repeated, particularly in relation to British Muslims. Back in 1993, in the same part of the East End, I was told this was a no-go area for non-whites. It was a time when racist murders and attacks were on the increase, and you would fear for your safety if you happened to be of Afro-Caribbean origin. This is now the reality for many British Muslims when far-right groups march into their neighbourhoods. I feared it then, being a newcomer to Britain, new to its particular strands of hostility and prejudices. Although years and years of activism on the part of anti-racist groups have largely chased the skinheads off the streets, it would be naive to think that the Macpherson Report has significantly reduced levels of institutional racism and racist ideologies in British society.

Far from it. The consistent anti-immigration policies implemented by successive governments, from the Tories to New Labour and the coalition, have ensured that those elements remain alive and are thriving, particularly in these economically straitened times. The study of public attitudes to immigration published by the National Centre for Social Research shows a growth in negative public sentiment: 75 per cent of respondents to the survey said they wanted to see a reduction in levels of migration and 60 per cent said settlement of migrants is bad for Britain. No wonder David Cameron's recent targeting of undocumented migrants, including giving police the power to confiscate their wages, kicked up no fuss.

Mainstream race politics has ensured that a corner of society is solidly in support of the far right. As communities affected by the 2008 economic crash and its aftermath have lost faith in the big parties and the establishment, these once marginalized political views are moving farther into the spotlight. For electoral gains, Britain's mainstream parties have promised to reduce net migration, and not to 'give in' to multiculturalism. Support for the BNP and its 'modernization programme' grew during the 2000s, peaking in 2008 when the party came fifth in the London mayoral election with 5.2 per cent of the vote, winning a seat in the London Assembly, and then in 2009 when it won its first county council seats and two seats in the European Parliament. In the past few years, many of its manual working-class votes have gone to the more modern-looking, apparently professional UKIP, which has done more than almost any other organization to shift the politics of race on to the mainstream agenda. This has been evidenced by the nearly four million votes (a 12.6 per cent share) UKIP won in the 2015 general election, in which the party came third nationally.

In the past six years, the English Defence League, formed in 2009, has emerged as a prominent voice by launching Britain's largest far-right street movement. It is particularly significant because some of its theories and practices have been endorsed by the centre-right media as well as by mainstream politicians. Deemed more 'acceptable' by society, the EDL's street movement has had a huge impact on Britain's political discourse in recent years. The National Domestic Extremism Unit, part of the Metropolitan Police, for instance, does not categorize the EDL as 'far right'. However, over the course of my two-year research, in which I spoke repeatedly with the movement's key members and those affected by their activities, I have found the movement to be ultra-nationalist, propagating a pro-Christian anti-immigration message, all of which are distinct features of the far right. While the EDL may not be a neo-fascist movement, many of its central ideas are racist in nature and contain elements that could develop into and overlap with neo-fascist ideologies.

The EDL has capitalized on the Islamophobia that has been growing in mainstream society since 9/11. As part of the modernization drive of the far-right, it propagates mainstream social prejudice against Muslims in a neutralized language. They have declared that they 'believe in freedom and democracy, and are in opposition to all forms of extremism'. Despite the majority of its activists and followers being white British, the EDL has attempted to present itself as a cross-ethnic street protest movement against Islam. Since 2009, they have been able to mobilize for demonstrations and riots in towns and cities all over the country, north to south, from Birmingham, Manchester, Leeds, Glasgow, Edinburgh, Nottingham, Dudley, Blackpool, Blackburn, Preston, Derby, Middlesbrough, Darlington, Bradford, Oldham, Leicester, Wolverhampton, Peterborough, Newcastle and Cardiff, to Luton, London, Rochdale, Cambridge, Reading, Bedford, Bristol, Brighton, Weymouth, Plymouth and Portsmouth. The list goes on.

The EDL has left traces of its violent attitude to Muslim communities across most of Britain, demonstrating that it has incorporated neo-fascist elements of the traditional far right. Stories told by some of the individuals involved in the street movement have depicted the relationship between the EDL and the rest of the far right.

When I talked to Tommy Robinson, the then-leader of the EDL, he said that 'the English way of life is being threatened' and that he was fighting for 'what is English'. When I realized that his ideas were nothing more than an amplified version of the British nationalism we've seen propagated for decades in mainstream media and politics, I knew that the significance of the EDL's street movement should not be underestimated.

The thinking behind such politics of irrationality has always fascinated me. Finding out why and how people choose a certain political path is always interesting to me. Naming racism 'madness' is too easy. Calling racists 'thugs' offers no real understanding. Talking about them as a social aberration is irresponsible. This book, I hope, has answered most of these questions: What makes it possible for the EDL leadership to pull in hundreds and thousands of people to take to the streets against a particular religion, its practices and its believers? What personal and social circumstances are leading these men and women – the grass roots of the movement – to come to such decisions based on prejudices and myths? What has motivated them? What lies behind their stated aims and what do they truly want to achieve through their action? And importantly, how can these racist ideologies be challenged? If merely countering that we should celebrate cultural diversity cannot provide an effective solution, what are the possibilities for change?

The growth of far-right activism in multicultural Britain poses one of the most important questions about the kind of society we live in. Instead of dismissing these racist ideologies as marginal and these social forces as irrelevant, this book has looked the street movement – a movement of individuals who feel like 'outsiders' – in its face, and attempts to offer an understanding and portrait of the marginalization and alienation that provide the breeding ground for the politics of despair.

INDEX

7/7 bombers, 121

Abdaly, Taimour al-, 121–2
Abdul, a resident of Bury Park, 124
Abdul, a sweet shop owner, 127–31
Abdullah Faliq, an activist 174–6
Ablitt, Tim, 224, 237
Abu Hamza, 94
Adrian, from Cyprus, 68–70
adultery, punishment for, in Islam, 347–8
Afghanistan, war in, 85
Al Hira Education Centre, attempted arson attack on, 125
Ahmed, Muktar, 169
Ahmed, Musaddiq, 169
Aked, Hilary, 293–4
Al-Khoei Foundation, 142
alcohol: consumption of, 139, 212, 282, 302, 281; culture of, 246 *see also* drunkenness
Alfredo, a barber, 50–61, 221
Ali, an ex-restaurant worker from Luton, 132–4
Ali, Altab, 169
Ali, Quddus, 169
Altab Ali Park, 169, 184
Amin, Afzal, 354–5
Andrew, a bus maintenance supervisor, 252–70, 280–1, 355
Andrew, a UKIP voter from Eastleigh, 304, 306

Angela, an anti-racist activist, 153–5
Ansar, Mohammed, 207
anti-abortion campaign, 276
anti-discrimination legislation, 357
anti-immigration perspectives, 144, 221–2, 227–8, 246, 252, 255, 278, 287, 296, 300, 301, 302, 304, 306, 310, 312, 315, 334, 365, 366; expressed by immigrants, 192; policies regarding, 356, 357, 365
anti-Islamic sentiment *see* anti-Muslim sentiment
Anti-Muslim League, 235
anti-Muslim sentiment, 2, 4, 6, 12, 13, 14, 17, 44–5, 50, 52–3, 67, 79–80, 87, 112–13, 116, 180, 206, 221, 235, 237, 243, 251, 253, 263, 275, 278, 281, 283, 288, 292, 293, 341; in Europe, 197; stereotypes, 126–7 *see also* Islamophobia
Anti-Nazi League (ANL), 97, 172–4, 360
anti-Semitism, 237, 239, 266; in Europe, 197
apprenticeships, 43, 47
Aron, an EDL activist, 24–5
Arsenal football club, 30
arson attacks, 124–5
Aryan Strike Force, 208

Asian-on-white violence, reporting of, 75
assimilationism, 222
Atkinson, Mark, 108–9
Australian points-based migration system, 144, 228, 313
Ayling, Alan *see* Lake, Alan

Bachmann, Lutz, 290
Baksh, Abdul Qadir, 134–5, 347
'Ban the Luton Taliban', 113
Bangladeshi Youth Movement, 171
banning of Muslim groups, proposed, 195
Barton, Jamie, 91
Barty, a West Indian, 33–4
Bates, Stuart, 102
Batten Gerard, 294
Battle for British Islam, The, 353
Beackon, Derek, 73
Begg, Moazzam, 186
Betsy, a laundry worker, 65–7, 70
BG Ben newspaper, 324
Big Issue sellers, Roma, 333–4
'black and white, unite and fight', 88, 90
Blair, Tony, 78, 81, 309
Blake, Billy, *EDL: Coming Down the Road*, 12
Blears, Hazel, 77
Blind Beggar pub, 177
Blood and Honor organization, 208
Bloom, Godfrey, 121
blue cards for immigrants, 325
Blunkett, David, 335
Bolton, Dave, 240–3, 281–2
Bolton football club, 241
Bone, Peter, 334
borders, strengthening of, 364
Borev, Filip, 332, 336
Boss Man, 238

Breivik, Anders Behring, 13, 116, 272
Brighton, unity demonstration of racists in, 265–6, 283
Britain First, 208, 219, 223, 227, 270, 275, 276–7, 278, 279–80, 292, 296, 346; growth of, 278–9
British Chinese people, 127–8, 130, 131
British Freedom Party (BFP), 67–70, 100; deregistration of, 70
'British jobs for British workers', 229, 255, 317, 357
British Movement, 37
British Muslims, 126, 130, 191, 192, 198, 199–200; identify with Britishness, 57
British National Party (BNP), xvi, 4, 14, 63, 67, 73, 101–5, 121, 157, 169, 170–1, 208, 219, 223, 227, 236, 246, 261, 262, 266, 275, 276, 278, 280, 282, 291, 292, 296, 306; and child exploitation issue, 56; entrism into EDL, 101–2, 213; in London mayoral election, 365–6; leafletting by, 152; resistance to, 104–5; seats in European Parliament, 366
British Patriotic Alliance (BPA), 280–1
British Patriots Against Islamic Extremism, 12
British Union of Fascists, 159
Britishness: definition of, 363; values of, 7, 132, 135 *see also* English way of life
Brixton, riots in, 43
Brons, Andrew, 197
Brown, Gordon, 47
Bryan, Ian, 299

Bulgarian people, 144, 228; immigration of, 294; in Southampton, 322–5

burglary, 158

burka, 69; campaigning against, 273

Bury Park (Luton), 34–6, 40, 58, 74, 111–49; as place of safety for Asians, 129

Bury Park Youth Posse (BPYP), 32, 44, 74

butchers, halal, importation of, 145

Buxton School, 350–1

Cable Street, battle of, 158–61, 191

Cadier, Paul, 311–15

CAGE organization, 78

Calvert, Shane, 181, 236

Cameron, David, 3, 56, 196, 199–200, 252, 365; attack on multiculturalism, 200

Camilo, Juan, 161–4

Candy, an EDL member, 265

Canning Town, xiii-xiv

Carare, Roxana, 322

care workers, immigrants as, 326

Carroll, Kevin, 13, 14, 36, 63, 67–8, 93, 99–103, 147, 149, 167, 179, 218, 226, 269, 285; denunciation of Catholicism, 100; involvement with BNP, 105–6; quits EDL, 193

Casuals see EDL Casuals

Casuals United, 11, 12, 44, 91, 271

Catholicism, 100, 116, 117, 218, 262

Cavendish Arms (East London), 152

census questionnaires, 363

Central Element, 44

Chalta, Rita, 164–7

Charlie Hebdo attack, 353

Chelsea football club, 253

Child Exploitation and Online Protection Centre, 54

child pornography, 214

China, racism in, 362

Chinese, use of term, 360

Chinese people: in Southampton, 318; 'Overseas', 360 see also British Chinese people

Chineseness, 362; definition of, 360–1

Choudary, Anjem, 8–11, 87, 94, 148, 278

Chris, a UKIP voter from Eastleigh, 306

Christian Patrol, 274, 275, 276, 278

Christianity, 218, 250, 285, 366

Christmas lights, lack of, 118

Church of the Templars, 272

Clash group, 172–3

Clegg, Nick, 335

Coborn Arms (East London), 152

cocaine, 139

Colombian people, 161–4

Combat 18 (C18), xvi, 108, 109, 208, 251, 281

Combined Ex-Forces (CxF), 214–15, 274

Communications Workers Union (CWU), 153, 155, 156

Communist Party of Great Britain, 160

Conde, Claro V., 316

Conservative Party, 175, 287, 295, 297, 301, 315, 348

Constantinescu, Razvan U., 328–31

construction industry, casual labour in, 314

Cooling, Davy, 101

Copeland, David, 109

Cordoba Foundation, 170, 175

Counter-Terrorism and Security Act (UK), 350
Cox, Caroline, 293
Cross, Scott, 311
cultural affinity, requirement for migrants, 313
curry, perceived as English dish, 145
Curtis, Tony, 102, 223–4
Cypriot people, in Luton, 68–9

Daily Bale website, 274
Daily Express, 334
Daily Mail, 55, 56, 121, 122, 159, 293, 334, 355
Daily Telegraph, 122
Dan, a non-voter from Eastleigh, 310
Darren, a painter and decorator, 25–49, 72–6, 78–96, 146–9, 282–6, 356–8; decides to vote Labour, 339–40; exits from EDL, 98, 148; joins Labour Party, 352; reticent about surname, 36
Dave, an anti-racist mentor, 341–3
Dave, author's boyfriend, 151–2, 170
David, a Polish immigrant, suicide of, 319–20
Davies-Dear, Glynn, 296, 298
Daz, a lorry driver, 180
defence league, use of term, 208
Demos think tank, 341
Derek, a road maintenance worker, 16–18, 65–72, 65
destitution of migrants, 165
dialogue, 205, 206, 208, 233, 354–5
Diddyman *see* Calvert, Shane
disenfranchisement, 233–4; among young people, 136
Dobson, Dave, 177–9

Dodd, Vikram, 55
Donaghy, Lee, 349–50
Donna, a friend of Andrew, 262–4
Donna, a single mother and friend of Andrew, 261–2
Dooley, Stacey, 122–3
Dowson, James, 275–6
dress, Islamic *see* Islamic dress
drugs scene, 36, 46–7, 48, 58, 63, 137–40, 300; associated with immigration, 59; in Grimsby, 256
drunkenness, 277, 278, 279
Duchness Community High School, 230–1
Duffy, Paul, 108
Dunt, Ian, 298

East End of London, 151–92
East Enders, identity of, 161
Eastern European migrants, 17
Eastleigh: heartland of UKIP, 297; industrial decline in, 297–8, 303
EasyJet, approached for cleaning contract, 229
Eddowes, Steve, 108, 224–8, 237–8, 345, 354
EDL Angels, 180–1, 182, 236
EDL Angels documentary, 181, 242
EDL Casuals, 43, 216–17
EDL News, 214, 271
education, value of, 130, 131, 200
emails, as means of communication for immigrants, 327
enforcement of immigration rules, 167
England, Bob, 272
'English culture', 246; erosion of, 118–19
English Defence League (EDL), xvi, 7, 11, 20, 21, 22–3, 45, 49–54, 67–72, 82, 83, 90–1,

95, 123, 127, 151–92 *passim*, 193–234 *passim*, 276–9, 286, 291, 292, 296, 306, 341, 344–5, 346, 351; and child exploitation issue, 56; demonstrations of (in Birmingham, 87, 88–9, 92, 265; in Blackburn, 108, in Bradford, 147, 271; in Dudley, 94, 97, 354; in Exeter, 273, 274; in Grantham, 236, 243, 270; in Leicester, 97; in Liverpool, 98; in Luton, 106, 261 (planned, 219–20); in Manchester, 93; in Newcastle, 268–9; in Peterborough, 240, 252, 254; in Preston, 96; in Slough, 223; in Stoke, 103; in Tower Hamlets, 151, 154, 167, 168–9, 174, 176–7, 248 (stopped at Aldgate, 179); in Walsall, 102; in Walthamstow, 177, 289; in Westminster, 264); divisions and splinter groups within, 197, 214, 215, 217, 220, 223, 227, 239, 280, 281, 283; drug usage among members, 140; elements of neo-fascism in, 107; establishment of, 84–96; Facebook page, 4; fight involving Asian people, 62; funding of, 115; growth of, 1–2, 96, 143, 225, 242, 251, 254, 344, 353; impact of, on British domestic politics, 366; in post-Robinson era, 235, 271; media security team, 226; members deal drugs, 138; membership of, 24, 86; mission statement of, 222, 227; neo fascist elements in, 101; not categorized as far-right, 226; rebranding of, 196, 220; registration of, 236; seek pub venues in East London, 154; Sikh Division, 221; support for,

61, 69, 157; Support Group, 236, 238; 'Walk of Honour', 2; women membership of, 180–1, 245–6, 268 *see also* BNP, infiltration of EDL; *and* Robinson, Tommy, quits EDL

English Democrats organization, 292
English heritage, 20–2
English language: lessons in, 321; standards of, 6
English Volunteer Force (EVF), 216, 261, 280, 283
'English way of life', 14–15, 148, 215, 367
'Englishman's house is his castle', 19
Englishness, 117, 231, 310
European Muslim Research Centre, 272
Exeter, targeted by EDL, 272
Exeter Together organization, 273
Exeter University, 272–3
extremism, 141, 189; 'combatting' of, 193, 205, 233; 'failing to protect children from effects of', 349; government policy regarding, 197, 349

Facebook, 142, 145, 220, 265, 266, 279
facilities, lack of, 63
factory employment, disappearance of, 230
Faisal, Mohammad, 135–6
Faliq, Abdullah, 170–2, 274, 275
Farage, Nigel, 227, 228, 229, 280, 287, 294, 295, 300, 304, 311, 338–9; claim of Muslim fifth column, 353; interview with Trevor Phillips, 353, 357; role as MEP, 296; trip to Bulgaria, 328

Farley Hill Estate (Luton), 11, 15, 25–49 *passim*, 50–1, 62, 81, 82, 138, 139, 140, 220–1, 232, 234; decline of, 47
fear, among Muslims, 186, 203
Female Footsloggers Division, 181
female genital mutilation, issue of, 244–5
Filipino people, in Southampton, 316, 321
Fitna film, 293
football, 28–34, 44–6, 74, 77, 87, 89–91, 129, 139, 163, 352; culture of, 37–9; in Farley Hill, 50; mobilization of fans, for EDL demonstrations, 89; school team, 28; violence in, 29–31, 171 (crackdown on, 39)
football hooligans, 216, 258, 269, 299
Ford, Robert, 300
Ford factory, in Southampton, layoffs at, 306–8
Forum, the, 236
Four Freedoms group, 115
Francesco, an Italian worker, 255
Freedom Party (Netherlands), 274
Fritz, Michael, 102
Front National (France), 274
Funky Junction club, 35

Gabinos gang, 44
Galloway, George, 183
gambling, 138
Game, Philip, 160
gang crime, 59
gang culture, 60, 77, 139
Gates of Vienna organization, 235
gays and lesbians: comments about, 237; opposition to, 239; possible EDL membership of, 238

Geller, Pamela, 2, 206, 209
Ghurabaa, Al-, organization, 8
Gianluca, an Italian worker, 255
'go home', use of phrase, 166
Go Home campaign, 164
Golden Dawn (Greece), 274
Golding, Paul, 275, 276–7
Goodwin, Matthew, 300
Gosia, a Roma dance teacher, 320–1
Gove, Michael, 348
Gower, Hel, 111, 235–9
Gradwell, Mick, 55
Gregor, Nick ('Nazi Nick'), 218–19
Griffin, Nick, 12, 13, 98, 102, 105–6, 197, 207, 223, 276, 296; UAF targetting of, 103
Griffin Must Go campaign, 155
Grimsby, 266; EDL membership in, 256; unemployment in, 254
grooming, accusations levelled against Muslims, 53–4, 74–6, 113, 121, 254, 274, 351, 355
Gulf War, 73, 74
Gurney, Mike, 273
Gypsies, use of term, 332

Hain, Peter, 217
halal meat, protests regarding, 108, 145
Half Moon pub, 153, 179
Hamilton, Neil, 296
Harper, Gary, 303, 310
Hasan, Usama, 76, 205–6
headscarf, wearing of, 136–7; as means of communication with people, 200–3; as rebellion, 188, 190
healthcare, paid for by immigrants, 325
heroin, 139, 140

hijab: pulled from women, 175; wearing of, 185, 349
Hill, John, 108
Hockwell Ring Masjid, 125–6
homelessness, 166
Honorary Consulate of Romania, 322
honour crimes, 68
Hooligans against Salafists (HoGeSa) (Germany), 290
Hoon, Geoff, 300
Hope Not Hate campaign, 42, 102, 287
Hoskins, Bob, 267
Hsiao-Hung Pai, politicization of, 359–64
Hughes, David, 349
Hughes, Gareth, 333–4
Human Rights Watch, 336

Icon Hotel, 211
illegal working, becomes criminal offence, 357
'I'm an immigrant' campaign, 357
Immigration Act (2014) (UK), 197, 325
Indo pub, 179
Indo-American Refuge and Migrant Organization, 162
Institute of Arab and Islamic Studies (University of Exeter), 273
integration, 63, 69, 94, 121, 126, 130, 167, 199–200, 205, 257; of Muslims, 53; racial, 57–8
International Slavery Museum (Liverpool), 342
Iraq war, 183; opposition to, 8, 10, 19–20
Irish people, 173, 218; in Luton, 23, 26–7, 35, 116, 124; racist treatment of, 206

Irish Republican Army (IRA), 239
Irish Republicans, planned demonstration against, 222
Islam, 2, 9, 10, 53–6, 93, 114, 115, 118, 119, 122, 131, 136, 140, 187, 201; charitable giving in, 131; conversion to, 141, 231; justice as basis of, 135; learning about, 189–90; perceived as threat, 143–4; political, 76; radicalism in, 135; Salafist, 347
Islam4UK organization, 8
Islamic dress, 184–92 *passim*, 199, 200–3
Islamic Education Research Academy, 205
Islamification, 227, 347, 353
Islamism Digest, 170
Islamophobia, 366; crimes of, 175; in state and institutions, 292–3 *see also* anti-Muslim sentiment
Israel, support for, 214, 219
Israeli flag, use of, 266
Italian people, in Luton, 50–1

James, Diane, 311
Jamie Masjid, arson attack on, 124–5
Japanese wife of Andrew, 257–60
Je Suis Charlie, 353
Jewish Defence League, 14
Jewish people, 30, 156–7, 242, 248, 328; in EDL, 221, 238
Jimas organization, 76
Joint Council for the Welfare of Immigrants, 357
Jones, Owen, *Chavs: The Demonization of the Working Class*, 229–30
June, wife of Darren, 25, 33, 39–40, 72, 75, 78, 80, 83–4, 87

Karamay, Xinjiang, banning of veils and beards in, 200
Kaydamov, Eugeniy, 324
Kemb, Joyce, 302
kettling of protesters, 84
Keyboard Warrior Everywhere, 265
Khan, Amir, 118
Khan, Dilawar, 176
Kick It Out organization, 91
Komorum, a teacher, 125–7
Ku Klux Klan, 109
Kundnani, Arun, 196–7; *The Muslims Are Coming!*, 77–8, 194, 343–4

Labour Party, 175, 287, 295, 297, 315, 352, 357; frustration with, 52; voting for, 49, 184, 226, 234, 256, 301, 302, 303–4, 306, 309, 312, 339–40 *see also* New Labour
Lady England, 180–1
Lake, Alan, 13, 14, 113–16, 293
Lam, Jabez, 317, 318
language proficiency, requirement for migrants, 313
Latif, Farasat, 348
Laura, a Romanian English teacher, 321
Lavalette, Michael, 96
Lawrence, Stephen, xvii, 17; murder of, 364
Lee Rigby Memorial March, 280, 292
leftists, resentment against, 254, 265–6, 270, 282
Lennon, Stephen, Tommy Robinson's use of name, 112 *see also* Robinson, Tommy
Leppard, an EDL activist, 156
Lewsey Farm estate (Luton), 60
LGBT activism, 156

Liberal Democrat party, 195, 296
Liddle, Rod, 55
Lincoln, 132–3
Lindsey oil refinery dispute, 255
Liogier, Raphael, 292
'Lionheart', a blogger, 116
Lithuanian people, 165
Little Driver pub, 153
Lizi, a UAF member, 273
London, as multicultural reality, 363
London Muslim Centre, 168, 170, 176
Luton, 27, 134, 215, 340, 352; allegiance to, 82; anti-Muslim demonstration in, 7; anti-war demonstration in, 7, 10–11; army parade banned in, 67; attacks on Muslims in, 124; development of, 229; forgotten town, 49; industrial decline in, 73; population of, 15; quality of life in, 128; regeneration of, 47; riot in, 42; seen as synonymous with Islamic extremism, 122; social change in, 16; unemployment in, 17–18
Luton Labour Club, 41
Luton Town Football Club, 28–34, 112; match against Braintree, 32, 32

Macpherson Report, 365
Mad Hatters nightclub, 29
madrasas, opposition to, 69
managed migration, 313
manufacturing, contraction of, 42
March for England, 13, 82–3, 265–6, 271, 283
Marchini, Ann, 13
Mark, friend of Darren, 75
marriage, cross-cultural, 134

Marsh, Jeff, 216
Marsh Farm estate, Luton, 59–61
Marsh Farm Gang, 60
Martin, a former Ford worker from Eastleigh, 307
May, Theresa, 347
Mazumder, Mohammed, 317
McQueen, Alexander, 199
McQueen, Nicholas, 199
media, role of, in fostering racism, 287–8, 335
Michael, a builder, 180
Migrants' Rights Network, 164
Migs (Men in Gear), 31–2, 33–4, 36, 39, 44, 46, 71, 77, 340
military-style organization, 279
Miller, David, 292
Millwall football club, 29–30, 38–9, 71, 90
Minquan organization, 318
mixed-race population of Britain, 364
Mohammad, a sweet shop owner, 131–2
Mohammad, Prophet, 140
Mohammed, a Muslim from Birmingham, 4
Moosavi, Leon, 57
Mosley, Oswald, 159
mosques, 122, 123, 124–5, 272, 273, 274; Aisha (Walsall), 142; al-Ghurabaa, attack on, 124; as social venues, 184; attacks on, 4, 274–5; Birmingham Central, 350; building of, 21, 57, 62, 144, 210–11, 355 (in Dudley, 94); defence of, 176, 198; East London, 143, 154, 167–70, 178, 189, 198, 201, 275, 279 (disliked by Muslim parents, 189); infiltration of, 355; invasions of, 279, 346; isolated, vulnerability of, 175; leadership of, 135; Medina, attack on, 124; opposition to, 69; regulation of, 210–11
Muhairoun, al-, organization, 8
multiculturalism, 43–4, 143, 144, 214–15, 151, 179, 200, 365
Muslim, term becomes synonymous with Asian, 55–6
Muslims: accused of grooming see grooming; accusations levelled against Muslims; British see British Muslims see also anti-Muslim sentiment; Islam and surveillance of Muslims

Naomi-Anne, an EDL member, 243, 262, 270
National Association of Schoolmasters Union of Women Teachers (NASUWT), 155
National Centre for Social Research, 365
National Domestic Extremism Unit, 208, 366
National Front (NF), xiii, xiv, xv-xvi, 10, 37–8, 42, 43, 87, 89, 91, 93, 97, 105, 109, 172–3, 208, 223, 236, 283, 353
National People's Party, 275
National Union of Rail, Maritime and Transport Workers (RMT), 155
National Union of Teachers (NUT), 88, 155, 176
Nawaz, Maajid, 193, 194, 196, 354
Nazism, 242
Nemesis, an EDL organizer, 236, 238
neo-fascism, 146–7, 181, 182, 209, 210, 213, 219, 227, 236, 237, 251, 261, 271, 367

neo-Nazism, 107, 108, 182, 194, 209, 214, 217, 224, 226, 227, 241, 278, 281, 290, 343
New Labour, 230, 309
New Voices festival, 163–4
Newcastle Unites, 291
Nielsen, Magnus, 294
niqab, 201; media campaign against, 199; wearing of (by EDL member, 251; in college, 202)
Northeast Infidels, 108, 208–9, 214, 219, 290
Northwest Infidels, 108, 147, 181, 208, 209, 210, 214, 217, 219, 220, 236, 239, 271, 283, 290

Odinites, 249–50
Ofsted, extremism inquiries in schools, 349
Olive Tree primary school, 347
Operation Nexus, 167
Operation Sleeping Bag, 166
Oppressed, The, group, 217
Order of the Knights Templar, 272

paedophilia accusations against Asian men, 214
Page Hall (Sheffield), Roma scaremongering in, 335
Paine, Joshua Bonehill, 273–4
Pakistani people, 127; in Luton, 31, 32, 74, 118, 119*
Palestine, 101
Palestinians, sympathy for, 85
Palmerston Park, Southampton, scene of racist attacks, 317
Park View Academy, 349–50
Parrot pub, 20, 22, 46, 51, 71
Peach, Blair, xvii
Pearson, Lord, 293
Pegida organization (Germany), 353

Pegida UK organization, 290–1; demonstration in Newcastle, 291
Peter, a hospital porter, 156–60
Petrova, Milena, 326–7
Phillips, Trevor, 353, 357
Piratin, Phil, 161
Pitt, Paul, 219, 270
police, xii, xii, xvii, 38, 42, 84, 106, 114, 133, 153, 159, 171, 175, 232, 241, 243, 254, 258, 276, 289, 365, 366; handling of EDL Tower Hamlets march, 176–7; one-sidedness of, 97
Polish people, 17, 133, 165, 304; in Eastleigh, 306, 309, 312; in Luton, 35, 62, 80; in Southampton, 316, 318–19
political correctness, 68, 278
politicians, anger with, 21
politicization of coming generations, 233
Posted Workers Directive, 255–6
poverty, 299
Praxis organization, 163
Preventing Violent Extremism programme, 77–8, 96, 122, 195
prison, 160, 258–9, 269; call for segregation of, 346; Muslims over-represented in, 346 *see also* Winchester prison *and* Woodhill prison
Prodromou, Paul, 283
Profir, Daniel, 322–3
Progressive Youth Organization, 171
Protestant Coalition, 275
Public and Commercial Services union (PCS), 88, 155, 176
pubs, 177–9; in East London, 151–3; refusal to serve EDL members, 178–9
punk music, xiii

Quilliam Foundation, 193–7, 204, 231, 232, 234, 341, 344–5, 354–5; loses government funding, 195; meeting in Luton, 207–8
Quran, 9, 10, 120, 187, 190

race, concept of, 363
Race Equality Forum (Eastleigh), 318
race hate incidents, reporting of, 74–5
race industry, xvii
Racial Volunteer Force (RVF), 108, 209, 216
racism, 17, 23–4, 27, 29, 30, 51, 132, 142–5, 163, 181, 225, 231, 241, 243, 244, 261, 263–4, 268, 270, 271, 279, 281, 283, 287, 296, 298, 315, 330, 332, 337, 353, 366; attacks, 42, 129, 169–70, 188, 198, 245, 272, 279, 318 (bombing plan, 215–16; in Southampton, 317–18; on Roma people, 333, 334; on women, 175, 198–9); class analysis of, 191; cultural aspect of, 174; deconstruction of, 342; disguised as defence of women's rights, 199; fuelled by official policy, 167; in Britain, 235–86; in China, 362; in police, 55; language of, 325, 326; mainstreaming of, 288; media complicity in, 198, 199, 287–8, 335; resistance to, 141–2, 174, 175, 191, 204–5, 359; verbal, 129, 133, 143, 166, 198, 225 (against women, 187–8)
radical right, changing faces of, 193–234
radicalization, Islamic, 135, 195, 350; theorization of, 76–7

Raff, Margaret, 299
Rafferty, Michael, 214–16
Ramadan: fasting for, 350; observance of, 142
Rastafarians, xiv
Ray, Paul, 13, 115, 116, 217–18
Red Action, xv
Refugee and Migrant Forum of Essex and London (RAMFEL), 164
Reggae, xiii, 45
religion, 249–50
Renton, Chris see Sheridan, John
Respect Party, 183
Rigby, Lee, killing of, 1–2, 4, 5, 10, 66, 125, 175, 213–14, 265, 268, 274, 276 see also Lee Rigby Memorial March
Riley, Steve, 267, 280
rioting, on Marsh Farm estate, 60
Robinson, Tommy (aka Stephen Lennon), 1–2, 12, 34, 20, 23, 54, 67, 89, 93, 95, 98–9, 102, 104, 107, 108, 111–21, 146–8, 149, 167–8, 179, 181–2, 193–234 passim, 235–8, 241, 251, 266, 269, 351–2, 353, 367; allegedly dealing drugs, 138; anti-Muslim activities of, 121; arrests and convictions of, 211–12; dresses as rabbi, 169; hoax story regarding mother, 218; imprisonment of, 284 351 (for mortgage fraud, 212; for visa offences, 209, 212–13); Mig Down, 33–4; post-prison, 147, 340–7; questioned about racism, 142–5; quits EDL, 193–6, 204, 223 (and faces accusations, 206–7); speech at Oxford Union, 354; tattoos of, 211; tweets sent to, 231–2 see also Lennon, Stephen

Rock Against Racism (RAR), 172–3
Rodd, John, 272
Roma people, 180, 270; allegation of baby-stealing, 335–6; attempted assimilation under Stalinism, 336; Bulgarian, 336–8; children not enrolled by schools, 337; distinctions between, 332; Polish, 320–1; racism against, 337; Romanian, 136–7, 331–5
Romanian Culture Centre (London), 329
Romanian people, 136–7, 144, 228; immigration of, 294; in Southampton, 316, 322–5 (allegations against, 323)
Rothermere, Lord, 159
Rotten, Johnny, 172
Royal Anglian Regiment, 81, 82, 109; protest at march by, 7, 52, 80–1, 85–6, 113
Rusev, Atanas, 336
Ruseva, Sasha, 336
Ruth, Tobias, 272

Salafism, 347
Sari Squad, xv
Save Luton, 12
Savile, Jimmy, 54
Scottish Defence League (SDL), 217, 291
Screwdriver music, 152
Seasonal Agricultural Workers Scheme, 295
'self-defence is no offence', xiv
self-employment, 314–15, 324
services, public, cutting of, 63, 70
Sex Pistols group, 172
Sham 69 group, 173
sharia law, 24, 52, 54, 93, 144, 167, 273

Sharia Watch UK, 293
Shaun, alleged conversion of, 87
Shaw, John, 108
Sheridan, John (aka Chris Renton), 14, 101, 181, 236
Sherratt, Robert, 105
Show Racism the Red Card, 90, 291
Sillett, Paul, 88–9, 90, 93, 172–4, 176, 291
Simmons, Steve, 236
Sisters Against the EDL, 182
skinheads, 39, 42–3, 45, 89, 91, 129, 130, 173, 194, 337, 365
sleeping bags, of migrants, confiscated, 166
Sleman, Mark, 271–2
smoking, 268–9
socialism, 191
Socialist Worker, 85
Socialist Workers Party, 183
Somali community centre, attack on, 4
SOS Polonia organization, 319–22, 333
Soul Crew, 217
Southampton, immigration into, 315–16
Southeast Alliance, 208, 219, 283
Speight, Gail, 181–2, 239
Spence, Alan, 101–2, 239
Spencer, Robert, 2, 206, 209
Spinwatch organization, 292
St George, cross of, 117
St George's Day, cancellation of, 118
St Margaret's Club, 23–4
Stand Against Far-right Extremism (SAFE), 356
Steve, a UKIP voter from Eastleigh, 301, 304–5
Steve White Band, 91

Stolipinovo (Plovdiv), Roma people in, 338
stoning, as punishment (in Bible, 348; in Islam, 347–8)
Stop the War Coalition, 184
Storey, Barbara, 319–22
Stormer, 109
Straw, Jack, 55, 335
Stuart, Graham, 350
surveillance, 96; of Muslims, 78, 186, 195, 198
'sus' law, xiii, 43
Susie, an EDL member, 265
sword, right to carry, 249–50
Syrian refugees, 285

Tahsin, an anti-racist woman activist, 182–92, 198–205
Taylor, Nathan, 271
Team Tommy, 238
Tebbit, Norman, 313
Tell Mama organization, 3
terrorism, 20; associated with Islam, 3, 5
Thatcher, Margaret, 158, 304, 313–14
The Non Violence Alliance (TNVA), 58, 106
This is My England video, 92
Toxteth, riots in, 43
trade unions, 153–5, 177, 316, 356
travellers, 61, 72
'Trojan Horse' operation of UK government, 348
Troxy Centre, Islamic conference at, 168

Ugandan Asian people, 312–13
Uighur people, in China, persecution of, 200, 361–2
UK Life League, 276

Ulster Loyalism, 103, 283
Ulster Unionists, 108
Umm Luqman, 9
undocumented people, 163, 164-5
'undocumented', use of word, 26
unemployment, 17–18, 63–4, 92, 157, 225, 229, 234, 254, 301, 303, 306, 308
Union Jack, 117–18
Union of Construction, Allied Trades and Technicians (UCATT), 356
unions *see* trade unions
Unite Against Fascism (UAF), 88, 90, 93, 154, 155–6, 168–9, 172–4, 176–7, 192, 217, 273, 289, 290; demonstration in Cardiff, 96; meetings attacked, 103–4; strategies of, 96–8, 103–4
Unite the Union, 104, 155, 176, 307
United British Patriots, 283
United East End (UEE), 154, 168–9, 170, 174, 176–7
United Kingdom Independence Party (UKIP), xvi, 197, 199, 228, 246, 247, 252, 256–7, 274, 280, 282, 287, 292, 293, 294–315 *passim*, 330, 356–7; base of support for, 299; electoral gains of, 366
United People of Luton (UPL), 7, 11, 12–13, 83, 235; website, 13
unity of the far right, moves towards, 197, 217, 219, 223–4, 265–6, 282–3 *see also* radical right
Urban Bar, 154–5

Vauxhall car plant, 18, 47, 116, 124
veil, Muslim: banned in Karamay, Xinjiang, 200; pulled off women, 198; wearing of, 184–9, 198–9,

200 (as political statement, 202, 203) *see also* hijab *and* niqab
Viking, an EDL organizer, 241–3, 244–52, 355–6
violence, 248 *see also* racism, attacks; *and* football, violence in
voting: abstention from, 302; revival of, 233

War on Terror, 78
Warsi, Sayeeda, 141–2
Waters, Anna-Marie, 293
Watterson, Kelly, 272
Wells, Hayley, 272
Welsh Defence League, 14, 216, 217
Welsh people: in construction trade, 229; in Luton, 48
Wendy, a woman from East London, 281
West Ham football club, 30, 37, 82
West Indian people, in Luton, 27, 104, 106, 124; involved with EDL, 90
West Midlands Police Force, xii
When Tommy Met Mo, 196, 207
white flight, 152
White Hart pub (East London), 178
White Horse pub (South London), 281
White House pub (Luton), 33
White Pride, 237
white working class, 18, 123, 229, 231, 234, 283; children, rate as underachievers, 233
Whitelaw, William, 43
whites-only pub in Glasgow, 109
Wilders, Geert, 274, 293
Wilson, Lenos, 50–9, 106, 139
Winchester prison, 285, 340–1, 346

Wolverhampton: EDL membership in, 225; industrial decline in, 225
women: as members of EDL, 180–1, 245–6, 268; in Islam, 245, 251, 263; Muslim (campaigning against racism, 182; prejudices against, 126) *see also* racism, attacks, on women
Wong, Denis, 299, 317, 318
Woodhill prison, 285, 346
Woodward, Raymond, 214
Woolwich Strong organization, 273
working class, 143, 158, 228, 230, 232, 247, 289, 299–300, 304, 305, 312, 315, 330, 357; breaking of, 148; unity of, 161 *see also* white working class
working hours, 326
Wright, Ian, 117

Xinjiang, 200, 362

Yaqoob, Salma, 87, 350
Yaxley, Stephen, 112
Yellas gang, 44
Yorkshire Infidels, 219
Young British National Party, 282
Young Muslim Organization UK, 171
Young National Front (YNF), 172
youth anger, 231–2
Youth Connection organization, 171
YouTube, 216, 218, 238, 265, 268
Yusif, a former drug dealer, 136–41

Zainabia Islamic Centre, Milton Keynes, 142
zero-hours contracts, 247, 307
Zionism, 13, 14, 85, 101

Z972471

Community Learning & Libraries
Cymuned Ddysgu a Llyfrgelloedd

This item should be returned or renewed by the
last date stamped below.

Newport
CITY COUNCIL
CYNGOR DINAS
Casnewydd

1 6 FEB 2017

07 OCT 2017

To renew visit:

www.newport.gov.uk/libraries

Hsiao-Hung Pai is a writer best known for her books *Chinese Whispers: The True Story behind Britain's Hidden Army of Labour*, which was shortlisted for the 2009 Orwell Prize, and *Scattered Sand: The Story of China's Rural Migrants*, which won the Bread and Roses Award in 2013. Pai's third book, *Invisible: Britain's Migrant Sex Workers*, was published in 2013. As part of her research for the book, Pai worked undercover as a maid in brothels all over the country. Pai's first work of fiction, *Hidden Army of Labour*, was published in the Chinese language in Taiwan and China.

Pai has lived in the UK since 1991. She is a contributor to the *Guardian* and many UK-Chinese publications.